Contributions to Economics

The series *Contributions to Economics* provides an outlet for innovative research in all areas of economics. Books published in the series are primarily monographs and multiple author works that present new research results on a clearly defined topic, but contributed volumes and conference proceedings are also considered. All books are published in print and ebook and disseminated and promoted globally. The series and the volumes published in it are indexed by Scopus and ISI (selected volumes).

Jakub Horák • Veronika Machová •
Valentina Vycheslavovna Mantulenko •
Tomáš Krulický

Development of World Trade in the Context of the COVID-19 Pandemic

A Case Study on the Czech Republic and the Russian Federation

Springer

Jakub Horák
Institute of Technology and Business
České Budějovice, Czech Republic

Veronika Machová
Institute of Technology and Business
České Budějovice, Czech Republic

Valentina Vycheslavovna Mantulenko
Samara State University of Economics
Samara, Russia

Tomáš Krulický
Institute of Technology and Business
České Budějovice, Czech Republic

ISSN 1431-1933 ISSN 2197-7178 (electronic)
Contributions to Economics
ISBN 978-3-031-27256-1 ISBN 978-3-031-27257-8 (eBook)
https://doi.org/10.1007/978-3-031-27257-8

This Springer imprint is published by the registered company Springer Nature Switzerland AG
The registered company address is: Gewerbestrasse 11, 6330 Cham, Switzerland

Contents

List of Abbreviations

AD	Anno Domini
ANN	Artificial neural networks
ARIMA	AutoRegressive integrated moving average
BC	Before Christ
BFGS	Broyden–Fletcher–Goldfrarb–Shanno
BMW	Bayerische motoren werke
BP	Backpropagation
CGE	Computable general equilibrium
CO_2	Carbon dioxide
COVID-19	Coronavirus disease 2019
CZK	Currency unit of the Czech Republic
DSGE	Dynamic stochastic general equilibrium
DT	Decision trees
EU	European Union
EU-27	27 European Union countries
EUR	Currency of the Eurozone
FDI	Foreign direct investment
GATT	General agreement on tariffs and trade
GDP	Gross domestic product
GIKDE	General intervalized kerned density estimator
IBRD	International Bank for Reconstruction and Development
ICT	Information and communication technologies
IMF	International Monetary Fund
IT	Information technology
MLP	Multilayer perceptron networks
MS Excel	Microsoft Support Excel
NAFTA	North American Free Trade Agreement
NATO	North Atlantic Treaty Organization
NN	Neural networks
NSC	Nash–Sutcliffe coefficient

PNN	Probabilistic neural networks
PQOL	Physical quality of life
Q	Quarter
RBF	Radial basis function networks
RBFT	Reputation-based Byzantine fault tolerance
RF	Random forests
RMB	Currency in the People's Republic of China
SET	Thai stock exchange
SW	Software
TTIP	Transatlantic Trade and Investment Partnership
UNCTAD	United Nations Conference on Trade and Development
US	United States
USA	United States of America
USD	United States dollar
USMCA	United States-Mexico-Canada agreement
WB	World bank
WHO	World Health Organization
WTO	World Trade Organization
XML	Extensible markup language

List of Figures

List of Tables

Chapter 1
Introduction

When thinking about the origin and history of external economic relations, it can be stated that their existence has been as long as the history of the state or its political and economic organization. Even today, the key part of the international economic cooperation or international division of labour in practically all countries in the world is foreign or international trade. International trade is often referred to as the most important aspect of the world economy, which plays a crucial role in its development. Moreover, the current period is characterized by a relatively high level of global specialization and standardization, which represents a very positive contribution to the creation of a strong basis for international trade and its development. In principle, the more economically developed a country, the more diverse the patchwork of its external economic relations is. The current world presents a picture of globalization determined by multilateralism and interconnection of social and economic processes. Thanks to globalization, the interconnection of the states by means of trade has been increasing notably and the economies of the countries are becoming mutually dependent on each other. Due to extensive application of communication and information technologies in practice, economic dimension can be perceived as one of the decisive factors. Economic thus represents a certain driver of globalization, whose immanent feature is a growth of mutual economic dependence of individual countries on a global scale through the growing volume and range of international transactions of goods, services, and capital.

However, the development of international trade has undergone a number of significant changes over the past few years, where the advent of the global financial and economic crisis, which resulted in stalling the process of the long-term development of international trade based on the opening of national markets, deepening the integration processes, and removing the obstacles to the movement of goods and capital, played an important role. The effects financial and economic crisis have brought many unexpected surprises to the globalized economy and also provided evidence on the degree of its interconnectedness. Negative effects have been recorded not only in international trade but also in the development of direct foreign

J. Horák et al., *Development of World Trade in the Context of the COVID-19 Pandemic*, Contributions to Economics,
https://doi.org/10.1007/978-3-031-27257-8_1

investments, as well as other forms of international economic cooperation. Since the second world war, the first significant year-on-year decline in the international trade was recorded in the years 2008–2009. This deep downturn was followed by a relatively fast recovery in 2010 but the long-term growth rate was not very encouraging. In 2012, the increase in the volume of international trade in goods did not exceed 2%. This was mainly due to the development of the advanced countries´ economies and the economic situation in the European Union, which showed decrease both in export and import. These results also reflected the mutual trade of countries within the EU; however, there were affected also the groups of states the EU traded with, especially the developing market economies. In the next period, the statistical results were optimistic. Developed countries experienced economic recovery and in terms of the development of the global economy, economic growth was predicted for the coming years. Similarly, positive development of the GDP was predicted in the majority of the geographical grouping. Certain prospect of the economic growth was brought by the achievement of the WTO Agreement on Trade Facilitation. Despite the above, there was still a lot of uncertainty concerning the development of the economic environment at the global, regional, and national level. The reason was seen especially in the newly introduced regulatory rules for certain business lines, approaches to solve problems related to high indebtedness of many states, and the manifestations of covert protectionism. In addition to other problems, the crisis caused a relatively high increase of competitiveness in the markets and erosion of trust between business entities, which was seen especially in the changes in the way of reflected especially in cross-border trade and its financing, as well as in the territorial direction of trade and investments. There is no doubt that these facts caused by the crisis have significantly influenced the behaviour of business entities, banks, financial institutions, and non-financial entities, often leading to the need to re-evaluate and adaptation of the strategies to new conditions.

The outbreak of the COVID-19 pandemic, whose consequences are often compared to the financial crisis in 2008–2009 by the experts, has had huge negative impacts on the international trade. The rapid spread of this respiratory disease and measures taken by the governments of individual countries to prevent its further spread has had very serious effects for the most important world economies. It has disrupted a wide range of productive activities, first in Asia, then in Europe, North America, and the rest of the world. Globally, restrictions concerning production, transport, and border closures were adopted, which has led to a sharp drop in both supply and demand, and finally to an unprecedented drop in GDP, a sharp increase in the unemployment rate in individual countries and the whole regions. In April 2020, the COVID-19 pandemic stopped the global economy, global production and consumption dwindled very quickly, and international trade seemed to be on the path to a steady decline; however, in the summer of 2020, the global trade in goods started to recovery slowly. This was mainly due to the support for exports of goods related to COVID-19 mainly from East Asian economies. Until the end of 2020, world trade recovered significantly in many countries and many sectors. The same growth was expected in the year 2021. As a whole, the estimates for the year 2021 say that the value of the global trade will be by 20%, or 28% higher than in the year 2019 and 2020.

The Russian-Ukrainian conflict became another source of major problems in international trade. This conflict started at the beginning of 2022 and significantly affected the entire world trade. Sanctions were imposed on the Russian Federation by almost the entire world, trade networks with the Russian Federation were stopped, and many products and services were stopped being exported from the Russian Federation. This fact showed how truly erratic and difficult to predict world trade is. That is why this publication tries to find a way to predict international trade at least in general terms. Unfortunately, the publication was created before the outbreak of this conflict and thus failed to take this point of view into account. Nevertheless, two chapters dedicated to the impact of the Russian-Ukrainian conflict and also the development of trade after the COVID-19 pandemic were retroactively inserted into the publication. The publication thus became more up-to-date and partially takes into account the new conditions.

It results from above that during its existence, international trade has faced a large number of unpredictable obstacles. What is worth mentioning is, among other things, the event that happened in March 2021 and that meant another severe blow to the global trade in the times when the supply chain had already been severely disrupted, specifically the Suez Canal blockage caused by a 400-metre-long container ship due to strong wind. About 30% of all container traffic passes through the Suez Canal; in general, it accounts for approx. 12% of the volume of all goods traded in the world. By way of illustration, in the previous year, approximately 19,000 ships used this waterway, which is more than 50 ships per day on average. Despite the fact that the ship was recovered in 6days, concerns of serious negative impacts on the international trade proved to be justified. According to the predictions made by analysts, the Suez Canal blockage was estimated to affect 10–15% of the global container traffic. The incident disrupted mainly the global supply chains, starting from oil through agricultural commodities to cars. Analysts also state that the sectors most affected by the blockage were European manufacturing industry and automotive. This can be explained by the fact that these sectors operate on the principle of just-in-time, which means that components and goods must be delivered at the moment when the customer needs them so that they do not have to be stored. Daily losses in the global trade were estimated at USD 5.1 billion (113.1 billion CZK) in the direction of the westbound cargo and USD 4.5 billion in the opposite direction. Based on these facts, in the near future, attention should be focused on the problems related to high and industrial demand, global lack of containers, and low reliability of transport companies´ services, which can make supply chains sensitive even to the slightest shocks and thus affect the entire international trade.

Chapter 2
World Trade Development

International trade between countries and across continents has existed for centuries. Traditionally, the international trade consisted only of tradable goods, which mainly represented food, textiles, spices, precious metals, precious stones and art or other objects. There are only few people that have not heard of the Silk Road or the Amber Trail or other famous paths that flourished precisely in connection with the history of trade. At that time, trading took place mainly through sea or land routes. However, since earlier times, the whole world has come a long way, and it can therefore be stated that today's international trade is taking on completely different dimensions. Due to technological progress and the impact of globalization, it is now essential for all countries to be involved in the international trade (Jawaid and Waheed 2017). According to Shoiw (2013), foreign trade and its components occupy a very important position in economic theory. In general, the term "foreign trade" is considered to be one of the forms of international relations. It can also be characterized as a tangible and intangible flow of goods, production and non-production services that crossed national borders. As a rule, foreign trade can be divided into two parts, namely import and export. In the case of import, we speak of a certain volume of goods (services) from abroad that crossed the state border for the purpose of its permanent or temporary retention in the country. Its contents include goods for the consumption of processing, repair, and re-export. In contrast to this, export can be understood as the volume of goods (services) that the state is able to produce and export abroad. In the last few decades, we have witnessed the emergence of exports and imports which usually have an increasing tendency. According to Kushnruk and Ivanenko (2017), international economic relations at the level of exports and imports of goods and services have an important influence on the development of the economy of each state. In this context, the international trade generally has a positive effect on technological change and innovation of domestic companies and it also supports the aggregate growth of industrial productivity. Through import and export, information, technology, and demands are indirectly transferred between economies. They also contribute to balancing markets and eliminating differences in the world.

J. Horák et al., *Development of World Trade in the Context of the COVID-19 Pandemic*, Contributions to Economics,
https://doi.org/10.1007/978-3-031-27257-8_2

Furthermore, growth in export volumes is aimed at increasing the employment rate in the domestic economy. Fürst and Pleschová (2010) express the opinion that foreign trade leads to an expansion of countries' consumption possibilities, while the reasons why a state chooses to open up to world trade vary depending on the natural conditions and resources at its disposal and the associated declining production costs, but also on the differences in consumers' taste.

2.1 History

There is no doubt that international trade has a very rich history. Based on archaeological findings, it can be stated that the origin of the international trade, which consisted in the free exchange of goods at that time, dates back to around 2500 BC. The then trade in metals and textiles was prosperous especially for the Sumerian inhabitants of Mesopotamia. Around 2000 BC, the ancient Greeks profited from the trade in wine, olive oil, and grain. Around 340 BC, the Greeks created a system of modern commerce based on a functioning banking system, contracts, insurance, and business credit. After the decline of the ancient Greek civilization, the ancient Rome flourished. From the first century AD to the fifth century AD, the Romans contributed to the creation of many trade routes, both by land and by sea, especially to the East (China, Egypt, India, and Syria). Up until the end of the fifteenth century AD, Rome was considered to be the centre and leader of trade. Over time, the centre of international trade shifted from the Mediterranean to Western Europe. The largest trading activity at that time was recorded in Spain, Portugal and later in the Netherlands.

The discovery of America in 1492 and, a little later, the discovery of a sea route to India subsequently contributed to the growth of trade and the colonization of the world. The primary goal of colonization was to increase national economic power by using the colonies for the benefit of the mother country. Through exports and the discovery of precious metals, they were considered the bases of a national treasure. The period of this first phase lasted until the advent of the Industrial Revolution in England, that is until 1750. Since then, Britain has been considered the largest industrial power and the most expanding colonizer and, until 1900, also the largest player in international trade (Seyoum 2014).

At the beginning of the twentieth century, the highly developed colonial system in particular was responsible for the high degree of liberalization of international trade. It was in the interests of the European industrialized countries to move products to the colonies as smoothly as possible, as well as raw materials and agricultural products back to Europe. The level of tariff and non-tariff barriers was very low. Countries such as Britain, France, Belgium, and Germany were among the most economically developed countries in Europe until the World War I. Apart from the European continent, the positions of the USA, Japan, and Russia also strengthened economically.

During the World War I, the established trade ties were severed and, on the contrary, support for domestic political and economic nationalism increased. The mobility of capital and goods has also been reduced and labour has declined as well. European countries thus lost not only their colonies, but also their export markets, after which new competition arose that was not involved in the war.

In the 1930s, the international trade was paralysed by the Great Depression that spread from the USA. The US stock market saw a sharp drop in stock prices, which resulted in a decline in household wealth and a decline in demand. Simultaneously with the decline in consumption on the US market, exports, on which a number of countries depended, decreased. The resulting crisis became global and had a negative impact on all international trade. There was a reduction in the willingness to cooperate in areas of international economic difficulties and an increase in national protectionist tendencies, such as setting customs and tariff barriers.

The Great Depression was exceptional due to its duration and depth of decline, with societal changes particularly in Germany, where it was more than obvious that the world was heading towards another war. Of course, World War II had a similar effect on international trade. It is also important to mention that even before the end of the war, the Allied countries held negotiations on international financial measures according to which foreign trade in the post-war world should be governed. The main reason for these measures was to prevent a recurrence of the economic situation after the World War I. In 1944, the International Monetary Fund (IMF) and the International Bank for Reconstruction and Development (IBRD) were established in Bretton Woods as part of a conference. While the IMF was established to ensure the growth of international trade through a system of fixed exchange rates, the IBRD was established to provide long-term investments. In 1948, the General Agreement on Tariffs and Trade (GATT) entered into force, which was to contribute to the free movement of goods through the reduction of tariffs and trade barriers (Hesselberg 2007).

2.2 Development of the International Trade Theory

According to Irwin (2001), the theory of trade policy and international trade is one of the oldest areas of economic thinking. As early as in the days of the ancient Greeks, intellectuals, economists, and officials considered the determinants of trade between nations, sought answers to the question of whether trade was more beneficial or detrimental to a nation, and sought to determine the best trade policy for a particular country. The perspective of ancient Greek philosophers on international trade was quite unsure. While acknowledging the benefits of international exchange, there were concerns that some domestic industries (or culture or workers) could be threatened or harmed by foreign competition. Depending on the importance placed on total trade profits or the losses of people impacted by imports, analysts have reached various conclusions on the appropriateness of free trade. However, many economists have shared the view that free trade can certainly be considered a technological advance. Although some interests may be harmed by it, the overall benefits to society are unquestionable. Based on today's intense trade debates, it can be said that the tensions associated with this dual view of trade have never been overcome.

Krugman et al. (2012) state that the effort of the theory of international trade consists in answering three main questions: (1) Are there benefits or profits from international trade? If so, what are they? (2) What should the structure of international trade look like? (3) How free should international trade between states be?

The following theories of international trade have gradually gone through a number of stages in connection with the development of trade. The author further states that the explanation of international trade on the basis of the principle of comparative labour costs was gradually replaced by differences which consisted in the equipment of human capital and factors of production in a given country. However, the greatest emphasis in theories is currently placed on capturing the changes that are taking place in the world economy and on the connection between international trade and external economic balance.

2.2.1 Mercantilism

Mercantilism can be seen as a systematic set of ideas that focuses on the international trade. Its origin dates back to the seventeenth and eighteenth century in Europe. According to Irwin (2001), for most of this period, the authors of mercantilism held the view that the primary goal of trade should be to promote a favourable trade balance. They explained the characteristic of a favourable trade balance as the value at which the value of exported domestic goods is higher than the value of imported goods from abroad. A trade was considered to be profitable on the basis of the extent to which the value of exports exceeded the value of imports, resulting in a trade surplus and the addition of precious metals and treasures to the country's stocks. Later on, scientists questioned the extent to which mercantilists confused the accumulation of precious metals with the increase in national wealth. Undoubtedly, however, mercantilists tended to perceive exports as favourable and imports as unfavourable.

The author further adds that the specific source of concern was not the trade balance, but the commodity composition of trade. Mercantilists considered the export of processed goods to be beneficial, but the export of raw materials (for its use by foreign producers) to be harmful. On the other hand, imports of raw materials were considered to be advantageous, but imports of processed goods were considered harmful. This sequence of activities was not only based on employment where processing and adding value to raw materials was considered to create better jobs than just mining or primary production of basic goods, but it was also based on building industries that would strengthen the national economy. The mercantilists sought to further seek a highly interventional agenda that applied trade taxes to manipulate the trade balance or the commodity structure of trade, for the benefit of the domestic market. However, this strategy can never work for all nations at the same time, as not every country can have a trade surplus and not every country can export manufactured goods and import raw materials.

Dorobăţ (2015) also describes mercantilist school as one of the primary complex approaches in the theory of international trade which emphasizes the usefulness of the international trade in the process of reproduction, i.e. from production, distribution, and exchange to consumption. The source further states that mercantilists considered foreign trade to be the so-called zero-sum game. This fact resulted in the accumulation of precious metals in the national economy, on the one hand, and the passive trade balance on the other. As outlined above, the direction of previous economic policy represented only the maximum possible distribution of existing wealth in favour of domestic economy. The enforcement of a restrictive trade policy was carried out through high import duties which replaced import embargoes, such as export subsidies, navigation acts, export monopolies, and foreign exchange regulations, which in turn led to a protectionist trade strategy.

2.2.2 *Traditional Political Economy*

This theory disproved the mercantilist considerations of the zero-sum game, while demonstrating the benefits of foreign trade for the wealth growth of all parties involved, regardless of their current trade balance. This fact was described as a game with a positive sum, which was also considered a valuable shift in the thinking at the time associated with the recognition that the essence of the benefits of international trade is not based on cash flows, but on the benefits of the division of labour between countries.

Undoubtedly, the most important contribution to the theory of international trade was made by Adam Smith (the founder of Political Economy), who formulated the principle of absolute benefits. According to this theory, countries should focus on producing such products that can be produced at a lower cost than in other countries. These products should then be exported to countries where their production is more expensive and, conversely, we should import such products that can be produced cheaper in those countries. Every state should specialize in a particular production branch that suits it the best. Although Adam Smith's theory was disproved relatively soon, it enriched the history of economic thinking significantly.

Following the above-mentioned theory, another British economist called David Ricardo appeared who elaborated Smith's ideas into the second classical theory, the so-called principle of comparative advantage. The definition of a comparative advantage can quite simply be described as the relatively largest absolute advantage or the relatively smallest absolute disadvantage. However, the primary purpose of this theory is to illustrate the benefits of involving economies in the international trade. Each country makes a profit by focusing on the relatively most efficient production. For this reason, this theory gives a strong argument to proponents of free trade—the focus and free exchange between economies means higher income for participants. Again, this theory has been re-examined and transformed into a more realistic form of economics as it is the case for the theories presented by John Stuart Mill, Alfred Marshall, and Gottfried Haberler. Thanks to these personalities, but also thanks to many others, the international trade has gradually taken the position of an independent scientific discipline within the broad macroeconomic theory (Dorobăţ 2015). For an easier and better idea, Krugman et al. (2012) present the most important conclusions of the classical model of international trade:

- The monitored state need not have an absolute advantage in order for international trade to be advantageous for it—a comparative advantage is sufficient.
- In the future, countries will focus on their comparative advantages, i.e. the goods the production of which has a comparative advantage will be exchanged in the process of international trading for goods that can be produced more efficiently in another state in terms of comparative advantages.
- The main disadvantage of this model lies in the assumption of full specialization of economies, which is impossible in the real economy.

2.2.3 Neoclassical Economics

Dorobăţ (2015) states that over time, the classical concept was followed by a number of new theories and models of international trade that modify or expand it. The author further adds that the new concept is focused mainly on the limiting assumptions of the classical model, especially on its constant and opportunistic costs, thanks to which the model requires a full specialization of the economy and the number of production factors. Representatives of neoclassical economics include the Swedish economists Eli Filip Heckscher and Bertil Gotthard Ohlin, who contributed the most to the addition of classical theories of international trade. The author Ohlin contributed to the creation of a neoclassical model, the so-called theory of equipment with production factors, which was later followed by the Stolper–Samuelson theorem on the change of world prices. The theorem on balancing the prices of production factors and the Rybczynski theorem, including the change in relative equipment, can be considered the most important innovation of the theory of comparative advantage, which responded mainly to the development of the real economy. These facts were also the starting point for the emergence of the so-called dynamic theory of comparative advantage, which states that countries will focus on the production and export of the kind of goods that are relatively undemanding to the factor of production with which the state is relatively best equipped.

Naturally, new modern theories of the international trade emerged over time, with the aim of greater real applicability to economic policy, or the inclusion of more factors of production, more commodities, and fewer simplified assumptions.

It can be stated that currently, the issue of world trade, including the factors that affect this trade, can be understood much better. The context of individual world markets has been guided by understandings and theories developed by economists based on natural resources available in various countries that give them a comparative advantage, mass economies, e-commerce technologies, and product life cycle change in line with technological advances and financial market structures. Currently, the issue of international trade is seen as part of the external economic balance (Krugman et al. 2012).

2.3 Current Trends in International Trade

There is a mass of transactions and daily international operations hidden under the term "international trade".

As outlined in the introduction, international trade is the trade that takes place across national or state borders through an importer and an exporter. The subject of foreign trade consists mainly of products (goods), services, or rights (for example, licenses or copyrights). Historically, the international trade is considered to be the oldest form of external economic relations, and its influence on the development of national economies has deepened throughout the post-World War II period. The development of the world trade in recent decades is one of the most dynamic elements in the development of the world economy. This means a dynamic development not only on a quantitative scale, but also a development in terms of the structure and changes in foreign trade flows of individual states, as well as the whole international trade as such. In accordance with the conclusions of theories of classical, neoclassical, and modern international trade, it can be stated that at present, the international trade is a decisive factor influencing the economic growth of individual economies and, after all, the whole world economy (Pacheco-Lopez 2005).

Havrlant and Husek (2011) state that the export and import of goods and services play a very important role in the international trade of individual countries. Exports are often seen as a function of international trade, where goods or services produced in one state are shipped for future sale or trade to another state. Factors influencing the size of each country's exports include mostly foreign demand, domestic and foreign price levels, and the exchange rate. The ability to export goods or services serves the economy for growth, as exports are a key component of the state's economy, as the sale of these goods or services contributes to gross domestic production. On the other hand, the term import stands for goods or services imported from one state to another. These two terms very often appear in connection with the term trade balance, which in turn represents the difference between the value of a given country's export and the value of that country's import. If the export indicator is higher than the import indicator of the given country, it means a positive trade balance together with the growth of the state's GDP. In the long run, this phenomenon exerts a positive effect on the country's economy. It can be stated that imports together with exports form the backbone of the international trade. Otherwise, when the indicator of total imports exceeds the indicator of total exports, it means a negative trade balance for the state. Businesses use the export of goods and services mainly because of their financial advantage or also because the goods, service, or technology are not available in the given country. For particular types of goods such as raw materials, imports are even inevitable.

2.3.1 Development of International Trade in Goods

The EU-27, China, and the USA have been the world's three largest players in international trade since 2004. In 2019, the total level of trade in goods (exports and imports) in the EU-27 was 4071 billion EUR (excluding intra-EU trade), which was 23 billion EUR less than the figure for China and 308 billion EUR above the figure recorded for the US. Japan had the fourth highest level of trade in goods, i.e. 1274 billion EUR.

The value of international trade in goods between the EU-27 and the rest of the world (the sum of exports and imports from non-EU countries) totalled 4067 billion EUR in 2019 (see Fig. 2.1). Both imports and exports were higher than in 2018, with an increase in imports (27 billion EUR) smaller than the increase in exports (73 billion EUR). As a result, the EU-27 trade surplus of 152 billion EUR in 2018 increased to 197 billion EUR in 2019.

Between 2009 and 2012, exports in the EU-27 increased rapidly from 1184 billion EUR to 1771 billion EUR. Between 2012 and 2016, exports remained relatively stable, nevertheless, they increased over the next three years from 1867 billion EUR in 2016 to 2132 billion EUR in 2019. Imports followed roughly the

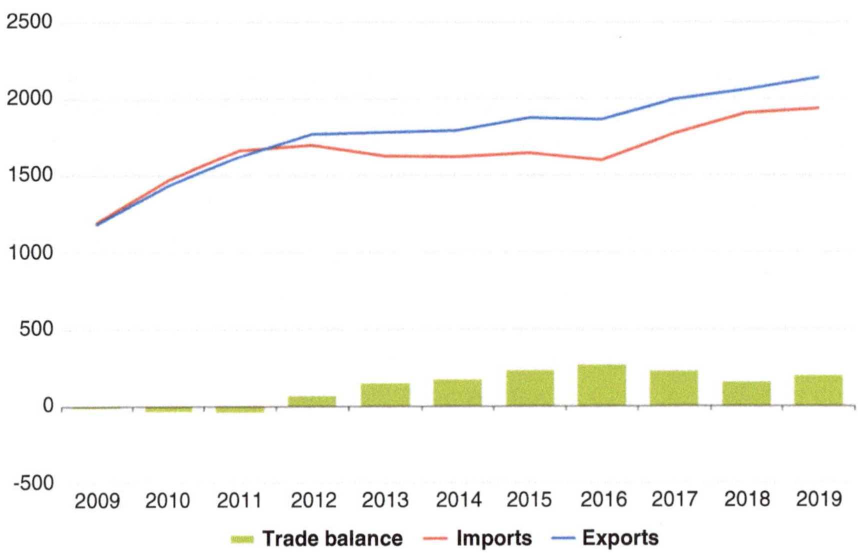

Fig. 2.1 Development of international trade in goods, EU-27, 2009–2019. Source: Eurostat (2020a)

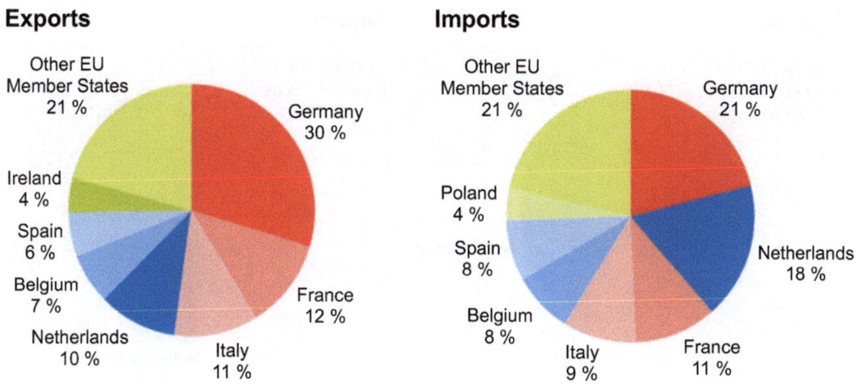

Fig. 2.2 Extra EU-27 trade in goods, 2019. Source: Eurostat (2020a)

same way as exports, rising from 1193 billion EUR in 2009 to 1666 billion EUR in 2011. Between 2011 and 2016, they remained relatively stable, but increased over the next three years from 1602 billion EUR to 1935 billion EUR in 2019 (Eurostat 2020a).

Of all the EU Member States, Germany took by far the highest share of non-EU-27 trade in 2019, contributing 29.6% to EU-27 exports to third countries and accounting for more than a fifth (21.0%) of EU-27 imports. The other three largest exporters, France (11.6%), Italy (11.0%), and the Netherlands (10.3%), were the only other EU Member States to account for the double-digit share of EU-27 exports. The Netherlands (17.5%), France (10.7%), and Italy (9.5%) followed Germany as the largest importers of goods from third countries in 2019. The relatively high share of the Netherlands can be explained, at least in part, by a significant amount of goods flowing into the EU via Rotterdam, the EU's leading seaport (Eurostat 2020a).

Trade in goods among the EU Member States (intra-EU trade) reached the value of 3061 billion EUR in terms of exports in 2019 (Fig. 2.2). This was 44% more than the value recorded for exports from the EU-27 to third countries, which totalled 2132 billion EUR (the trade outside the EU).

Intra-EU-27 trade—again measured by exports—increased by 1.5% between 2018 and 2019 across the EU-27. In terms of exports, double-digit growth between 2018 and 2019 was recorded only in Cyprus (16.4%), while the intra-EU exports decreased only in Sweden (−0.6%), Belgium (−0.3%), and in Slovakia (−0.1%). Only Croatia (7.8%) and Portugal (7.4%) had an increase in imports above 5%, while imports from Ireland (−3.9%), Belgium (−1.4%), Malta (−1.3%), and Sweden (−0.9%) reported loss values.

As in the case of the non-EU-27 trade, Germany was also the one EU Member State with the highest level of the intra-EU-27 trade in 2019, contributing 22.8% to exports of goods from the EU-27 to other Member States and 23.2% of EU-27 imports of goods from other Member States. The Netherlands (13.5%) was the only other Member State to contribute more than one tenth of intra-EU exports, again due to the Rotterdam effect, while France (12.5%) was the only other Member State,

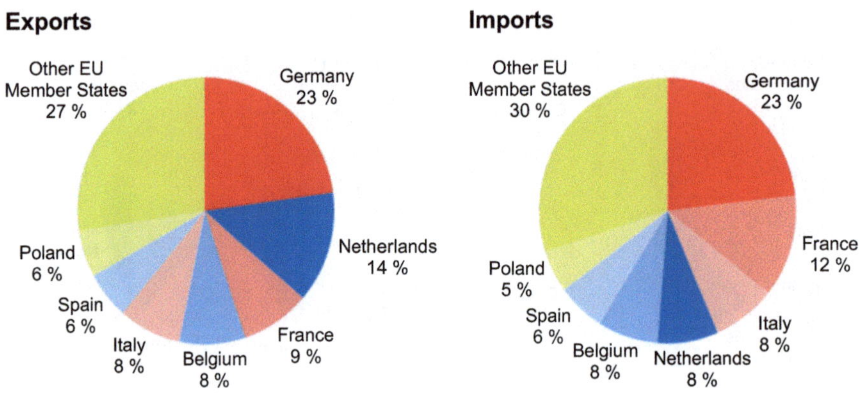

Fig. 2.3 Intra EU-27 trade in goods, 2019. Source: Eurostat (2020a)

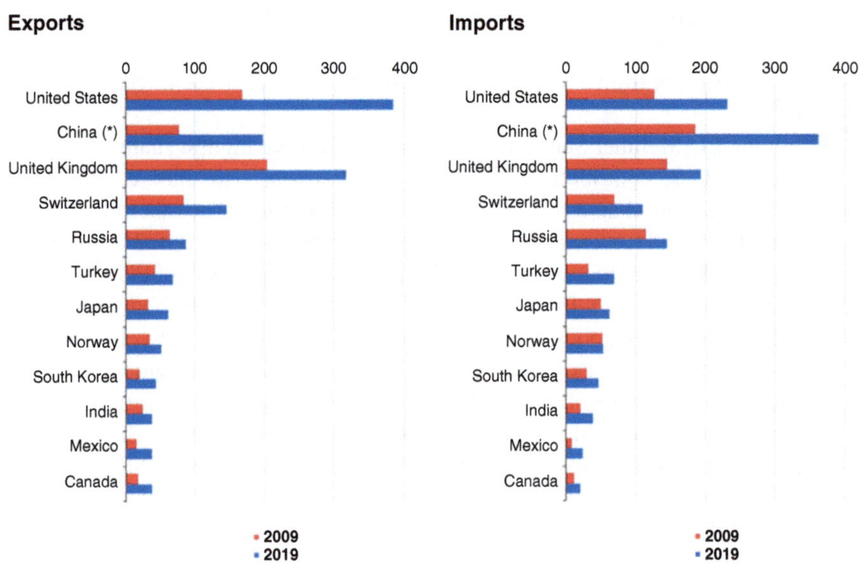

Fig. 2.4 Extra EU-27 trade in goods by main trading partners, 2009–2019. Source: Eurostat (2020a)

which accounted for more than one tenth of intra-EU imports (Eurostat 2020a) (Fig. 2.3).

The following Fig. 2.4 illustrates the trade in goods outside the EU-27 by major trading partners in 2009–2019.

As can be observed above, between 2009 and 2019, according to the main trading partners, the development of exports of goods from the EU-27 varied considerably. Of the main trading partners, the highest average annual growth was recorded for

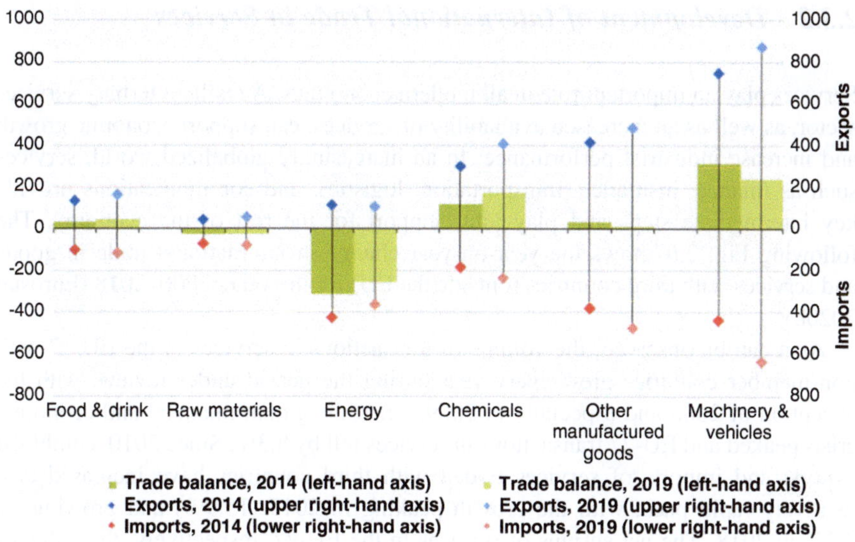

Fig. 2.5 Extra EU-27 trade by main products, 2014–2019. Source: Eurostat (2020a)

exports to China (9.9%) and Mexico (9.5%). The lowest growth was recorded for exports to Russia (3.3%) and Norway (4.1%).

On the import side, imports of goods from Mexico (10.5%) and Turkey (8.1%) had the highest average annual growth rate between 2009 and 2019. The lowest growth rates were recorded for imports from Norway (0.3%), Russia (2.3%), and Japan (2.2%) (Eurostat 2020a).

The following Fig. 2.5 illustrates the trade in goods by the main products.

Between 2014 and 2019, the value of exports from the non-EU-27 increased for most product groups listed, with the exception of energy exports which fell by 8.2%. The highest growth rate of exports was recorded for chemicals with an increase of 35.8%. An increase of more than 20% was also recorded for food and beverages (22.7%) and raw materials (20.1%).

On the import side, a similar pattern was observed with a large overall decrease in the level of energy imports from the non-EU countries (−15.2%) between 2014 and 2019. On the other hand, imports of machinery and transport equipment from the non-EU countries increased by 45.4%. Chemicals (28.6%) and other industrial products (24.1%) also recorded a high growth rate.

The EU-27 trade surplus with goods in the EU totalled 197.1 billion EUR in 2019 due to large trade surpluses in machinery and vehicles (237.1 billion EUR) and chemicals (171.6 billion EUR) and smaller surpluses in areas of food and beverages and other manufactured goods. They cannot be offset by a large energy trade deficit (−258.2 billion EUR) and a smaller raw material deficit (−26.1 billion EUR) (Eurostat 2020a).

2.3.2 Development of International Trade in Services

Services play an important role in all modern economies. A resilient tertiary services sector, as well as an increased availability of services, can support economic growth and increase industrial performance. In an increasingly globalized world, services such as finance, insurance, transportation, logistics, and communications provide key intermediate steps and play vital support for the rest of the economy. The following Fig. 2.6 shows the year-on-year change in international trade in goods and services with third countries (outside the EU) for the years 2000–2018 (Eurostat 2020b).

As it can be observed, the volume of transactions in services in the EU-27 with non-member countries grew every year during the period under review, with the exception of 2003 and especially in 2009, when the global financial and economic crisis peaked and EU-27 transactions in services fell by 8.3%. Since 2010, combined exports and imports of services traded with third countries have increased at a relatively rapid pace, with the growth peaking in 2015 (15.9%) and growing by 2.2% in 2018. The net surplus of services in the EU-27, respectively, the value of exports minus the value of imports, increased significantly between 2000 and 2018.

From 2013 to 2018, the exports of EU-27 services to non-member countries grew annually, from 695 billion EUR in 2013 to 969 billion EUR in 2018. On the other hand, imports of services from third countries increased from 575 billion EUR in 2013 to 824 billion EUR in 2018, leading to an increase in the trade surplus in services from 120 billion EUR to 145 billion EUR. This phenomenon is illustrated in the Fig. 2.7 (Eurostat 2020b).

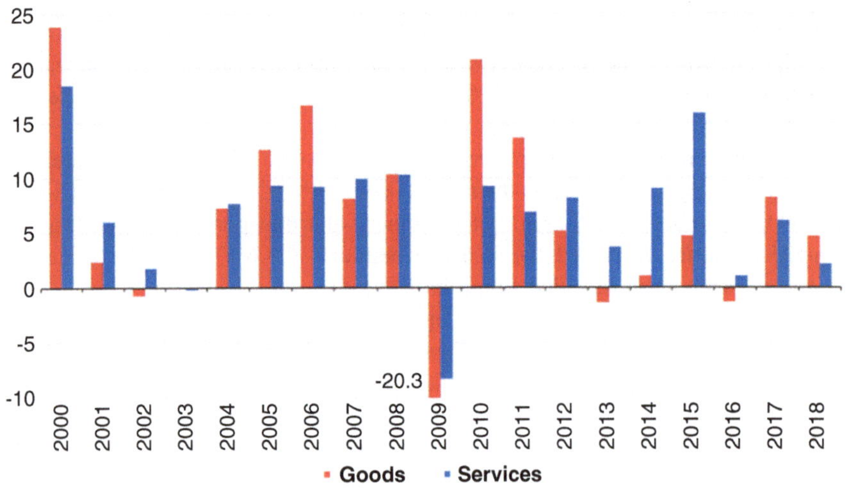

Fig. 2.6 Annual change in international trade with non-member countries (extra-EU), EU-27, 2000–2018. Source: Eurostat (2020b)

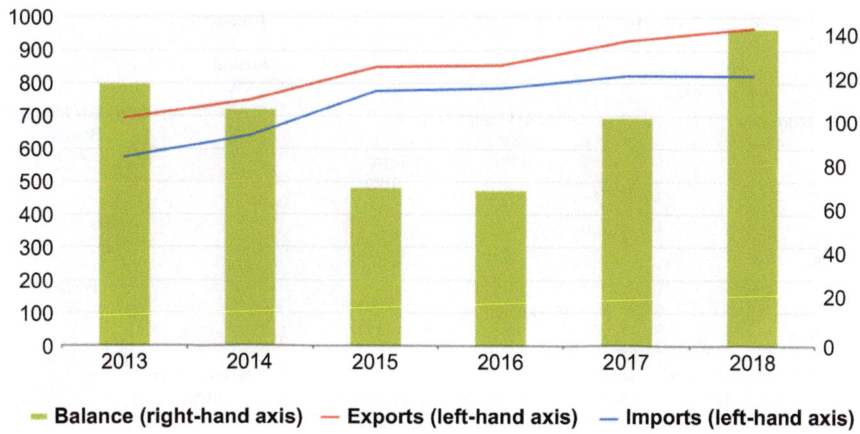

Fig. 2.7 International trade in services with non-member countries (extra-EU), EU-27, 2013–2018. Source: Eurostat (2020b)

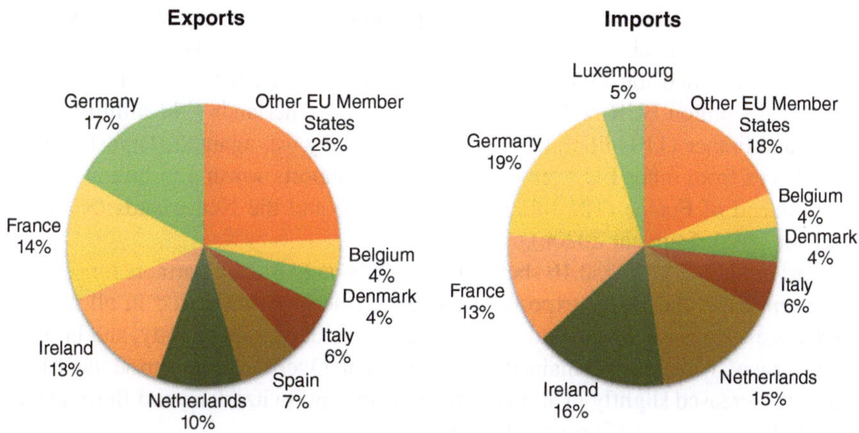

Fig. 2.8 Share of EU Member States in international trade in services with non-member countries (extra-EU), 2018. Source: Eurostat (2020b)

The data from 2018 shows that Germany was the EU Member State with the highest value of exports of services to third countries, with exports of 167 billion EUR corresponding to 17% of the total EU-27—see the Fig. 2.8. The next highest levels of exports to third countries were recorded in France (139 billion EUR or 14%), Ireland (127 billion EUR or 13%), and the Netherlands (99 billion EUR or 10%). Germany also had the highest level of imports of services from third countries totalling 156 billion EUR or 19% of the total EU-27. This was followed by countries such as Ireland (136 billion EUR or 16%), the Netherlands (120 billion EUR or 15%), and France (104 billion EUR or 13%) (Eurostat 2020b).

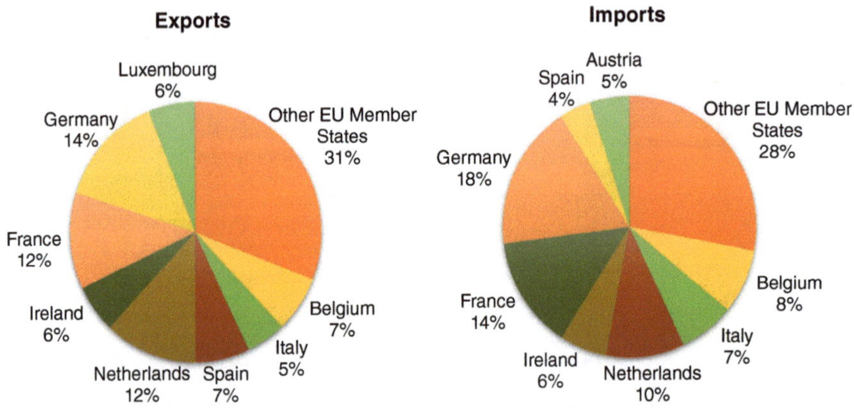

Fig. 2.9 Share of EU Member States in international trade in services within the EU (intra-eu), 2018. Source: Eurostat (2020b)

Subsequently, the following Fig. 2.9 presents an analysis of trade in services among the EU Member States (intra-EU trade)—rather than with third countries. Germany recorded the highest value of exports of services to other EU Member States (124 billion EUR or 14%), followed by the Netherlands (111 billion EUR or 12%) and France (110 billion EUR or 12%). Germany was again the largest importer of services from other EU Member States, with imports worth 155 billion EUR or 18%, ahead of France (121 billion EUR or 14%) and the Netherlands (88 billion EUR or 10%) (Eurostat 2020b).

Last but not least, Fig. 2.10 shows the EU-27's main trading partners for services. Between 2017 and 2018, exports of the EU-27 services increased in all its main partners except Switzerland and Russia, where they decreased slightly, and in Brazil and Norway, where they remained almost constant. Over the same period, the EU-27 imports increased slightly in all major partners except Switzerland and Bermuda, for which they decreased (Eurostat 2020b).

2.4 Chosen Leaders in the International Trade Sphere

The following text will be devoted to the three most important leaders in the field of international trade which show large trading volumes. Specifically, the USA and China, as the most important representatives of the world trade scene, will be analysed. Furthermore, attention will be paid to Germany, as the European player in the trade giants. The above-mentioned economies of these three countries together account for up to 1/3 of all world trade in goods and about ¼ of all trade in services. Each state comes from a different continent, which is clearly dominated by it as far as trade volumes are concerned. The following Fig. 2.11 shows the comparison of the sizes of the countries' economies and their development according to GDP.

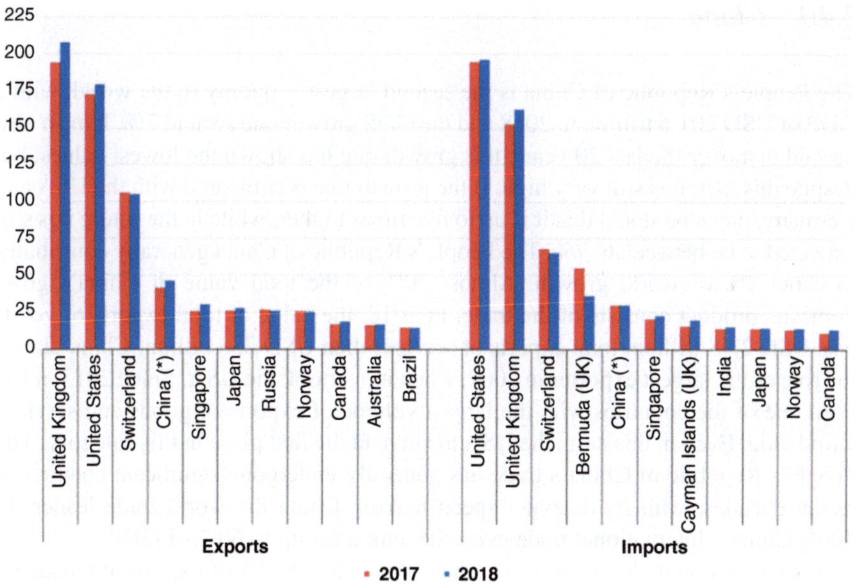

Fig. 2.10 Trade in services with non-member countries (extra-EU), main partners, EU-27, 2017 and 2018. Source: Eurostat (2020b)

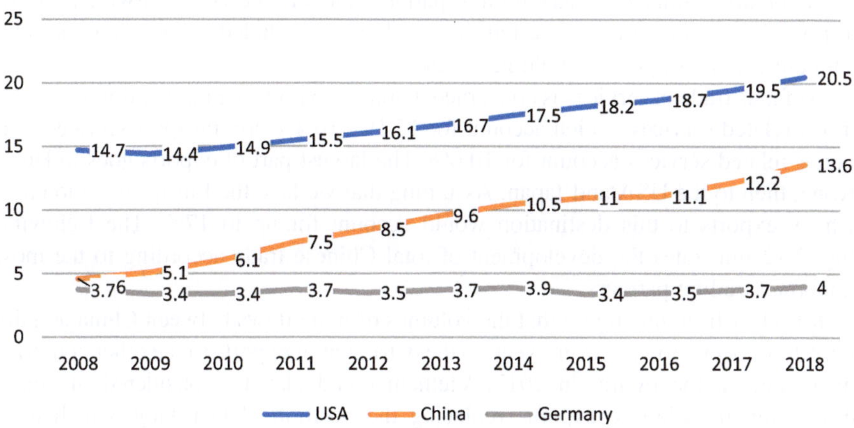

Fig. 2.11 Development of national economies according to GDP. Source: The World Bank (2019), own processing

In the following figures illustrated for the respective trade leaders, only data relating to the export indicator is given below, as it is the most appropriate reflection of the country's production.

2.4.1 China

The People's Republic of China is the second largest economy in the world, with a GDP of USD 201.6 trillion in 2018 and the GDP growth rate around 7%. It must also be said that over the last 20 years, this growth rate has shown the lowest values, but despite this fact, it is still very high. If the growth rate is compared with the USA and Germany, it can be stated that it is up to five times higher, while in the future it is still expected to be between 6–7%. The People's Republic of China generally contributes to about 2% of world growth. Almost 20% of the total value of China's gross domestic product consists of the trade. In 2018, the value of total exports of goods was USD 2.48 trillion, total exports of services then USD 233 billion. China played the role of the largest exporter in 2007, when it overtook the USA. Since 2013, it has been one of the countries with the largest volume of exports of goods and services worldwide. Even in this case, the USA again held the first place in this category. The People's Republic of China's trade has generally undergone significant changes in recent decades, with its dizzying speed making China the world trade leader. In 2006, China's international trade even accounted for up to 60% of GDP.

If we focus on trade in goods, it can be stated that 93.7% of exports are made up of manufacturing products, 3.6% are made up of agricultural products, and 2.4% are minerals and fuels. The most important exported products include broadcast equipment with 9.6 exports, as well as office equipment and computer components. Undoubtedly, China's primary trading partners include the USA, to which almost a fifth of all production is exported. If the EU were included in the statistics, total Chinese exports of goods would be 16.2%.

As far as trade in services is concerned, Chinese exports are mainly dominated by travel-related services, which account for 17.1%, 16.4% are transport services, and goods-related services account for 10.6%. The largest part of exports goes to Hong Kong, then to the USA and Japan. Assuming that we take the European Union as a whole, exports to this destination would account for up to 17%. The following Fig. 2.12 illustrates the development of total Chinese trade according to the most important trading partners.

It is clear from this figure that the volumes of trade flows between China and the USA have been growing every year, to the detriment of exports to the other countries mentioned in the figure. In 2017, Vietnam could also be considered the main destination for Chinese exports, replacing the position of Germany, which until then held the fifth place in the volume of exports (Zhang et al. 2018).

2.4.2 The United States

The USA is one of the countries with the second highest volume of foreign trade and is considered the largest economy in the world with a total GDP of USD 20.5 trillion. In 2018, this GDP increased by 2.85% and is expected to increase further by 2–3% in

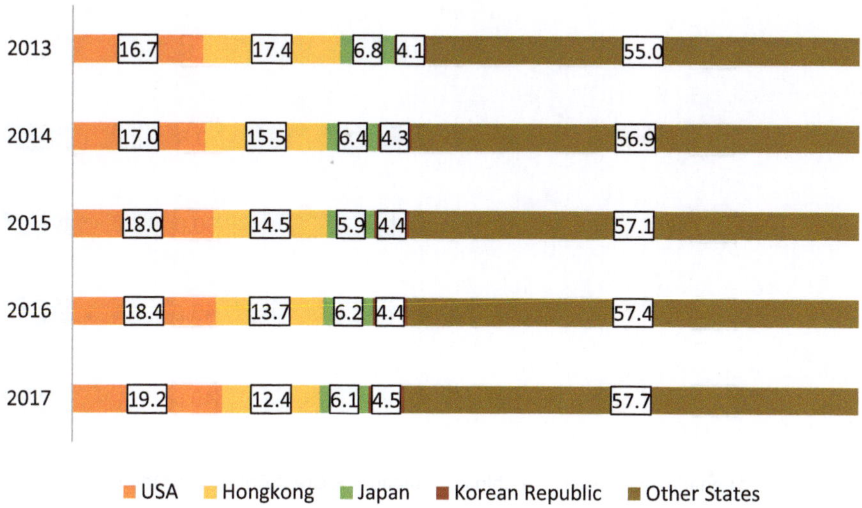

Fig. 2.12 Development of total exports of China's goods and services by trading partners. Source: The World Bank (2019), own processing

the future. The GDP of the USA of America accounts for approximately ¼ of the world's GDP. Overall, trade accounts for about 12% of US GDP, with 2/3 of this coming from trade in goods in the amount of USD 1.66 trillion and the rest consists of services worth USD 826 billion.

Based on the economic openness index, which assesses the state's ability to interact and reap the benefits of trade in foreign and domestic markets, the USA is the ninth most open country in the world. In this ranking, for comparison, Germany is right behind the USA, i.e. on tenth place, China then on place 51. If we focus on the structure of trade in goods, it can be stated that 75% consist of manufacturing products, 11% of agricultural production, and 7.8% are minerals and fuels. The main export products include refined oil, aircraft, automobiles, space rockets, and helicopters. For several decades, the USA has been a leader in trade in services, with world exports reaching around 15%. The most important part includes services related to travelling occupying about 26.7%, transport services total 11.4%, and 3.4% of goods-related services. The main importers of American services are Canada and China. If we took the European Union as one economy, it would be in first place with 31.4% (Nwoke 2020). The following Fig. 2.13 shows, for example, the development of total exports of US goods and services. These statistics do not include the European Union, which would clearly rank first among the destinations, as the shares after the breakdown by the individual countries are less significant.

Based on the figure above, it can be stated that the US trade is relatively stable, except for small shifts from exports to Canada and Mexico, which change to exports to the EU. Nwoke (2020) states that the US keeps the closest trade relations with the geographically closest countries. Interestingly, although Israel is not culturally or geographically related to the USA, it plays a very important role in its international

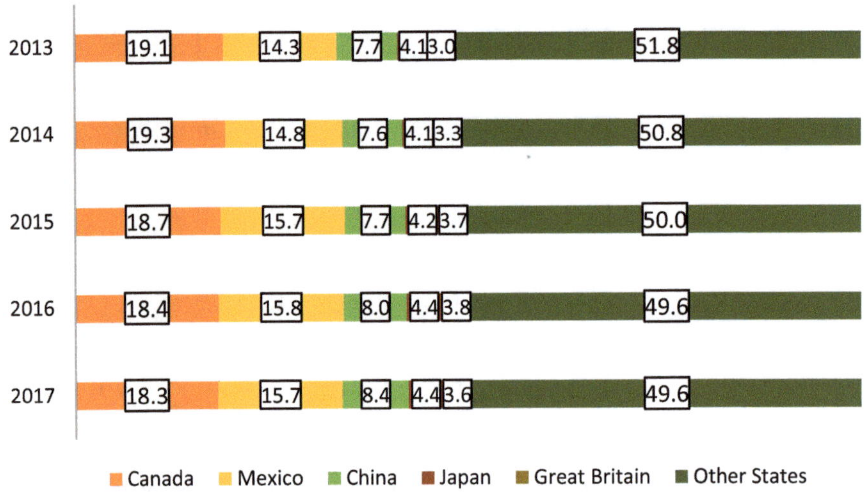

Fig. 2.13 Development of total exports of US goods and services by trading partners. Source: WITS (2019), own processing

trade. This fact can be explained from the historical point of view, when the USA was one of the first countries to recognize Israel as a state in 1948, but also from the political point of view, as Israel is currently one of the USA's most reliable partners in the Middle East.

The passionate debate that was provoked during the negotiations on TTIP (Transatlantic Trade and Investment Partnership) is also worth mentioning. TTIP was intended to be a free trade agreement between the EU and the US. Its essence was to reduce tariff and non-tariff barriers on both sides. Undoubtedly, this would be the largest bilateral agreement in the world, as these two countries together represent about 45% of the world trade. However, the agreement was criticized mainly by the EU member states which were afraid of the import of genetically modified food, chlorinated meat from farms, or banned pesticides. Although the conditions that would allow this were in fact never determined, the wave of resentment was very intense. After a number of negotiations, however, the agreement did not reach a consensus and was withdrawn, which many countries praised as a result.

2.4.3 Germany

The Federal Republic of Germany is one of the largest economies in Europe and has a strong influence on its neighbouring states. Together with Italy, Spain, and France, it is one of the main powerhouses of the EU countries. According to the data from 2018, the German GDP was USD 3.99 trillion, with 30% of international trade in goods and services. Of all exports, 80% are goods with a volume of 1560 billion; the

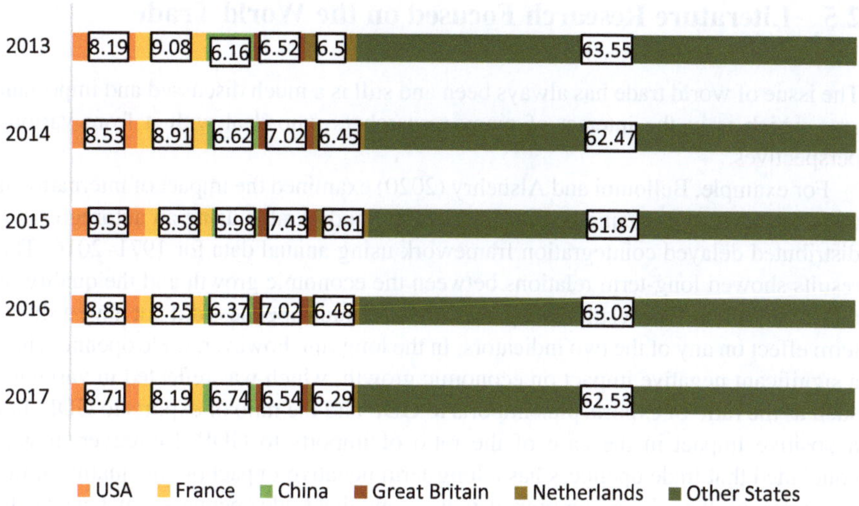

Fig. 2.14 Development of total exports of goods and services of Germany by trading partners. Source: WITS (2019), own processing

remaining 20% are services with a volume of USD 342 billion. 86.9% of exported goods represent products of the manufacturing industry, 6.6% of agricultural products, and 4.2% of minerals and fuels. In the case of focusing on specific products, it can be stated that 12% of exports are cars, about 5% automotive parts, and 4% belong to packaged drugs. The most well-known car groups include, for example, Volkswagen, Mercedes, and BMW. The Federal Republic of Germany exports almost 60% of the total goods produced to the EU, but from the point of view of individual states, the role of the closest trading partner is occupied by the USA. In the case of trade in services, 20% of services are transport services, 13.3% are travel services, and 5.4% are goods-related services. The remaining part of the services consists mainly of financial, business, or security services. More than half of them are exported to the nearest neighbouring states within the EU and then to Switzerland and the USA (Dziubanovska 2019). The following Fig. 2.14 shows the development of the total trade volume in goods and services of Germany by business partners.

As can be observed from the figure above, there is no predominant trade partner for Germany as it is the case for China and the USA. For this reason, the position of individual destinations changes only minimally over the years. In 2017, German trade with the United Kingdom weakened due to the withdrawal of the United Kingdom from the EU (Brexit) in 2016. This fact caused the United Kingdom to fall by two places in the list of Germany's most important trading partners in 2018. From the point of view of the intensity of foreign trade, it can be stated that, for example, Germany's trade with the USA with which it achieves the largest bilateral trade flows is below average. On the other hand, despite all expectations, the trade intensity increases with a country's proximity, which is influenced also by the common membership in the EU (Dziubanovska 2019).

2.5 Literature Research Focused on the World Trade

The issue of world trade has always been and still is a much discussed and important area which is in the interest of many researchers who deal with it from various perspectives.

For example, Belloumi and Alshehry (2020) examined the impact of international trade openness on sustainable development in Saudi Arabia using an autoregressive distributed delayed cointegration framework using annual data for 1971–2016. The results showed long-term relations between the economic growth and the quality of the environment. The results also proved that the trade openness did not have a short-term effect on any of the two indicators. In the long run, however, trade openness had a significant negative impact on economic growth, which was reflected in variables such as the ratio of exports plus imports to GDP and the ratio of exports to GDP, but a positive impact in the case of the ratio of imports to GDP. Moreover, it was concluded that trade openness has a long-term negative impact on the quality of the environment. It has been comprehensively found that trade openness may have led to a deterioration of sustainable development in Saudi Arabia over the last 14 years. Gil-Pareja et al. (2017) examined again to what extent the degree of economic development of a country affects the impact of banking crises on the international trade. For these purposes, the authors estimated the gravitational model of trade through a sample of 13 countries for the period 1975–2012. Their research showed that middle-income countries were most negatively affected. Furthermore, the financial turmoil has been proved to have a smaller impact on bilateral trade flows between high-income countries and, more specifically, between low-income countries. This is mainly due to the level of financial development, the enforcement of contracts, and the extent of the use of bank loans in international trade.

Based on the integration of theories from macromarketing, economics, and sociology, Mullen et al. (2009) proposed a conceptual model that was able to assess the impacts of international trade and economic development on physical quality of life (PQOL), individual freedom, and the environment (carbon dioxide [CO_2] emissions and environmental impact). The results of the survey showed that the international trade is linked to economic growth, which results in an increase in the well-being of people and their environment, but also has a detrimental effect on global warming as it increases CO_2 emissions. Individuals are associated with lower CO_2 emissions and improved environmental performance, and these findings are particularly important for public policy makers, marketing academics, and practitioners.

Fu (2011) states that due to the development of Chinese foreign trade, the commodity structure of imports and exports has changed. Based on this fact, the author used Markov's model to analyse in detail the changing rules of the Chinese structure of imports and exports and predicted the commodity structure of imports and exports and its final distribution in 2012–2020. The results of the research showed that there are three main categories of the total Chinese export: means of transport, miscellaneous manufactured articles, and industrial goods classified according to raw materials, with the total share in total exports exceeding 90%. As far as total Chinese imports are concerned, its main categories included machinery and transport equipment, non-food raw materials and manufactured goods classified by raw materials and chemicals and related products. Machová and Mareček (2020) dealt with the import of the People's Republic of China to the Czech Republic, specifically examining the effects of the imposed sanctions on the international trade between the PRC and the USA. Based on the analysis of data on the development of imports and exports between the PRC and the USA, and the PRC and the Czech Republic, the authors did not find any negative effects of the imposed sanctions on imports from the PRC to the Czech Republic. Jawaid and Waheed (2017) examined the relationship between the international trade and the human development. The authors specifically addressed the impact of aggregate and disaggregated trade on human development in Pakistan through data from annual time series for the period 1980–2013. A cointegration test was performed to verify the long-term relationship between human development and trade. A sensitivity analysis confirms that initial results are robust. Causality analysis has also been done for the causal relationship between international trade and human development.

Based on current evidence, it can be stated that many methods and models have been used for the international trade research. In recent years, however, new techniques that have to do with artificial intelligence and that surpass traditional methods have come to the forefront of interest. We are talking about machine learning, which also includes artificial neural networks (ANN) suitable for the needs of various predictions. For example, Ozbek et al. (2011) focused on predicting the export of denim trousers from Turkey through artificial neural networks and an autoregressive integrated moving average model. The results of their research showed that ANN models are more successful than ARIMA models. Through ANN, Vochozka and Rowland (2020) specifically predicted the trade balance between the Czech Republic and the People's Republic of China with the help of multilayer perceptron networks (MLP) and radial basis function networks (RBF). The authors also took into account seasonal fluctuations. The results of their survey showed that MLP networks performed better. Based on monthly data from the years 2000–2018, Krulický and Brabenec (2020) again compared the possibilities of predicting the Czech Republic's exports to the PRC through a regression analysis and ANN. The results showed that ANNs were evaluated as more useful for prediction. Zhang et al. (2019) investigated whether it is better to use econometric models or artificial neural networks (ANN) to predict international trade. The authors concluded that through time series data, economic prediction models produced better predictions compared to ANN algorithms. It should be noted, however, that ANN algorithms produced fewer errors and showed a higher degree of agreement than econometric models using long-term data. The best predictions were achieved by the generalizing model of autoregressive heteroskedasticity and the model of back propagation of LV. In their research, Bartl and Krummaker (2020) examined the ability to accurately predict export credit financing requirements for four machine learning techniques. Specifically, it was the technique of random forests (RF), probabilistic neural networks (PNN), neural networks (NN), and decision trees (DT). Based on their results, it was found that although all of the above-mentioned techniques performed well, the decision tree technique converted its verification performance into the test most reliably. The prediction of export was also addressed by Li et al. (2008). Specifically, the authors examined the prediction of Taiwanese polyester fibre exports using teaching methods with small data sets. For this purpose, they used the GIKDE (General Intervalized Kerned Density Estimator) methodology, which is considered to be a new method used to predict small data sets of future exports. This method provides a more accurate estimate that can help managers create plans for products, markets, and capacities. The aim of Narayan's (2006) paper was to examine the relationship between China's trade balance and the real exchange rate vis-à-vis the USA. Using a borderline testing approach to cointegration, the author proved that China's trade balance and the real exchange rate vis-à-vis the US are cointegrating. Furthermore, with the help of the autoregressive model of distributed delays, he came to the conclusion that the devaluation of the Chinese RMB in the short and long term improves the trade balance. The effort of Rowland et al. (2019) again consisted in comparing the accuracy of the alignment of time series, for example, the trade balance of the Czech Republic and the PRC, with the help of regression analysis and neural networks. Based on the results, the authors came to the conclusion that the best of the linear regression for this purpose appears to be the LOWESS curve. Out of the neural networks, the best choice is the RBF 1-24-1 network.

No less interesting is Zhang's research (2016). He used six different input variables and the total export of China as the output variable to create the BP neural network, which could be used to predict the country's total exports. In order to test the accuracy of the BP model, the Nash–Sutcliffe coefficient of the model efficiency factor (NSC) was introduced, after which the model was found to have a high accuracy of 99%.

References

Bartl M, Krummaker S (2020) Prediction of claims in export credit finance: a comparison of four machine learning techniques. Risks 8(1):2–27

Belloumi M, Alshehry A (2020) The impact of international trade on sustainable development in Saudi Arabia. Sutainability 12(3):5421

Dorobăț CE (2015) A brief history of international trade thought: from pre-doctrinal contributions to the 21st century heterodox international economics. J Philos Econ: Reflect Econ Soc Issues VIII(2):106–137

Dziubanovska N (2019) Multifactor models for studying the EU countries' international trade. Econ Ann-XXI 175(1–2):29–34

Eurostat (2020a) International trade in goods. Dostupné z. https://ec.europa.eu/eurostat/statistics-explained/index.php?title=International_trade_in_goods

Eurostat (2020b) International trade - services. Dostupné z. https://ec.europa.eu/eurostat/statistics-explained/index.php?title=International_trade_in_services

Fu H (2011) The prediction of China's imports and exports structure based on Markov model. In: Recent advance in statistics application and related areas, pts 1 and 2, pp 593–597

Fürst R, Pleschová G (2010) Czech and Slovak relations with China: contenders for China's favour. Eur Asia Stud 62(8):1363–1381

Gil-Pareja S, Liorca-Vivero R, Martinez-Serrano JA (2017) Does the degree of development matter in the impact of banking crises on international trade? Rev Dev Econ 21(3):829–848

Havrlant D, Husek R (2011) Models of factors driving the Czech export. Prague Econ Pap 20(3): 195–215

Hesselberg Y (2007) Eli Heckscher, international trade and economic history. Scand Econ Hist Rev 55(3):309–311

Irwin DA (2001) A brief history of international trade policy. The Library of Economics and Liberty. https://www.econlib.org/library/Columns/Irwintrade.html

Jawaid ST, Waheed A (2017) Contribution of international trade in human development od Pakistan. Glob Bus Rev 18(5):1155–1177

Krugman PR, Obstfeld M, Melitz M (2012) International economics: theory and policy. Prentice Hall, New Jersey. isbn:978-0-13-214665-4

Krulický T, Brabenec T (2020) Comparison of neural networks and regression time series in predicting export from Czech Republic into People's Republic of China. In: Paper presented at Innovative Economic Symposium 2019 – Potential of Eurasian Economic Union (IES2019)

Kushnruk V, Ivanenko T (2017) Analysis of trends and prospects for development of export and import of goods and services by enterprises of Ukraine at the regional level. Balt J Econ Stud 3(5):252–259

Li D, Yeh C, Li Z (2008) A case study: the prediction of Taiwan's export of polyester fiber using small-data-set learning methods. Expert Syst Appl 34(3):1983–1994

Machová M, Mareček J (2020) Machine learning forecasting of CR import from PRC in context of mutual PRC and USA sanctions. SHS web of conferences: innovative economic symposium – potential of Eurasian Economic Union (IES) 73. ISBN: 978-2-7598-9094-1

Mullen MR, Doney PM, Ben Mrad S, Sheng SY (2009) Effects of international trade and economic development on quality of life. J Makromarketing 29(3):244–258

Narayan PK (2006) Examining the relationship between trade balance and exchange rate: the case of China's trade with the USA. Appl Econ Lett 13(8):507–510

Nwoke (2020) Imposition of trade tariffs by the USA on China: implications for the WTO and international trade law. J Int Trade Law Policy 19(2):69–84

Ozbek A, Akalin M, Topuz V, Sennaroglu B (2011) Prediction of Turkey's Denim trousers export using artificial neural networks and the autoregressive integrated moving average model. Fibres Text East Eur 19(3):10–16

Pacheco-Lopez P (2005) The effect of trade liberalization on exports, imports, the balance of trade, and growth: the case of Mexico. J Post Keynes Econ 27(4):595–619

Rowland Z, Suler P, Vochozka M (2019) Comparison of neural network and regression time series in estimating the Czech Republic and China trade balance. In: Innovative economic symposium 2018 - milestones and trends of world economy (IES2018), 61

Seyoum B (2014) Export-import theory, practices, and procedures, 3rd edn. Routledge, New York. isbn:978-0-415-81837-7

Shoiw MT (2013) Trade flows between Czech Republic and East Asia. Rev Econ Perspect 13(3): 146–158

Vochozka M, Rowland Z (2020) Forecasting trade balance of Czech Republic and People's Republic of China in equalizing time series and considering seasonal fluctuations. In: Paper presented at Innovative Economic Symposium 2019 – Potential of Eurasian Economic Union (IES2019)

WITS – World Integrated Trade Solution (2019) World trade statistics: exports, imports, products, Tariffs, GDP and related development indicator. https://wits.worldbank.org/CountryProfile/en/WLD

World Bank (2019) Data 2019. https://data.worldbank.org/
Zhang Q (2016) Prediction on China's merchandise exports based on BP neural network associated with sensitivity analysis. In: Modern computer science and applications, pp 351–356
Zhang HS, Meng B, Ma SZ (2018) Determinants of China's bilateral trade balance in global value chaos. J Int Trade Econ Dev 27(5):463–485
Zhang X, Xue T, Stanley HE (2019) Comparison of econometric models and artificial neural networks algorithms for the prediction of Baltic dry index. IEEE Access 7:1647–1657

Chapter 3
Development of the World Trade in the Context of the COVID-19 Pandemics

Nowadays, the world's population is facing a number of unprecedented situations arising from the COVID-19 pandemic recognized worldwide by the World Health Organization (WHO) on 11th March 2020. Since it was first detected in Wuhan, China, on 17th November 2019, it has expanded to a total of 213 countries and territories (Khanthavit 2020). According to Vidiya and Prabheesh (2020), the disease had a stressful impact, especially on the world economy. World GDP and world trade have fallen sharply recently. The authors further state that the pandemic originated in China, but its spreading already affects the whole world. As of 16th May 2020, more than 300,000 deaths worldwide have been reported on the WHO website. In connection with this fact, a number of countries have begun to slow down further spreading of COVID-19 by introducing certain restrictions both for the population and the business. Several states have even declared an entire city or even the whole country to be locked down, and in some countries, foreigners have been banned from entering. It is therefore quite logical that such restrictions have seriously damaged the world economy. The Chinese economy serves as an example, having fell by 6.8% in the first quarter of 2020. This decline is the first decline since 1992 when China first published its GDP data.

Many economists and experts have sought to respond to the pandemic as quickly as possible and to examine its economic implications and its impact on international trade (Hayakawa and Mukunoki 2020). Mention may be made, for example, of Baldwin and Tomiura (2020). These include in particular the simulation of results and the conceptual framework for the economic impacts of COVID-19. The Centre for Economic Policy Research has again launched an online review of COVID-19 studies entitled "COVID-19 Economics: Vetted and Real-Time Papers". The content of this review is a formal investigation into the various impacts of COVID-19, including finance, human mobility and, last but not least, gender equality (Obayelu et al. 2020).

J. Horák et al., *Development of World Trade in the Context of the COVID-19 Pandemic*, Contributions to Economics,
https://doi.org/10.1007/978-3-031-27257-8_3

3.1 International Trade in the COVID-19 Era: Theoretical Viewpoint

Worldwide trade allows countries to access goods and services that are not available on the domestic market or to provide goods or services that are produced in large quantities on the domestic market. As already mentioned, this trade has been significantly affected by the COVID-19 pandemic and will undoubtedly remain afflicted in the future as well. Vidiya and Prabheesh (2020) even consider the COVID-19 pandemic to be the most serious global economic crisis since the one that troubled the world in the 1930s. For most countries, the scope for complacency is somewhat limited as a result of the disease as the whole world faces a downturn—there is a slowdown in trade and economic growth, global imbalances grow, and weakening financial markets lead to a freeze of the monetary system. For many developing countries, for example, the emergence of COVID-19 has been associated with adverse conditions of trade shocks, reduced remittances and foreign direct investment (FDI) flows, increased debt vulnerability and capital flight. According to Obayelu et al. (2020), the immediate effect of an ongoing pandemic can be seen, for example, in poverty, employment rate, service-based enterprises, and the informal economy. Manufacturers and retailers receive fewer orders and are subsequently forced to limit their production and the banking sector facing stressed loans is also affected. Reduced demand on global markets also affects a number of different sectors, such as the oil industry. However, tourism, gastronomy, and aviation suffer from the consequences the most due to restrictions in various countries and limited public movement. Aydin and Ari (2020) consider the power industry to be the most critical sector affected by COVID-19, specifically the sector focused on oil production. Since the recognition of COVID-19 as a global pandemic, the global demand for oil has begun to decline. The authors also state that, for example, in the first quarter of 2020, oil consumption numbered 94.4 million barrels per day on average, which is 5.6 million barrels less than in the previous year.

We can say that all economic activities are very important in terms of international trade, with aggregate growth in trade volumes being positively correlated with GDP growth. As it can be seen in Fig. 3.1, according to the World Bank's projection (2020), the world Gross Domestic Product was expected to decline significantly in 2020 due to COVID-19.

The original assumption was that advanced economies will decline by 7% in 2020 while in emerging economies, the decline will represent 2.5%. Similarly, the global trade was expected to decline by more than 13% in 2020, which is slightly more than in World War II, as Fig. 3.2 shows.

From the theoretical point of view, it was relatively clear that COVID-19 will have an impact on international trade in various ways. On this account, it can be stated that the higher burden of COVID-19 in the exporting countries logically reduces the volume of production, which results in a reduced supply for export. Exports will also be reduced, especially in industries and countries where remote work (home office) is less feasible. The effect of the COVID-19 burden in importing

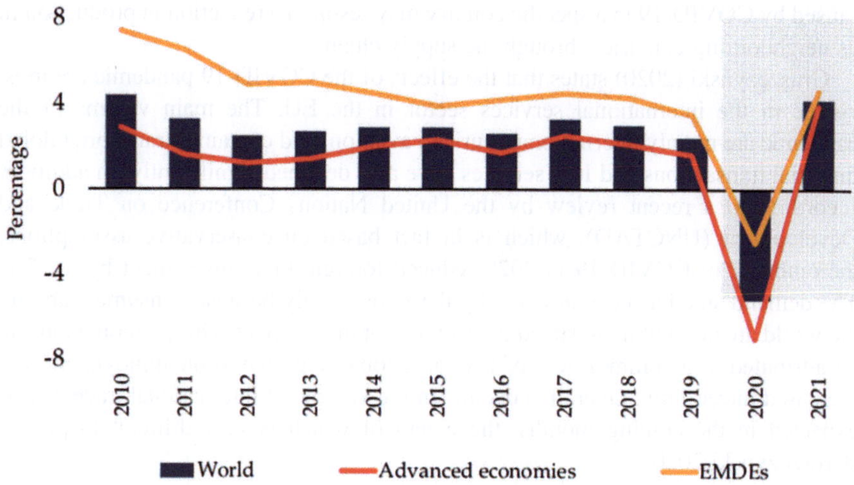

Fig. 3.1 Global GDP growth trends. Source: World Bank (2020)

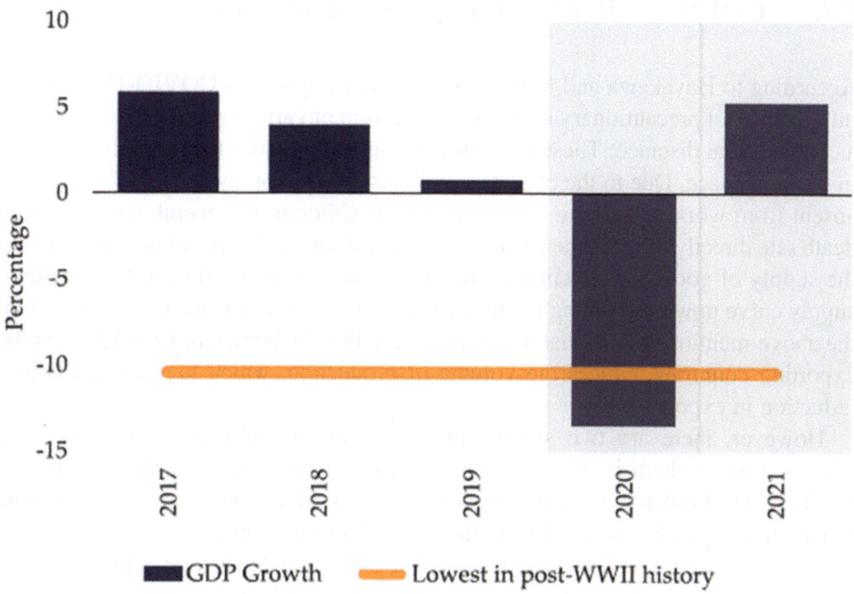

Fig. 3.2 Global trade growth trends. Source: World Bank (2020)

countries lies mainly in reduced aggregate demand in these countries. Reduced earnings and retail trade will lead to lower demand. The international trade of one particular country can also be affected by the burden of COVID-19 in its neighbouring countries. For example, one country's reduced exports create export opportunities for its neighbours. On the other hand, negative production shocks caused by COVID-19 in a specific country may result in a reduction in production in its neighbouring countries through the supply chain.

Gruszczynski (2020) states that the effects of the COVID-19 pandemic are most visible in the international services sector in the EU. The main victims of the pandemic are mainly international tourism, aviation, and container transport. Global financial transactions and ICT services have also declined significantly. In addition, according to a recent review by the United Nations Conference on Trade and Development (UNCTAD), which is in fact based on conservative assumptions, the outbreak of COVID-19 in 2020 reduced foreign direct investment by 5–15%. The demand side has been affected by the virus mainly because consumers around the world are not willing to spend their money at the moment. This phenomenon can be attributed to a common fear of loss of income (e.g. due to unemployment) and increased uncertainty. Overall, a decline in the volume of international trade can be expected in the coming months, the extent of which is very difficult to predict (Gruszczynski 2020).

3.1.1 COVID-19 Burden in Exporting Countries

According to Hayakawa and Mukunoki (2020), the spread of COVID-19 led to the introduction of precautionary measures in the form of various restrictions and thus to a certain social distance. These measures undoubtedly reduce the mobility of people in the workplace. Due to the closure of schools, many employees were forced to be absent from work in order to take care of their children. In general, the increasing death rate directly reduces the workforce. These changes also result in a reduction in the supply of goods, a reduction in the price elasticity, and a shift in the country's supply curve upwards leading to an increase in its steepness as well. It follows from the above-mentioned facts that it is only natural that the burden of COVID-19 in the exporting countries reduces the volume of production, which logically leads to a reduction in export supply.

However, there are two significant criteria in determining the net effect on exports. One of them is, for example, the reduced domestic demand for exported products. The burden of COVID-19 can therefore result not only in a reduction in the production of goods, but also in a reduction in domestic demand for these particular goods. If the decline in domestic demand is greater than the decline in production, a net increase in exports can be achieved by redirecting "unused" products from the domestic market to the export market. In other words, the ratio of the relative volume of production to the size of domestic demand plays a key role in determining the net effect on exports.

The second criterion is the impact of home office work regimen on work productivity. The undeniable fact is that a number of countries have tried to maintain their economic activity precisely through the implementation of remote work from home. If these systems increase productivity or efficiency, export may have an increasing tendency. On the other hand, however, there may be a rapid reduction in the volume of production in countries or industry branches where home office regimen is less feasible. For example, it is very difficult to carry out these operations in labour-intensive industries requiring personal presence of the employees. This also applies for countries with a less developed IT infrastructure. It follows from the above-mentioned facts that there is a strong likelihood of an export decrease in these sectors and countries due to reduced productivity.

3.1.2 COVID-19 Burden in Importing Countries

Hayakawa and Mukunoki (2020) state that as far as the impact of the COVID-19 burden on the trade of importing countries is concerned, it will come mainly from reduced aggregate demand in these countries. Strict restrictions at the national level will result in a reduction in entrepreneurs' earnings, and if the government does not provide sufficient compensations for their losses, aggregate demand will logically fall. Despite the fact that many people manage to maintain their earnings, the fear of infection reduces their visits to retail stores or supermarkets, and consequently, the demand decreases. As stated by Eaton et al. (2016) examining the impact of the global recession on trade in 2008–2009, negative demand shocks often reduce expenditures on consumer durables more than expenditures on non-durable goods. Baldwin and Tomiura (2020) explain this phenomenon by stating that purchases of durable goods can often be postponed. On the other hand, uncertainty about the future or "panic purchases" may lead to an increase in demand for consumer durables. Among other things, there may be an increase in demand for hygiene products such as disinfectants, face masks, or other products preventing the COVID-19 infection.

3.1.3 COVID-19 Burden in Neighbouring Countries

The international trade of one country may also be affected by the COVID-19 burden in its neighbouring countries and consequently be impacted in numerous ways. First, there can be a positive influence. This means that reduced exports of some countries caused by COVID-19 may create export opportunities for their neighbouring countries, as importing countries can change their suppliers. This situation is often called the substitution effect. Furthermore, reduced imports in neighbouring countries affected by the pandemic may lower market prices due to lower demand levels. This reduction in trade prices on international markets may increase imports to other countries. However, the impact of the pandemic can also be negative and is often referred to as the contagion effect. Negative production shocks in a particular country caused by COVID-19 can result in reduced production in other countries through the supply chain (Hayakawa and Mukunoki 2020). Boehm et al. (2019), whose research proved that international trade and foreign direct investment play a greater role in transferring shocks to other countries' domestic production, as the substitute flexibility of imported intermediate products and domestic factors is lower, agree with this statement. Also, Halpern et al. (2015) state that the decline in imported inputs leads to a decline in producers' productivity. The findings of Blaum et al. (2018) show that reduced imported inputs increase product prices due to the interconnection of outputs and inputs. Based on the above-mentioned, it can be stated that a country's exports are declining if they rely only on materials or products imported from neighbouring countries suffering from COVID-19.

3.2 International Trade Impacted by COVID-19 in Numbers

As already mentioned, in order to prevent the further spreading of the COVID-19 pandemic, countries all around the world have been forced to introduce a number of restrictive measures. The following figure below shows the data from March 2020 and their significant impact on the international trade. In March 2020, compared to January 2020, total seasonally adjusted trade outside the EU (imports + exports) decreased from 252 billion EUR to 228 billion EUR.

As it can be seen from Fig. 3.3, a decrease in exports was recorded for all five key trading partners with the following values: Switzerland (−8.5%), China (−7.1%), Russia (−6.8%). The United Kingdom (−6.2%), and the USA. In the case of imports from these partners, there was a decrease in the values for Switzerland (−1.2%), the

Fig. 3.3 Development of European imports and exports of goods with five main trade partners. Source: Eurostat (2020a)

USA (−2.6%), Russia (−8.2%), China (−10.9%), and The United Kingdom (−17.0%).

Naturally, this decline was also reflected in the total trade volume, with the largest declines for The United Kingdom (−10.4%) and China (−9.6%), while smaller reductions were recorded for trade with the USA (−3.6%), Switzerland (−5.3%), and Russia (−7.6%). Of the EU's 11 main trading partners, Turkey (−13.0%), India (−11.8%), and Norway (−11.7%) saw the largest decline in the total trade volume, while the trade with South Korea fell by only 1.9%. In March 2020, the trade balance increased with eight of the EU main partners. Turkey, the USA, and Switzerland showed declines in the trade balance (see Fig. 3.4).

It should also be noted that the impact of the COVID-19 pandemic differed widely as far as different groups of products are concerned (see Fig. 3.5).

The figure shows that in the case of exports outside the EU, the largest decreases in absolute terms compared to January were recorded for machinery and vehicles (−14 billion EUR, −20%) and for the group of processed goods (−7 billion EUR, −16%). In relative terms, there was the largest decrease in energy (−2 billion EUR, −25%). During this period, despite a general decline, exports of chemicals increased (+4 billion EUR, + 4%). Imports developed in a similar way, i.e. exports of machinery and vehicles (−8 billion EUR, −15%) and other processed goods (−7 billion EUR, −16%) fell again. The largest decrease in relative and absolute terms was recorded for products' energy (−9 billion EUR, −31%).

Figure 3.6 further shows the development of total trade and the trade balance.

As it can be seen, the total trade volume decreased for all products except for chemicals, with the largest decreases for machinery and vehicles, other industrial goods and energy. Logically, these changes also had an impact on the trade balance in various ways. For example, the increase in the trade with chemicals had a positive effect on its trade balance. On the contrary, the decline in the total trade volume in machinery and vehicles had a negative effect on the trade balance, while the energy sector again had a positive effect. With regard to other industrial products, the decline in total trade between exports and imports was almost evenly balanced. For this reason, there was not much change in the trade balance (Eurostat 2020b).

The fact that the COVID-19 pandemic has negatively affected international trade with goods is unquestionable, but there are also notable exceptions on which the pandemic has had the exactly opposite effect. We are mainly talking about goods used in direct connection with this pandemic. These are sterilization products including disinfectants, protective clothing, medical vehicles and furniture, diagnostic test equipment, various types of medical devices, oxygen equipment and medical consumables or other so-called COVID-19 related products (see Fig. 3.7).

The development of individual products related to COVID-19 can be observed according to the respective categories illustrated by Fig. 3.8.

The figure shows that, compared to March 2019, imports of COVID-19-related products outside the EU increased by 2% in March 2020. On the contrary, the trade in other similar product branches decreased by 5%. Over the same period, the exports of non-EU COVID-19 related products increased by 18%, while exports of other similar products from non-EU countries decreased by 6%.

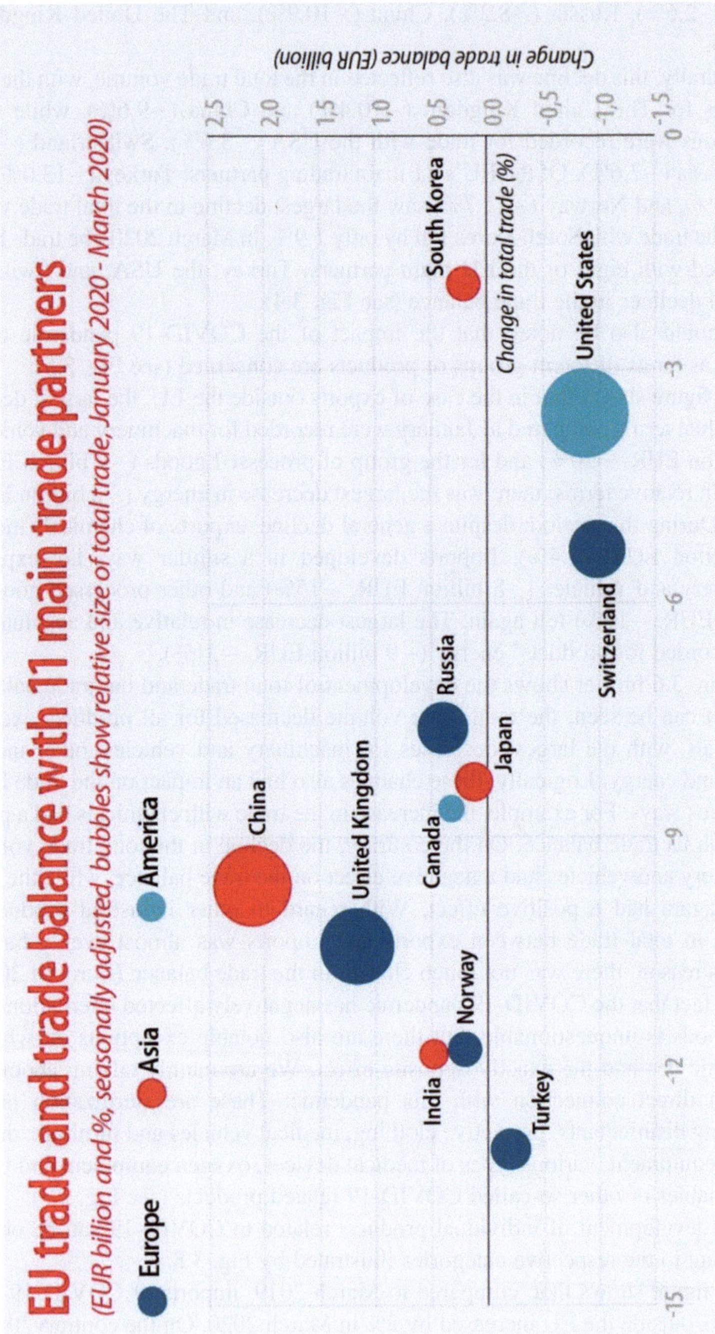

Fig. 3.4 Development of European total trade and trade balance with 11 main trade partners. Source: Eurostat (2020a)

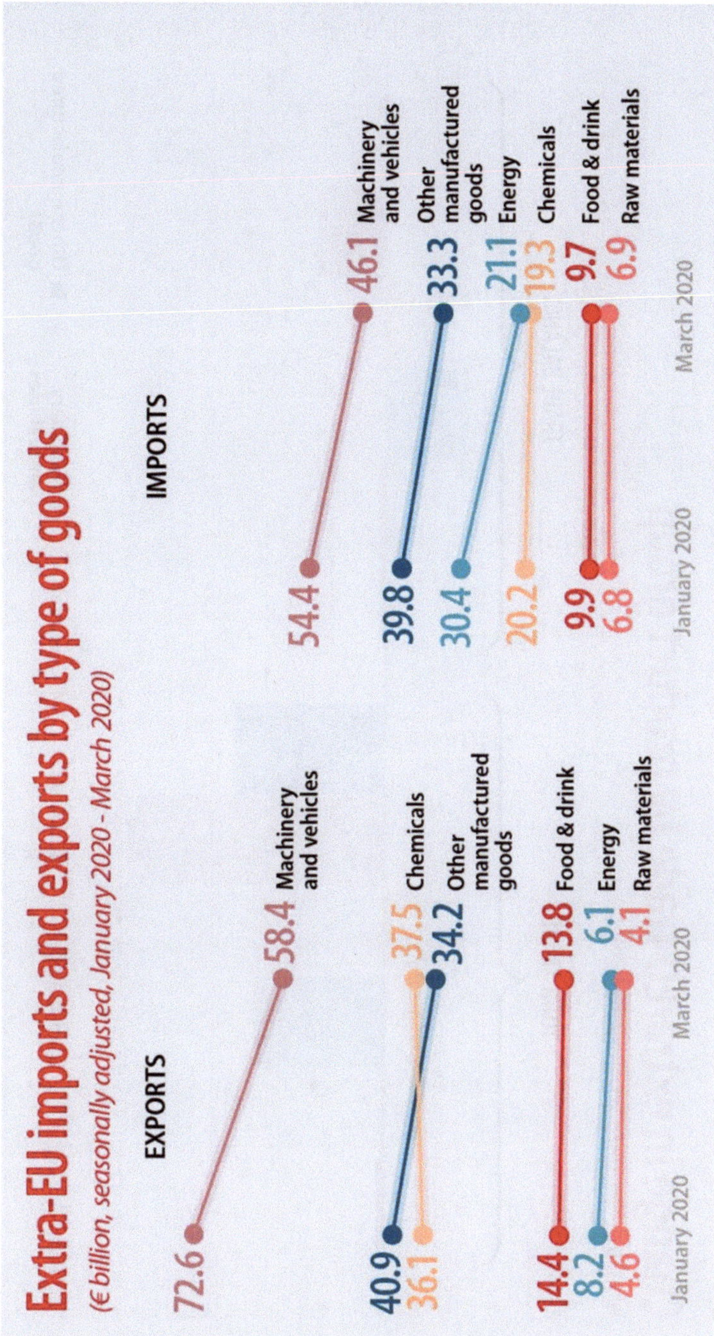

Fig. 3.5 Development of exports and imports of various types of goods. Source: Eurostat (2020b)

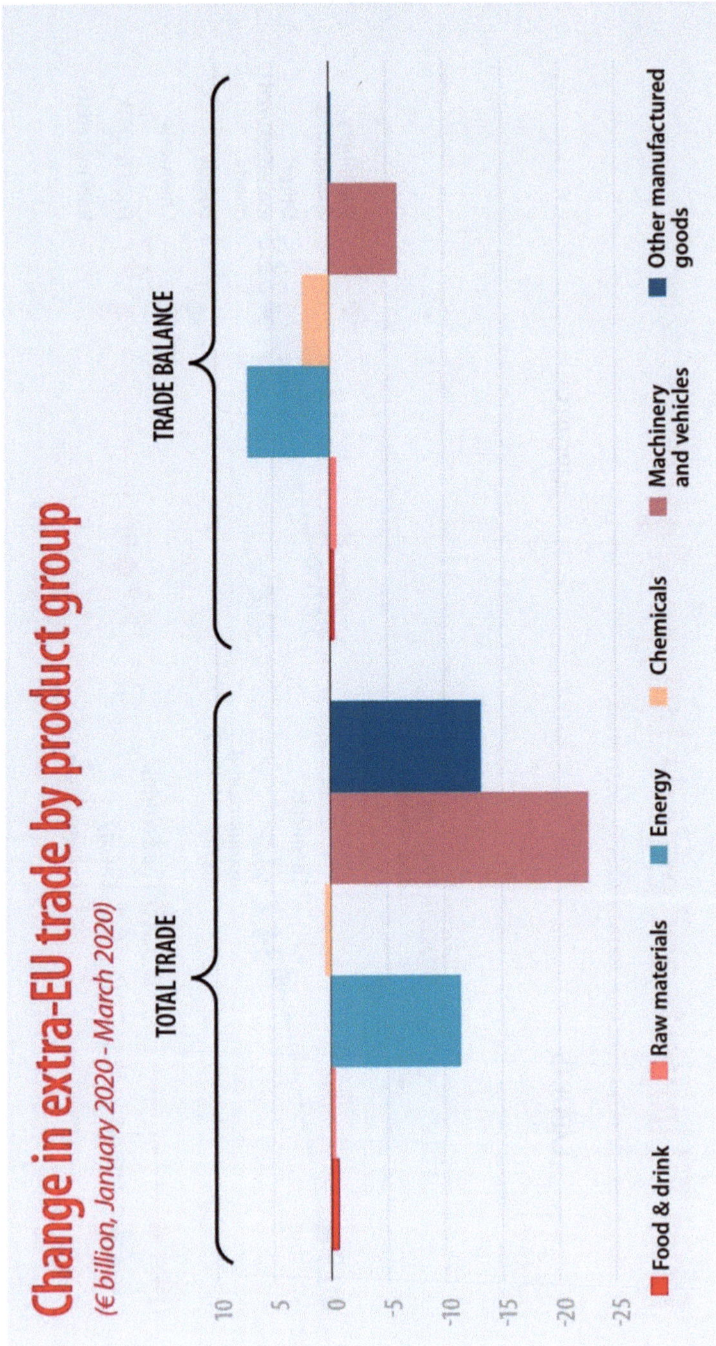

Fig. 3.6 Development of total trade and trade balance. Source: Eurostat (2020b)

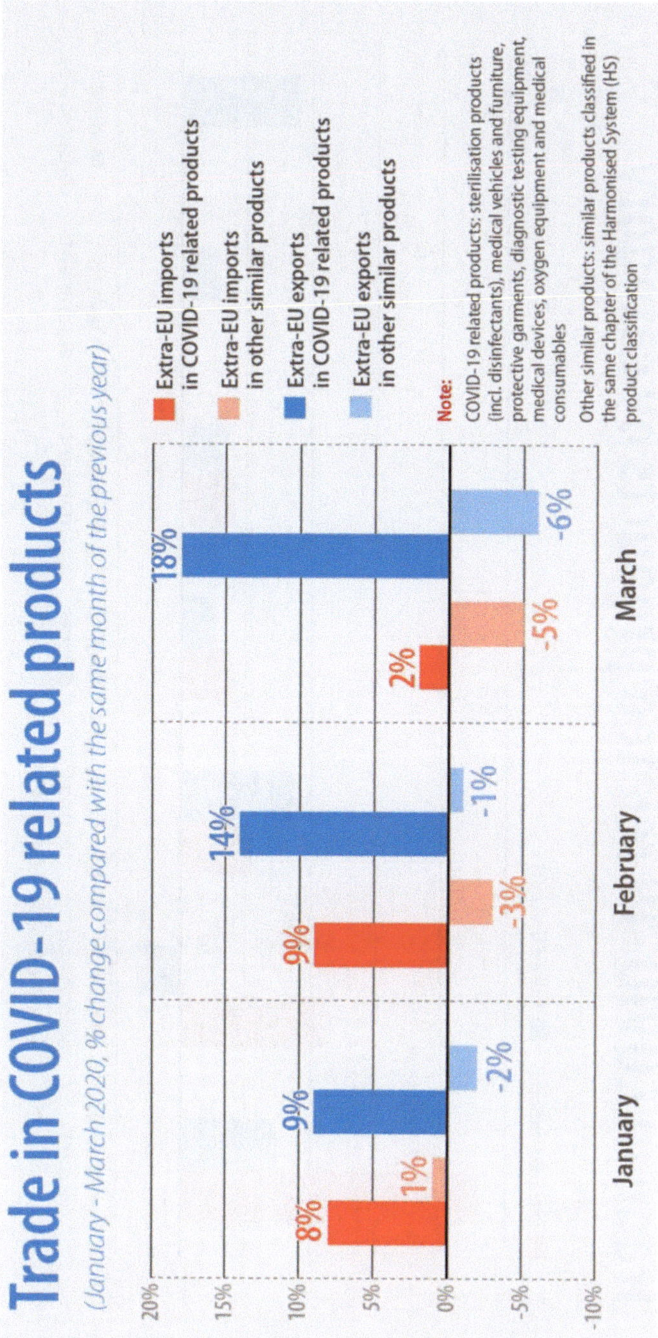

Fig. 3.7 Overall product development related to COVID-19. Source: Eurostat (2020c)

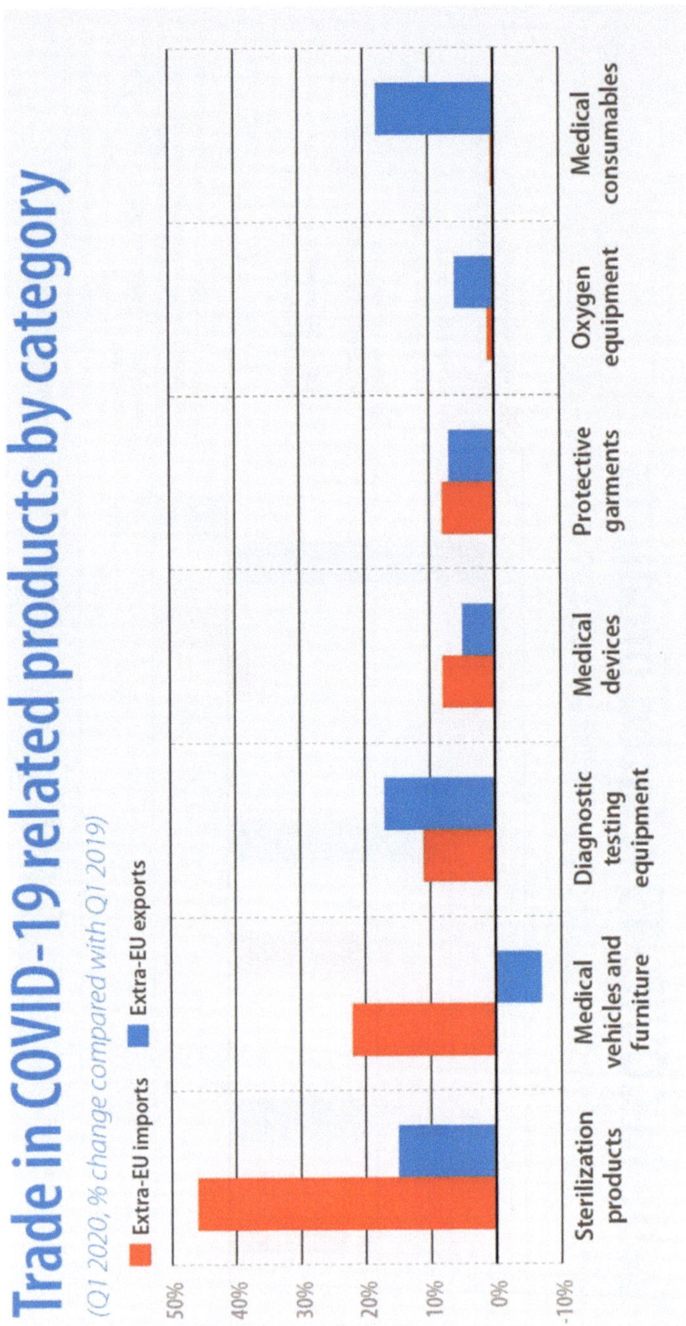

Fig. 3.8 Development of individual products related to COVID-19 by category. Source: Eurostat (2020c)

As it can also be observed further, exports of these products increased faster in March 2020 than in January and February 2020, while imports of these products increased more slowly than in January and February. This may be due to the fact that EU member states have acquired sufficient stocks until then, or also to the fact that local production has increased, thus reducing the need for imports. Although the overall economy and the total trade volume outside the EU declined, trade in all types of COVID-19-related products increased in the first quarter of 2020. The highest increase among these types of products was recorded by imports of sterilizers (+46% compared to Q1 2019). In the case of exports, the highest increase was seen in medical consumables (+18%) and diagnostic test equipment (+17%) (Eurostat 2020c).

3.3 International Trade Restrictions Connected with COVID-19

Obayelu et al. (2020) states that, according to the World Trade Organization (WTO), approximately 80 countries have introduced various export bans or restrictions as a result of the pandemic, with most measures affecting health-related products but also certain food products. Based on this, export restrictions were expected to have an impact on world prices, as an effective post-market trading will require a complete restructuring of the debt package to ensure that all companies survive their current negative development and restart successfully. However, Gruszczynski (2020) points out that it is a mistake to think that the current epidemiological situation has only resulted in a wave of trade restrictions and barriers, as the reality is actually far more complex. With regard to COVID-19, a number of countries have relatively recently started to remove or suspend some trade controls. An example is Argentina, which has suspended its anti-dumping duties on imports of certain medical products from China or Canada, which has temporarily abolished duties on specific categories of products if they are imported into hospitals or other public health facilities. The aim of all these measures is to ensure a sufficient supply to domestic markets (either by means of increasing the imports or reducing the exports). Interestingly, some trade restrictions have also been temporarily removed between the USA and China, the two major rivals who have been waging trade war with each other in recent years. In particular, China has decided to temporarily eliminate customs for the US on certain products (e.g. disinfectants). The USA responded in a similar way.

The pandemic has also slowed the pace of various planned international trade initiatives all around the world, as all countries are very concerned about the current crisis. It is also necessary to state that, on the other hand, new agreements have emerged. An example is the new agreement between the USA, Mexico, and Canada (the so-called USMCA), which was intended to replace the NAFTA agreement. Although the agreement has been ratified by all three parties, its entry into force depended on a successful implementation of the countries' commitments at the national level. The mentioned trade between the USA and China faced similar problems as well. On 1st January 2020, the two countries concluded a preliminary agreement, which set out temporary conditions for ending the trade war. Under the agreement, China has committed to purchase more goods and services in the USA, while the USA has agreed to reduce some of its established customs on Chinese products. However, it is not clear whether, in the current situation, both China and the US will be able to meet the requirements of the agreement. It is also worth mentioning the suspension of negotiations on future relations between Great Britain and the EU. Based on the Brexit agreement, the transitional period ended on 31st December 2020. Notwithstanding the conclusion of the EU-UK Trade and Cooperation Agreement, the trade between the two entities will be governed by a new regime.

3.4 Specific Examples of Surveys on World Trade Issues Connected with COVID-19

Hayakawa and Mukunoki (2020) examined the effects of the coronavirus on the international trade. The authors used data on trade between 186 countries from the first quarter of 2020. The following conclusions emerged from the results of their research. First, the burden of COVID-19 in exporting countries had a negative impact on the international trade but this did not apply for importing countries. Second, this negative impact was reflected in exports in developing countries but not in developed countries. Furthermore, the burden of COVID-19 in the neighbouring countries of an exporting country had a positive effect on its exports. The authors also concluded that the coronavirus burden on importers had a positive effect on the trade in the agricultural industry, while the burden on exporters negatively affected the plastic, footwear, and textile industries. Vidiya and Prabheesh (2020) measured the relationships between countries before and after the outbreak of COVID-19. In addition to that, the authors further focused on predicting the future direction of trade using neural networks. This study analysed the density and trade links between the world's leading economies, i.e. the economies of Canada, the USA, Great Britain, Germany, France, Italy, Japan, South Korea, India, China, Hong Kong, Indonesia, Russia, the Netherlands, and Singapore. For this purpose, the analysis of the sales network for two specific time periods was applied, namely the year 2018 and the first quarter of 2020. On the basis of the data, it was discovered that the trade density decreased significantly from 0.833% to 0.429%. Although China was the core of trade during 2018, by 2020 it was only slightly relocated "within the centre". The results clearly showed that although the COVID-19 pandemic occurred in China in 2019 and thus affected its trade, the country's relative position in the trade network has not changed significantly. As for projected imports and exports, the results of the research showed a significant decline by the end of December 2020. Overall findings have shown that there will be a significant decline in trade in all economies due to the adverse impact of the COVID-19 pandemic. The aim of Khanthavit (2020) was again to examine the behaviour of foreign investors on the Thai Stock Exchange (SET) during the coronavirus illness. Specifically, the author examined whether the trading behaviour of investors was unusual, whether the established strategies were followed or whether a "herd behaviour" was present and whether the market was destabilized. The trading behaviour of foreign investors was measured by the share of net purchase volume and market capitalization, while the behaviour of the stock market was measured by the recorded return on the SET index portfolio. The data set contained daily data from August 2018 to May 2020. The results of the research showed that the abnormal trading volume of foreign investors was negative and significant. According to the analysis of the abnormal volume of trading in stock returns, foreign investors were not among the investors with positive feedback, but rather, they self-herd. Although abnormal trading by foreign investors did not destabilize the market, it did cause volatility in stock returns of a similar size as in normal trading. Gruszczynski (2020), who studied the short-term and long-term effects of the COVID-19 pandemic on the international trade, states that although some of the short-term effects of the COVID-19 pandemic on the international trade are severe, they do not appear to be unmanageable. Based on this claim, it could therefore be concluded that once the pandemic disappears or is at least under control, international trade will return to normal operations. However, in the long term, the impact of the pandemic may be deeper than originally expected, which will certainly lead to structural changes in the process of economic globalization. While the seeds of such a process have been sown some time ago, the COVID-19 pandemic may exacerbate existing tendencies for states to turn inwards and compete more openly for economic and political dominance in the world. If this actually happens, it will very much depend on the severity and especially the duration of the disease. However, it is now clear that the greater its impact, the more likely it is that the paradigm shift in international trade relations and governance will occur.

The COVID-19 pandemic and the resulting economic crisis represent, according to White et al. (2021), a global disruption that is being felt in all sectors, including the seafood sector. For this reason, these authors investigated the early effects of COVID-19 on US fisheries and seafood consumption. To this end, the authors synthesized a large number of data sources from the entire seafood supply chain, including unconventional real-time data sets that showed initial responses and recovery indicators during the COVID-19 pandemic. News articles were synthesized from January to September 2020, covering the US seafood sector, including shortening of the fishing season and revenue losses. In the case of production, trade, unloading, and distribution, both past and current data were assessed. The results of the research showed that compared to the previous year, there was a significant decrease in the fresh seafood production by about 40%, imports decreased by 37%, and exports showed a decrease of 43%, while frozen seafood was significantly less affected. Furthermore, according to trends and traffic data from the seafood markets, it was found that consumer demand for food from restaurants fell by as much as 70% during lockdown, with a recovery varying according to the situation. However, these declines were partially offset (270%) by increased supply and demand searches. The results of this research have clearly shown the widespread but heterogeneous implications of COVID-19 in the seafood sector, which encourage policy makers to focus on supporting the states and sub-sectors affected by pandemics the most, i.e. communities dependent on fishing, fish processing and fishing and aquaculture cities focusing on fresh sea food production.

The impact of COVID-19 on trade, specifically on African trade, was addressed by Obayelu et al. (2020). Their study relied on data and information provided by organizations such as the WTO (World Trade Organization), WB (World Bank), Organization for Economic Co-operation and Development, International Monetary Fund, European Union, international trade statistics, and trade and national statistical publications of various African countries. The analysis was divided into two phases. In the first phase, the impact of the COVID-19 outbreak on the African trade was observed. The second phase focused on the potential business impacts, with COVID-19 spreading more intensively than expected. Based on this analysis, it was concluded that the COVID-19 outbreak affected several aspects of international trade, although the full effects of the outbreak were not yet visible in the data. Some key indicators showed that maintaining the trade flows could support the fight against COVID-19 and thus have a detrimental effect on the African trade. COVID-19 has resulted in a profound decline in transactions, both internationally and within regions. Tariffs and other import restrictions have hampered the flow of critical products to African countries. Non-cooperative trade policies have led to higher commodity prices in the fragile and vulnerable African countries. According to Norouzi et al. (2020), the issue of oil and electricity supply is very often linked to the international trade. For this reason, their aim was to perform quantitative analyses by means of auto-regression elasticity and neural network-based sensitivity analyses to determine the importance and vulnerability of different economic sectors, with a special focus on oil and electricity demand. The output of the research was the creation of a comparative regression and neural network model that was able to analyse the impacts of COVID-19 on electricity and oil demand in the People's Republic of China. The results of the model showed that the elasticity of demand for oil and electricity to the infected population was -0.1% and -0.65%, respectively. Moreover, Cardwell and Ghazalian (2020) proposed a very interesting contribution to the research by discussing how the COVID-19 pandemic affected the demand and supply of international food aid and provided three proposals for policy changes that could ensure the flow of food to the ones in need. All these proposals were only regulatory changes that could be made without the need to increase spending. First, the authors suggested that donor countries prioritize humanitarian spending when deciding on aid delivery. Second, governments can free food aid from trade barriers that prevent procurement (export restrictions) and supplies (import tariffs). Third, donor countries can allow flexibility to implementing agencies by releasing food aid from domestic purchasing and shipping restrictions. Last but not least, there is Muhammed et al. (2020) who examined the demand for imported cotton by its product form (raw cotton and yarn) and by its source (e.g. the USA, India), as well as dynamic price relationships between countries. The impact of COVID-19 on Chinese imports and supplying countries was assessed using year-on-year trade data, demand estimates, and price forecasts. The results of the research showed that, depending on the projections, the most serious impacts of COVID-19 on Chinese cotton imports were already overcome or that the second half of the year would be potentially as bad as at the beginning of the year. The result will depend mainly on the impact of the price of the manufactured products on imports, the effects of which are large but insignificant. Although imports from certain countries are expected to fall significantly, the projection intervals suggest a negligible decline or even a positive result. As it can be seen from the previous facts, there are a number of surveys related to the COVID-19 trade and infection, but very few studies have examined the trade consequences of the COVID-19 pandemic using analytical tools. For example, McKibbin and Fernando (2020) used these tools by specifically employing the global computable general equilibrium (CGE) models to estimate pandemic losses. These models offer a rich sectoral disaggregation that allows for different effects across industries to be taken into account, as well as an estimate of trade spillovers and endogenous policy responses. In addition to that, these authors have developed a dynamic stochastic general equilibrium (DSGE) model that can be applied to multiple countries and sectors. Furthermore, the authors also observed a negative impact of the pandemic on production networks and trade. Simulations of the potential impact of COVID-19 on trade through the global CGE model were also performed by Maliszewska et al. (2020). In this study, a shock is modelled as an underutilization of labour and capital, rising costs of international trade, declining travel services, and a shifting demand from activities that require proximity between people. Based on the study, the authors found that the greatest negative shock is recorded in the output of domestic services affected by the pandemic, as well as in traded tourist services.

3.5 Development of Trade After the COVID-19 Pandemic

In 2020, global trade declined significantly due to the COVID-19 pandemic and the future growth is expected to remain below the trend before the pandemic. Has the pandemic changed the relative importance of individual countries within the global trade network? Kiyota (2022) mentions the resilience of these countries' trade structure. The pandemic has significantly affected the Asian economies. The trade war between the USA and China stalled after the first phase of the trade agreement and the pandemics but the future development remains unclear (Heo 2021).

At the beginning of 2020, the COVID-19 pandemic appeared for the first time in the history, followed by national lockdowns. These lockdowns had significant impact on the international trade of the affected countries, especially during the lockdowns. It is also widely acknowledged that the spread of the COVID-19 pandemic has changed the lives of individuals. During the pandemic, several industries have been significantly affected. The above implies that the sector of services played an important role before as well as after the pandemic. According to Zhao (2022), the pandemic has had an impact on the sector of services, businesses, and other organizations contributing to the economic growth of countries. Furthermore, Zhao (2022) identified the negative impact of the pandemic on both private and public businesses. The coronavirus has hit all industries in an unimaginable way, with the tourism and hospitality sectors, which account for 9% of the total GDP, being considered the worst affected ones (Mehta and Panse 2022). The construction sector has experienced an extreme disruption, with many projects being suspended, many employees losing their jobs, and many building companies going bankrupt (Gamil et al. 2022).

In their research, Ahn and Steinbach (2022) analysed the determinants of temporary non-tariff measures (NTM) as a response to the COVID-19 and their effects for trade in agricultural products and food. Using a control function approach, they found that the economic and pandemic aspects played an essential role in implementing these NTM. Based on the differences identified between treated and untreated varieties, they estimate the post-event dynamic trade response being 5.4% for facilitation of import and −27.5% for the restriction of export by NTM. Once repealed, the trade effect of the measurements will disappear, which means that these temporary trade policies have been effective in achieving the set policy goals, disrupting the long-term trade only to a limited extent.

The international trading system has shown sufficient maturity and the ability to remain stable even in extreme conditions. The negative impact of COVID-19 on trade has been caused by the general decrease in demand, disruption of the global value chains, restrictions on exports, increase in trade costs, tightening of hygiene requirements, and the restrictions on tourism and business trips. The pandemic has accentuated the need for cooperation not only in the narrow aspect of coordinating anti-pandemic measures but also in the broader sense of supporting the development and reduction of differences in well-being, health care, and the quality of life in general both in different countries ad within individual economies. In the field of trade policy, the pandemic pointed to the urgent need for closer cooperation in removing the barriers to trade (reduction of tariffs, removal of technical barriers, mutual recognition of sanitary certificates, interconnection of the digital regulation systems) (Zagashvili 2021).

Bing and Ma (2021) found that during the COVID-19 crisis, foreign investors play a stabilizing role in the market and exhibit significant negative feedback to trading while institutional investors are not able to stabilize the market. Compared to the pre-COVID-19 period, foreign investors are showing even stronger negative trade feedback. Bing and Ma (2021) further confirm that the negative trading feedback of foreign investors is given mainly by their response to negative returns. Moreover, both institutional and foreign investor trading shows more precise predictability of future returns during the pandemic; the negative returns after selling by foreign investors and positive returns after buying by institutional investors are much higher in the period of crisis. The impact of the COVID-19 pandemic has been detrimental for all countries, despite the continuous efforts of governments on all continents to mitigate its harmful effects, and all social and economic indicators have worsened. Ugurlu and Jindrichovska (2022) found that the impact of COVID-19 can be seen in all countries but its intensity is different. As for the countries outside the

V4 group, there can be seen strong trade relations with Germany, which appears to be the strongest European economy.

According to Golovin (2022), Thailand has been affected by the pandemic more than the neighbouring countries due to the larger share of tourism on GDP, problems with supply and local production of vaccines in the initial phase, as well as the sharp decrease in foreign trade. After the difficult start, the Thai authorities managed to launch a mass vaccination campaign and continue the measures to support businesses and vulnerable groups of inhabitants. Moreover, Golovin (2022) found that the demand recovery in developed countries has helped to boost import. However, the recovery of the Thai economy is expected to be long and uneven. Firstly, the global tourism sector is not likely to return to the preceding level, which will also depend on the situation concerning the spread of COVID-19. However, further intensification of international trade will be limited due to the disruption of the global supply chain. Moreover, it will be difficult to enhance GDP growth through private and public consumption, since the indebtedness of households and government has grown significantly in the last 2 years. This could have a negative impact on the economic growth in 2022 and in the long run. Thai authorities will thus need to pursue prudent policy and try to support household incomes while reducing the growing unemployment, since the fiscal space for new borrowings shrinks.

The research by Yang (2022) identified the changes in the Korean ICT industry in the post-COVID period. The sectors related to non-physical and contactless technologies in the ICT sector, such as semiconductors, show the exponential growth. With the USA becoming a new key player, the causal relationship with China, which was a key player in the GVC (Global Value Chain) disappeared in the pre-COVID-19 period. The GVC in the ICT sector is not a rigid, one-direction vertical structure but is changing into a flexible structure influenced by cooperation and competition between countries. Yang (2022) suggests that in the post-COVID period, it is necessary to continuously develop new ICT sectors that use contactless and technologies; the main strategies in response to the changed GVC would be to take the initiative by ensuring source technologies and expansion by means of cooperating with other GVC and sharing resources.

In the early stages of the COVID-19 pandemic, small enterprises were more often closed compared to large enterprises. Although they recovered afterwards to large extent, market concentration remains higher than before the pandemic. Fairlie et al. (2022) suggest that at the beginning of the crisis, COVID-19 lead to a large decrease in the number of businesses continuing their activities; however, surprisingly little is known about whether these temporary shutdowns turned into permanent closures and whether small enterprises have been abnormally affected. The trading behaviour of short sellers attracts a lot of attention, especially in the case of negative shocks. He et al. (2022) found that a larger number of new confirmed cases of COVID-19 in the location of listed companies' headquarters is connected with greater subsequent short selling of these companies. In addition, the impact of the local COVID-19 pandemic on short selling is stronger in the case of companies in more difficult financial situation, operating in vulnerable sectors, and with higher risk of stock price collapse. This impact is weaker after the repeal of the closure measures in Wuhan and becomes insignificant in later outbreaks.

Kasim and Muslimin (2022) examined the market response to the COVID-19 pandemic through the stocks listed on the LQ45 index using the method of event study to calculate and analyse the difference in the average abnormal revenue and the trading volume activity (TVA) during the COVID-19 pandemic in Indonesia. The first finding was that the LQ45 stock market responded positively from the confirmation of the outbreak of COVID-19 in Wuhan, since investors did not consider the information to be bad news. Second, the stocks of LQ45 have seen a decline since the confirmation of the first cases of COVID-19 in Indonesia. Third, the notification of the World Health Organization (WHO) concerning the pandemic continued until the regional lockdown in Jakarta in April 2020, which caused a negative response from the company LQ45. The market started to respond positively after the launch of vaccination in Indonesia (January 2021). Overall, the results show that the LQ45 stock market responded quickly to the COVID-19 pandemic from its very beginning, and the response changed over time depending on the events during the pandemic. Investors tend to respond quickly to any event; therefore, the movements of stocks are very difficult to predict. The conclusion of the presented research is that the negative impact that occurred in the stock market in Indonesia can be attributed to the COVID-19 pandemic.

References

Ahn S, Steinbach S (2022) The impact of COVID-19 trade measures on agricultural and food trade. Appl Econ Perspect Policy

Aydin L, Ari I (2020) The impact of Covid-19 on Turkey's non-recoverable economic sectors compensating with falling crude oil prices: A computable general equilibrium analysis. Energy Explor Exploit 38(5):1810–1830

Baldwin R, Tomiura E (2020) Thinking ahead about the trade impact of COVID-19. In: Baldwin R, di Mauro BW (eds) Economics in the Time of COVID-19, pp 59–71

Bing T, Ma H (2021) COVID-19 pandemic effect on trading and returns: evidence from the Chinese stock market. Econ Anal Policy 71:384–396

Blaum J, Lelarge C, Peters M (2018) The gains from input trade with heterogeneous importers. Am Econ J Macroecon 10(4):77–127

Boehm CE, Flaaen A, Pandalai-Nayar N (2019) Input linkages and the transmission of shocks: firm-level evidence from the 2011 Tōhoku earthquake. Rev Econ Stat 101(1):60–75

Cardwell R, Ghazalian PL (2020) COVID-19 and international food assistance: policy proposals to keep food flowing. World Dev 135:105059

Eaton J, Kortum S, Neiman B, Romalis J (2016) Trade and the global recession. Am Econ Rev 106(11):3401–3438

Eurostat (2020a) COVID-19 impact on EU international trade in goods. https://ec.europa.eu/eurostat/en/web/products-eurostatnews/-/ddn-20200519-2

Eurostat (2020b) Which trade goods are affected the most by COVID-19? https://ec.europa.eu/eurostat/en/web/products-eurostatnews/-/ddn-20200522-1

Eurostat (2020c) Extra-EU trade in COVID-19 related products. https://ec.europa.eu/eurostat/en/web/products-eurostat-news/-/ddn-20200618-2

Fairlie R, Fossen FM, Johnsen R, Droboniku G (2022) Were small businesses more likely to permanently close in the pandemic? Small Bus Econ:1–17

Gamil Y, Al-Sarafi AH, Najeh T (2022) Post COVID-19 pandemic possible business continuity strategies for construction industry revival a preliminary study in the Malaysian construction industry. Int J Disaster Resil Built Environ

Golovin SN (2022) Influence of Covid-19 pandemic on the economy of Thailand. Mirovaya Ekonomika I Mezhdunarodnye Otnosheniya 66(8):52–60

Gruszczynski L (2020) The COVID-19 pandemic and international trade: temporary turbulence or paradigm shift? Eur J Risk Regul 11(2020):337–342

Halpern L, Koren M, Szeidl A (2015) Imported inputs and productivity. Am Econ Rev 105(12): 3660–3703

Hayakawa K, Mukunoki H (2020) "Impacts of covid-19 on international trade: evidence from the first quarter of 2020," IDE Discussion Papers 791. Institute of Developing Economies, Japan External Trade Organization(JETRO)

He J, Ma X, Wei Q (2022) Firm-level short selling and the local COVID-19 pandemic: evidence from China. Econ Model 113:105896

Heo U (2021) Asia in 2020 the COVID-19 pandemic and the US-China trade war. Asian Surv 61(1):1–10

Kasim MY, Muslimin DIKB (2022) Market reaction to the Covid-19 pandemic: Events study at stocks listed on LQ45 index. Cogent Bus Manag 9(1):2024979

Khanthavit A (2020) Foreign investors' abnormal trading behavior in the time of COVID-19. J Asian Finance Econ Bus 7(9):063–074

Kiyota K (2022) The COVID-19 pandemic and the world trade network. J Asian Econ 78:101419

Maliszewska M, Mattoo A, van der Mensbrugghe D (2020) The potential impact of COVID-19 on GDP and trade: a preliminary assessment. In: Policy Research Working Paper, 9211

Mckibbin W, Fernando R (2020) The global macroeconomic impacts of COVID-19: seven scenarios. In: Baldwin R, di Mauro W (eds) Economics in the time of COVID-19. Centre for Economic Policy Research, London, pp 45–51

Mehta K, Panse C (2022) Effect of Covid-19 pandemic: tourism and hospitality industry. Cardiometry 22:406–414

Muhammed A, Smith SA, Yu THE (2020) COVID-19 and cotton import demand in China. Agribusiness 37(3):24

Norouzi N, de Rubens GZ, Choupanpiesheh S, Enevoldsen P (2020) When pandemics impact economies and climate change: exploring the impacts of COVID-19 on oil and electricity demand in China. Energy Res Soc Sci 68:101654

Obayelu AE, Edewor SE, Ogbe AO (2020) Trade effects, policy responses and opportunities of COVID-19 outbreak in Africa. J Chin Econ Foreign Trade Stud 14(1):44–59

Ugurlu E, Jindrichovska I (2022) Effect of COVID-19 on international trade among the Visegrad Countries. J Risk Financ Manag 15(2):41

Vidiya CT, Prabheesh KP (2020) Implications of COVID-19 pandemic on the global trade networks. Emerg Mark Financ Trade 56(10):2408–2401

White ER, Froehlich HE, Gephart JA, Cotrell RS, Branch TA, Bejarano RA, Baum JK (2021) Early effects of COVID-19 on US fisheries and seafood consumption. Fish Fish 22(1):232–239

World Bank (2020) Global economic prospects, June 2020. Washington, DC: World Bank, 238 p. ISBN 978-1-4648-1553-9. https://openknowledge.worldbank.org/handle/10986/33748

Yang C (2022) A study on the changes in the ICT industry after the COVID-19 pandemic. Ind Manag Data Syst 123(1):64–78

Zagashvili VS (2021) International trade in the aftermath of the Covid-19 pandemic. Mirovaya Ekonomika I Mezhdunarodnye Otnosheniya 65(10):15–23

Zhao S (2022) Impact of COVID 19 pandemic and big data on China's international trade: challenges and countermeasures. Front Public Health 10

Chapter 4
Development of International Trade Between the Czech Republic and the Russian Federation

According to Il'jičeva et al. (2013), the economic and political relations between the Russian Federation and the Czech Republic are marked by historical conflicts, the impact of which is reflected in both countries even today. One of the most important events is undoubtedly the year 1968, when the intervention of Soviet troops in Czechoslovakia took place, which fundamentally affected mutual relations. The situation did not improve until 1991, when the USSR collapsed and the Czech-Russian cooperation agreement was initiated by the foreign ministers of both countries and was signed by the Russian President Boris Yeltsin and Czechoslovak President Vaclav Havel. This agreement represented a kind of a compensation for the intervention of Soviet troops. However, based on the expression of dissatisfaction from the Russian side at the Czech Republic's accession to NATO, Russia's position remained the same.

Based on the scientific literature, it can be stated that since 2000, the development of trade relations between the Czech Republic and Russia has been alternating, as during this time period, their business relations have repeatedly improved, but also cooled. The undoubted cause of the deterioration of mutual relations was, in particular, the accession of the Czech Republic to the EU and the already mentioned accession to NATO. However, other factors, such as the discussion on the construction of an American radar base in Brdy or the issue of the memorials of World War II soldiers, may have caused the mutual relations to tense up. These above-mentioned difficulties even resulted in the loss of the position of Czech companies on the Russian market, despite the fact that historically, they had a good reputation there (Il'jičeva et al. 2013).

Heinrich (2005) states that the Czech Republic considers Russia to be a viable and growing market with the existence of a precondition for long-term development. Furthermore, Russia is a market that has an important raw material base, available workforce, and at the same time, a reliable market for Czech products. The advantageous starting position for the goods and services of the Czech Republic is based on a long tradition of exports, knowledge of the market environment in Russia,

J. Horák et al., *Development of World Trade in the Context of the COVID-19 Pandemic*, Contributions to Economics,
https://doi.org/10.1007/978-3-031-27257-8_4

knowledge of Russian business partners and often the ability to communicate in the Russian language. The positive reputation of Czech products on the Russian market is certainly a benefit. In addition to that, in a number of areas of modern and efficient industrial production, the Czech Republic is capable of a technological response to the requirements and needs of the Russian market. However, the business environment on the Russian side can be considered a weak point in some regions that do not yet reach the level of European standards. Furthermore, it is also possible to meet with great differentiation in terms of economic level or existing differences in the availability of skilled labour, in the application of legal standards and the occurrence of a large number of trade barriers. A significant obstacle to mutual cooperation is often seen in the insufficient knowledge of the Czech business environment about the realities and possibilities of the Russian market environment, together with the insufficient capital opportunities of companies in the Czech Republic.

Kontsevaya (2017) sees the opportunities of the Russian market for the Czech side mainly in the dynamic growth of its economy together with the improved position of public finances or in the support of the process of structural reforms by Russia. Among other things, Russia has recently seen an increase in real incomes and a corresponding increase in consumer spending, which has resulted in new consumer demand for imported goods. Gradually, the market environment was opened up together with the privatization of the energy sector, payment morale and investment capacity of Russian partners improved. It is also worth noting that on the Russian side, the obsolete production base has been modernized in recent years and new technologies have been implemented in a number of industries, such as metallurgy and metalworking, energy, agriculture and food production, heavy engineering, chemicals, and raw materials. The telecommunications and transport infrastructure developed relatively quickly in the Russian Federation, as well as less competition and market saturation in the Russian regions. Russia's participation in the World Trade Organization and in the Russia-Belarus-Kazakhstan Customs Union certainly has a positive effect. In this case, however, it must be said that the Russian economy is highly dependent on the extraction and export of raw materials, which can have negative effects if world prices of raw materials fall sharply. In addition, Russia is insufficiently diversifying its economy, resulting in structural imbalances, such as uneven and undersized logistics, energy, telecommunications, transport and distribution infrastructure. Thus, the Russian economy often has to deal with high levels of corruption, a large number of state interventions in the economy, and low law enforcement. For this reason, Czech businesses may face a number of administrative barriers and a decline in the price advantage of products, as well as limited access of foreign entities to selected sectors of the Russian economy (Coufalová and Žídek 2017).

Liuhto (2018) also expresses the opinion that Russia represents one of the most promising markets for the Czech Republic, despite considerable specifics requiring a high degree of prudence and knowledge. The author further adds that without proper preparation and without the possibility of on-site production or subcontracting, the penetration of Czech companies into the Russian market is very difficult and very costly. Increasing international competition and changing conditions in the Russian

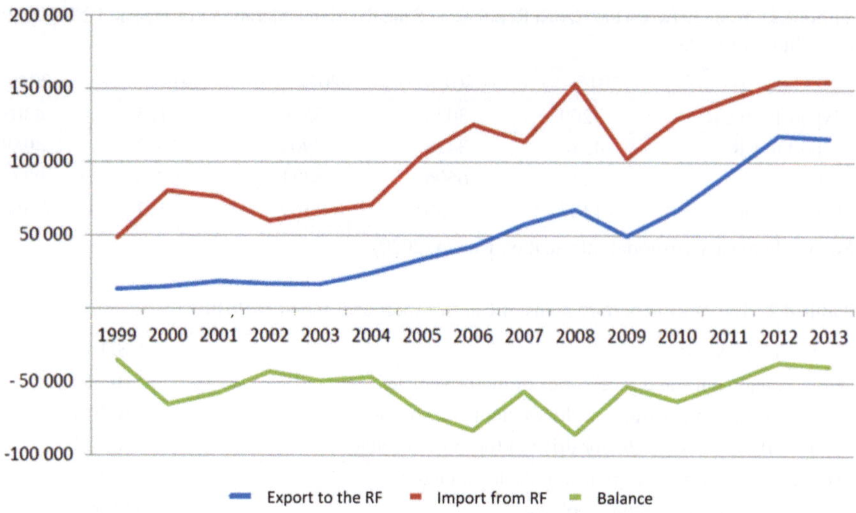

Fig. 4.1 Trade exchange between the Czech Republic and the Russian Federation, 1999–2013. Source: CSO (2014)

market result in a shift in value from the goods market to the investment market. The interest of the Russian Federation in modern production at a high technical level, in the establishment of joint ventures and cooperation is constantly increasing. Business entities of Czech origin also belong to the ranks of major investors in Russia, especially in the fields of insurance, finance, but also food, mining of precious metals, etc. On the other hand, there are a number of major Czech companies that own companies with Russian roots.

Given the current and expected development of the Russian economy as well as the structure of the Czech Republic's export opportunities, the most promising areas for Czech exporters appear to be mining, engineering (machinery), manufacturing, pharmaceutical and chemical industries, municipal services, energy, agriculture, textile industry, glass production, construction industry, and public transport. Deliveries of consumer goods and sanitary products are also considered to be very promising.

Regarding the specific development of trade between the Czech Republic and Russia, reference may be made, for example, to the following figure, which illustrates trade between the Czech Republic and Russia in the period 1999–2013.

From the Fig. 4.1, it can be observed that the mutual trade between Russia and the Czech Republic increased very significantly throughout the period under review. Since 1999, exports to the Russian Federation have increased almost nine times, specifically in 1999 from 13,185 million CZK to 116,165 million CZK in 2013. The very highest value was recorded for exports in 2012, namely 118,025 million CZK. As for imports from the Russian Federation, they have increased almost three and a half times since 1999, i.e. from 48,146 million CZK in 1999 to 155,302 million CZK in 2013. In the same year, these imports also showed the highest value. As it can be

Table 4.1 Trade between the Czech Republic and the Russian Federation in the period 2015–2019 (in millions of USD)

	2015	2016	2017	2018	2019
Export from CR	3209	3078	3536	4125	4303
Import to CR	4210	3428	4905	5642	4969
Sales	7413	6506	8441	9768	9272
Trade balance	−1107	−350	−1369	−1517	−666

Source: Summary territorial information Russia (2020)

Table 4.2 The most important items of Czech export and import in 2019

Item: Czech export	USD (thousand)
Parts, components, and accessories of motor vehicles	670,716
Automatic data processing machines, units, sensors, etc.	310,913
Bodywork (including cabs for drivers) for motor vehicles	178,134
Tricycles, scooters, dolls prams, dolls, toys, puzzles	154,527
Medicines, antisera, cotton wool, etc.	115,593
Item: Czech import	**USD (thousand)**
Mineral oils	1,760,611
Natural gas and other gaseous hydrocarbons	1,597,016
Semi-finished products from steel and iron	217,884
Passenger cars and other motor vehicles designed primarily for the transport of persons, including vans and racing cars	207,771
Hydrazine and hydroxylamine salt	190,179

Source: Summary territorial information Russia (2020)

seen, the Czech Republic had a long-term negative trade balance in the period under review, but it has a declining trend.

In 1999 and 2013, similar values were recorded for the trade balance, −34,960 million CZK in 1999 and −39,137 million CZK in 2013. The highest value is recorded in 2008, when the balance totalled 85,825 million CZK (CSO 2014).

Table 4.1 then provides an overview of trade between the Czech Republic and the Russian Federation over the last 5 years.

As it can be observed, since 2016, Czech exports have had an increasing tendency. As far as imports from Russia are concerned, there are obvious fluctuations, mainly due to changes in oil, gas, and imported volumes of these raw materials. As indicated above, the negative balance of the Czech-Russian trade is a relatively permanent issue.

The five most important items of Czech exports and imports of goods are provided in Table 4.2.

As for the information on mutual exchange in the field of services of the two states over the last 5 years, it can be explored in Table 4.3.

The large surplus of trade in the services of the Czech Republic with the Russian Federation is caused by the provision of tourist and travel services to Russian

Table 4.3 Development of the exchange of services between the Czech Republic and the Russian Federation in 2015–2019 (in billions of CZK)

	2015	2016	2017	2018	2019
Export CR	25.5	26.4	29.7	27.3	28.0
Import CR	12.9	8.7	10.9	10.6	10.0
Sales	38.4	35.1	40.6	37.9	38.0
Trade balance	12.6	17.7	18.8	16.7	18.0

Source: Summary territorial information Russia (2020)

citizens in the Czech Republic whose expenditure reached more than 14 billion CZK in 2019. The most important services on the import side include telecommunications, computer and information services, exported by the Russian Federation to the Czech Republic in 2019 for more than 2 billion. One of the most key Czech companies for mutual trade in services are Czech Airlines and SmartWings which in cooperation with codeshare offers 46 flights to Russia. In the long run, they represent one of the strongest foreign carriers on the Russian market. With the exception of the Prague-Moscow connection, flights to Samara, Kazan, and Rostov-on-Don are operated. Thanks to the air transport of Russian tourists, conditions are being created for other Czech service providers in the Czech Republic.

Most of all Czech service providers operate on the market independently or with the help of local partners, while in recent years, some Czech companies have established branches in the Russian Federation.

4.1 Impacts of Russian Invasion of Ukraine on Global Trade

Regional cooperation involves a viable alternative to the ongoing globalization process, allowing countries to respond effectively to the changes in the external environment through regional integration. Although strong global markets usually sell better, the sustainability of international trade is under enormous pressure (Strielkowski et al. 2022). On top of encumbered logistics and disrupted production chains, sustainable world trade suffers from severe sanctions given the Russian-Ukrainian conflict (Cabelková et al. 2022).

Tajoli (2022) shows that, unlike China, Russia did not develop or diversify its trade flow after joining the WTO. Rather than that, the country increased its fuel and raw material production only to become highly dependent on European demand and the rest of the world. Russia also fell short of exploiting its trading potential and favourable geographic position, failing to support and improve the welfare of its inhabitants. Although increasingly dependent on Russian fuels, old and new EU members (former members of the Soviet Bloc) got their hopes up integrating the single European market with the rest of the world. Tajoli (2022) argues that these contrasts and related economic meltdowns created high tension between Russia and the EU. Ranjan (2022) suggests that after imposing economic sanctions against the invading country, the states may appeal to national security exceptions within the WTO.

The international community responded to the Russian "special military intervention" against Ukraine remarkably fast and in unison, imposing strict trade and financial sanctions to isolate the invader. The change in long-run relationships between Russia and most countries caused by the invasion is still unpredictable. Mardones (2022) revealed that Russia suffered severe production cuts by 10.1% induced by the EU sanctions, expecting a rise to 14.8% if Australia, Canada, Japan, the USA, and Great Britain adopt the same measures. Mardones (2022) predicts that European countries in the immediate vicinity and lively trade with Russia will sustain a drastic production decline, including Lithuania, Latvia, Estonia, Finland, Hungary, and Poland. Re-export, re-import, mining, and extraction are the most stricken Russian sectors. Estimated impacts count only with lower limits, ignoring repercussions from financial sanctions, exchange rates, and commodity prices.

Liadze et al. (2022) argue that the war involves enormous costs equal to 1% of the global GNP in 2022, approximating 1.5 T dollars. Europe is the most afflicted region, given its close vicinity to Ukraine and Russia and its dependence on energy and food supply from the countries. We expect a slump in the European GNP by more than 1%. The most struck western European states include Germany, France, and Italy. The GNP in the "developing Europe", primarily represented by Ukraine, will fall by 30%, whereas the global inflation will soar by about 2% in 2022 and 1% in 2023. Since the military invasion in Ukraine in February 2022, Russia has been facing severe economic sanctions, including financial, trade, visa, transport, and other punitive measures. Although the last 30 years have seen a transit from "economic carpet bombing" to "smart sanctions", the economic punishment for Russia is of the old school. Timofeev (2022) argues that rather than changing the paradigm, the severity and effectiveness of the sanctions are what matter. Smart sanctions still carry weight, yet resemble "economic carpet bombing". Threatening their economies is the only sound reason for instigators to refrain from imposing sanctions. They must fall back on smart sanctions to avoid tremendous losses.

Smutka and Abrhám (2022) found that an embargo on Russian food imports significantly, yet differently, impacted all EU countries, violently shaking with so far compact state clusters. Apart from attempting counter-sanctions, the imposed ban on imports aims to reduce Russia's dependence on food imports and support national food security. The international trade with agricultural commodities in the Euro-Asian region has recently been thriving, given the sanctions hindering foreign trade activities between Russia and selected world countries. Krivko et al. (2022) argue that the sanctions swayed the food market, affecting items on the sanction list and items not directly included in the restrictive import measures. Krivko et al. (2022) also claim that entries not involved in the embargo list have only an indirect, punitive effect, aiming at the Russian trade with sugar and its price movement. The authors (2022) suggest that the import ban has a long-term, negative impact on consumer sugar prices. On the flip side, the market shock caused by the sanctions pushed the sugar consumer price, hitting its original state after 9 months of the depression. We may say that import restrictions and other crucial aspects comprise decisive factors for the Russian trade with sugar.

The Russian invasion of Ukraine has depressed markets with agricultural commodities, disrupting wheat supplies and pushing food prices. Global trade came to harm, suffering from dramatic nationwide impacts (Hellegers 2022).

Astrov et al. (2022) predict a damaging effect on Russian national finance and the economy caused by the sanctions. Although the central bank partly suffered from freezing most Russian assets in the EU and G7, an effective combination of inspiring loyalty and repressive measures led to stabilizing financial markets. Although disciplinary actions include penalties like capital controls, foreign exchange controls, relaxing the regulation of financial institutions, and doubled base interest rates, the medium- and long-term expectations are negative. The conflict and imposed sanctions fuelled galloping inflation in Europe, halting real incomes and economic growth. Many European countries rely heavily on imported natural gas and oil from Russia. The former commodity covers more than 75% of the import in Czechia, Latvia, Hungary, Slovakia, and Bulgaria, while the latter involves the same amount in Slovakia, Lithuania, Poland, and Finland. Fossil fuels will be lacking in Cyprus, Estonia, Latvia, Denmark, Lithuania, Greece, and Bulgaria. In the event of other commodities, the rest of Europe will not sustain severe losses, as non-energetic and investment relations between Russia and many European countries have declined since 2013. The Russian invasion of Ukraine will make Europe force four draconian structural changes as follows:

- Europe will streamline its defence system.
- The transition to the green economy will pick up the pace.
- The EU will encourage Euro-Asian integration.
- Hopes of South European countries for early admission to the EU will be higher.

Afontsev (2022) suggests that a political-economic approach may resolve many undesired outcomes, frequently occurring when inspecting sanctions like ineffective sanctions, adverse reactions of the target country, escalating the ineffective punishment by their initiators and taking retaliatory measures. The author (2022) revealed that tightening economic sanctions against Russia cannot nudge national foreign policy in the desired direction. On the contrary, escalating costs of sanctions lead to supporting Russian national politics and foreign policy decisions. Rather than economic sanctions, Afontsev suggests a multilateral constructive political dialogue to settle the conflict, which has weakened the global financial system. Quereshi et al. (2022) found that the costs of system instability significantly exceed Russian and Ukrainian financial possibilities, threatening the economic stability of European countries and the USA. The author warns about increasing the systemic risk when sanctions can also damage the rest of the world.

4.2 Impacts of Invading Ukraine on Czech-Russian Business Relationships

Czech companies have sustained significant losses since the Russian invasion, as they heavily relied on importing goods to Russia, including Škoda Auto or Plzeňský Prazdroj. We estimate that up to 150 Czech firms have subsidiaries in Russia. Nosek (2022) revealed that Czech export declined by 5.5% after the conflict, peaking at 79.6 B CZK. Before the onset of the COVID-19 pandemic and the outbreak of war, the export was roughly 85.7 B CZK. The Czech export to Russia tops 2%, equal to shipments to Belgium. Supplies imported from Czechia to Russia mainly involve industrial devices and machines, causing Škoda Auto tremendous losses. Nosek (2022) further argues that the prominent Czech car company imported up to 90 k cars to Russia. Zetor Company also terminated production in the invading country, losing 14% of its sales, compared to 2020, when the enterprise topped 1.9 B CZK.

Kovanda (2022) proves substantial drops in export to Russia in the last year. In 2015, shipping from the Czech Republic to Russia ranged from 1.9 to 2.4%, peaking at 3% in 2012–2014 and 4% in 2013. The ongoing conflict led to a decline caused by the imposed sanctions. Although the Czech Republic sees Russia as an essential energy source of oil and natural gas, Czechia is considering importing unconventional shale oil and compressed natural gas from the USA. Kovanda (2022) further predicts that the growing tension in Ukraine will not directly affect the Czech economy, given the rising gas prices and Czech Crown devaluation.

CzechTrade (2022) argues that Russian and Ukrainian markets involve hundreds of firms negotiating with 128 B CZK total. Many companies rely heavily on these markets, although the Czech export does not exceed 2.6%. The Russian-Ukrainian conflict discontinued business relations between both countries, imposing existential problems on many Czech firms which depended on both warring states. Russia is a Czech essential exporter, ranking among 13 prominent shippers for Czech companies in 2021. The same year saw Russia as the sixth largest importer to the Czech Republic, witnessing an increase in the total foreign trade turnover to 230 B CZK.

Since Europe lacks raw materials, Russia has become its major exporter. The EU has cornered the global market in the agriculture and food industry. Although the movement of grain, raw material, and fertilizer prices troubles aggregate producers and consumers, supplies are ample, unlike in the event of oil and gas. The current crisis will only add fuel to the fire, as Ukraine and Russia contribute more than 20% to the world market with wheat and barley, having even a majority share in sunflower oil production (Žižka 2022).

Galloping inflation and energy price rise made us tighten our belts. Experts predict even sharper cuts in economic growth rates, blaming huge household heating bills and exorbitant energy prices. The Russian-Ukrainian conflict made fuel prices sky-high, disrupting global trade and investments. No country or region was left intact, making poorer people live from hand to mouth to cover essential needs. Voženílek (2022) argues that the financial slowdown also affected the Czech economic growth, peaking at 1.9%. No later than February 2022, experts forecast the GNP to reach 4.4%. The author attributes the financial decline to increased economic insecurity and rampant inflation. Specialists estimate the average price rise will top 11.7% in 2022, slumping to 4.5% in 2023, given the Czech Crown's appreciation and settled energy prices.

References

Afontsev SA (2022) Political paradoxes of economic sanctions. Zhurnal Novaya Ekonomicheskaya Assotsiatsiya-J Econ Assoc 3:193–198

Astrov V, Ghodsi M, Grieveson R, Holzner M, Kochnev A, Landesmann M, Pindyuk O, Stehrer R, Tverdostup M, Bykova A (2022) Russia's invasion of Ukraine: assessment of the humanitarian, economic, and financial impact in the short and medium term. Int Econ Econ Policy 19(2): 331–381

Cabelkova I, Smutka L, Rotterova S, Zhytna O, Kluger V, Mares D (2022) The sustainability of international trade: the impact of ongoing military conflicts, infrastructure, common language, and economic wellbeing in Post-Soviet Region. Sustain For 14(17):10840

Coufalová L, Žídek L (2017) The impact of sanction on Czech economic relations with Russia. In: Cingula M, Przygoda M, Detelj K (eds) Economic and social development: 23rd international scientific conference on economic and social development. Varazdin Development and Entrepreneurship Agency, Madrid, pp 208–220

CSO - Czech Statistical Office (2014) Database of foreign trade. 2014. Dostupné z. https://www.czso.cz/csu/czso/databasesregisters

CzechTrade (2022) CzechTrade spouští krizové poradenství pro firmy vyvážející na Ukrajinu a do Ruska. Pomůže dostat se na jiný trh. [CzechTrade launches crisis consultancy for companies exporting to Ukraine and Russia. It will help to reach another market.] BusinessINFO.cz. https://www.businessinfo.cz/clanky/czechtrade-spousti-krizove-poradenstvi-pro-firmy-vyvazejici-na-ukrajinu-a-do-ruska-pomuze-dostat-se-na-jiny-trh/

Heinrich A (2005) Economic politics in Eastern Europe between economic culture, institutional formation and actor behaviour. Comparison of Russia, Poland and the Czech Republic. Osteuropa 55(2):138–139

Hellegers P (2022) Food security vulnerability due to trade dependencies on Russia and Ukraine. Food Secur 14(6):1503–1510

Il'jičeva L, Komarovskij V, Prorok V (2013) Rusko ve 21. století: politika, ekonomika, kultura. [Russia in the 21st century: politics, economy, culture.] Plzeň: Vydavatelství a nakladatelství Aleš Čeněk, 515 p. ISBN 9788073804367

Kontsevaya S (2017) Comparable financial analysis and control procedures of agricultural companies in Russia and the Czech Republic. New dimensions in the development of society home economics finance and taxes. Econ Sci Rural Dev 46:264–271

Kovanda L (2022) Pro Česko je Rusko méně důležitý vývozní trh než třeba Belgie. Případná válka Ruska s Ukrajinou a související sankce by se Česka přímo dotkly jen omezeně, třeba ve formě dražších pohonných hmot. [For the Czechia, Russia is a less important export market than, for example, Belgium. A possible war between Russia and Ukraine and related sanctions would directly affect the Czech Republic only to a limited extent, for example in the form of more expensive fuel]Kurzy.cz. https://www.kurzy.cz/zpravy/635548-pro-cesko-je-rusko-mene-dulezity-vyvozni-trh-nez-treba-belgie-pripadna-valka-ruska-s-ukrajinou-a/

Krivko M, Smutka L, Pulkrabek J, Timoshenkova I (2022) Development of Russian sugar market in 2010-2019 in context of European economic sanctions and import ban. Listy Cukrovarnicke a Reparske 138(5–6):206–211

Liadze I, Macchiarelli C, Mortimer-Lee P, Sanchez JP (2022) Economic costs of the Russia-Ukraine war. World Econ

Liuhto K (2018) The economic relations between the Czech Republic (Czechia) and Russia. 10.13140/RG.2.2.14618.95688

Mardones C (2022) Economic effects of isolating Russia from international trade due to its 'special military operation' in Ukraine. Eur Plan Stud

Nosek M (2022) České firmy zarazily obchod s Ruskem. Nejvíce utrpí strojaři a výrobci vozidel. [Czech companies stopped trade with Russia. Engineers and vehicle manufacturers will suffer the most.] E15.cz. https://www.e15.cz/byznys/prumysl-a-energetika/ceske-firmy-zarazily-obchod-s-ruskem-nejvice-utrpi-strojari-a-vyrobci-vozidel-1388244

Qureshi A, Rizwan M, Ahmad G, Ashraf D (2022) Russia-Ukraine war and systemic risk: who is taking the heat? Financ Res Lett 48:103036

Ranjan P (2022) Russia-Ukraine war and WTO's national security exception. Foreign Trade Rev

Smutka L, Abrhám J (2022) The impact of the Russian import ban on EU agrarian exports. Agric Econ-Zemedelska Ekonomika 68(2):39–49

Souhrnná Teritoriální Informace Rusko [Summary Territorial Information Russia] (2020) Obchodní a ekonomická spolupráce s ČR [Business and economic cooperation with the Czech Republic] (s. 30). 2020. http://publiccontent.sinpro.cz/PublicFiles/2020/05/13/Nahled%20STI%20(PDF)%20Lotyssko%20-%20Souhrnna%20teritorialni%20informace%20-%202020.142502210.pdf

Strielkowski W, Kulagovskaya T, Panaedova G, Smutka L, Kontsevaxa S, Streimikiene D (2022) Post-soviet economics in the context of international trade: opportunities and threats from mutual cooperation. Econ Res-Ekonomska Istrazivanja 36(1):2021–2044

Tajoli L (2022) Too much of a good thing? Russia-EU international trade relations at times of war. J Ind Bus Econ 49(4):807–834

Timofeev IN (2022) Policy of sanctions against Russia: newest stage. Zhurnal Novaya Ekonomicheskaya Assotsiatsiya-J Econ Assoc 3:198–206

Voženílek L (2022) Všechny jistoty pryč. Jak ruská invaze na Ukrajinu změnila ekonomiku. [All certainties gone. How Russia's invasion of Ukraine changed the economy]. https://www.seznamzpravy.cz/clanek/ekonomika-finance-vsechny-jistoty-pryc-jak-ruska-invaze-na-ukrajinu-zmenila-ekonomiku-203426

Žižka J (2022) Globální agrární obchod nebyl nikdy volný a férový. Válka odhalila jeho slabiny. [Global agricultural trade has never been free and fair. The war exposed his weaknesses.] E15.cz. https://www.e15.cz/byznys/obchod-a-sluzby/globalni-agrarni-obchod-nebyl-nikdy-volny-a-ferovy-valka-odhalila-jeho-slabiny-1391975

Chapter 5
Methodology

For the analysis, data on the size of exports, imports, and the trade balance of Russia and the Czech Republic for the period from 31 January 1993 to 31 July 2020, i.e. for more than 27 years, will be used. These are monthly data representing the value on the last day of the respective month in millions of USD. The values will therefore also include the period of the two major global economic crises, i.e. the great financial crisis around 2008 and the crisis caused by the COVID-19 pandemic which erupted in full in 2020. The data is available at https://data.imf.org/regular.aspx?key=61013712.

The calculation will take the form of an experiment. First, we will predict the values of exports, imports, and the trade balance based on the date. Furthermore, we will take the seasonal effect into account and make predictions based on three variants (day, month, year). For each variable, the same number of steps will be used as the input for the calculation, namely 1 step, 3 steps, 6 steps, and 12 steps. We will work with a time series delay. In total, the following outputs will be generated:

1. Prediction based on date
   (a) Trade balance
      - 1 step
      - 3 steps
      - 6 steps
      - 12 steps

   (b) Export
      - 1 step
      - 3 steps
      - 6 steps
      - 12 steps

   (c) Import

J. Horák et al., *Development of World Trade in the Context of the COVID-19 Pandemic*, Contributions to Economics,
https://doi.org/10.1007/978-3-031-27257-8_5

- 1 step
- 3 steps
- 6 steps
- 12 steps

2. Prediction according to the seasonal effect (three variables)

   (a) Trade balance

   - 1 step
   - 3 steps
   - 6 steps
   - 12 steps

   (b) Export

   - 1 step
   - 3 steps
   - 6 steps
   - 12 steps

   (c) Import

   - 1 step
   - 3 steps
   - 6 steps
   - 12 steps

The data file will first be modified in MS Excel so that it can be applied to SW Statistica. The calculation will be performed using the tool Data Mining - > Neural Networks - > Time series (regression). Then we select the data to be processed. The continuous predictor will be Date, the continuous target variable will be Export, Import, or Trade Balance, and the categorical predictor will be the day, month, and year in the second variant. We also determine the sampling by dividing the data into three files. A total of 70% of the input data will be included in the training sample of data, and this set will be used for the actual training of the artificial neural networks. The second sample of data—the testing set—will contain 15% of the input data, while the third sample—the validation set—will also contain 15% of the input data. Both of these files will be used for testing, checking, and verification of the obtained results. Two available types of neural networks will be generated, namely multilayer perceptron networks (MLP) and basic radial function networks (RBF), while the minimum and maximum numbers of hidden neurons will be set by default.

MLP is the most widely used neural network using iteration in training. A larger number of hidden neurons or data increases the computational time. The basic building block is a neuron, or perceptron. This element was already described by Rosenblatt (1957), while the MLP network learning algorithm itself was described by Rumelhart et al. (1986). The network contains neurons interconnected in such a way that they form a layered network as a result. The perceptron is a special type of a formal neuron, a general element of neural networks, where the internal potential is

Table 5.1 Activation function of hidden and output layers of MLP and RBF

Function	Definition	Range
Identity	a	$(-\infty; +\infty)$
Logistic sigmoid	$\frac{1}{1+e^{-a}}$	(0;1)
Hyperbolic tangent	$\frac{e^{a}-e^{-a}}{e^{a}+e^{-a}}$	(−1;+1)
Exponential	e^{-a}	$(0; +\infty)$
Sine	sin(a)	[0; 1]
Gaussian	$\alpha e^{\frac{-(x-b)^2}{2c^2}}$	Different for each variable

Source: Own research

calculated as a weighted sum of inputs. Neurons in one layer are directly connected to neurons in the next layer.

The RBF network is a three-layer forward neural network. RBF neural networks are among the youngest models of neural networks and are an alternative to classical models, such as the MLP networks.

Motivation to study them can be found in numerical mathematics, specifically in the study of interpolations and approximations of data. The solution to the approximation problem is usually sought as a linear combination of basic functions in some particular form, for example as a combination of polynomials.

The radial function is determined by its centre and its value depends on the distance of the argument from this centre. If we imagine a radial function in a two-dimensional space with a Euclidean metric, then sets of points with the same functional value form a circle.

RBF. This network realizes a linear combination of radial basic functions. If we look at the network as a classifier, we can say that the task of the first layer is to transform the input vector so that it can be evaluated by a linear combination of its new coordinates. Cover (1965) addressed this problem in the mid-1960s and showed that the number of hidden units should be chosen to be larger than the number of input units.

Functions will be chosen as activation functions in the hidden and output layer: identity, logistic, hyperbolic tangent, exponential, and sine. Table 5.1 shows the activation functions used in the hidden and output layer of MLP and RBF neural networks.

The identity function is one of the simplest linear functions. It is a function that always returns the same value that was used as its argument. Logistic sigmoid is a function often used to model development over time. In the initial phase, the growth is approximately exponential, later it slows with an increasing saturation, and finally, it stops asymptotically. The logistic function is often used in empirical sciences, for example, to model population growth and concentrations. The hyperbolic tangent is surprisingly similar to geniometric functions, although it has nothing to do with triangles. The exponential function is a purely monotonic function, as it is increasing or decreasing throughout the domain. The function is simple and limited from below, it has no maximum or minimum. The exponential function can be used, for example, in statistics when modelling exponential trends. For example, sales of a newly introduced product to the market may grow exponentially in the first years. The sine is a trigonometric function of some angle. It is written as *sin (a), where (a)* stands for the magnitude of the angle. For acute angles, it is defined in a right triangle as the ratio of the opposite perpendicular to the hypotenuse (longest side). The definition can be consistently extended to all real numbers as well as to the field of complex numbers. In the Gaussian function α, b, c are arbitrary real constants. The graph of a Gaussian is a characteristic symmetric "bell curve" shape in which α represents the height of the curve's peak, b is the position of the centre of the peak, and c (the standard deviation) is the parameter for controlling the width of the "bell".

As an error function, the method of least squares will be used. The least squares method refers to the fact that the regression function minimizes the sum of the squares of the variance from the actual data points. In this way, it is possible to draw a function which statistically provides the best fit for the data. Note that a regression function can either be linear (a straight line) or non-linear (a curving line):

$$E_{SOS} = \frac{1}{2N} \sum_{i=1}^{N} (y_i - t_i)^2 \tag{5.1}$$

where N is the number of trained cases, *yi* is the prediction of target variable *ti*, *ti* is the target variable of the i-th case.

For the calculation, the BFGS (Broyden–Fletcher–Goldfrarb–Shanno) and RBFT (Reputation-based Byzantine Fault Tolerance) algorithms will be used. For unconstrained optimization problems, there are many methods for them, where the BFGS method is one of the most effective quasi-Newton methods. The normal BFGS update only exploits the gradient information, while the information of function values available is neglected (Yuan and Lu 2011). RBFT is an algorithm that incorporates a reputation model to evaluate the operations of each node in the consensus process. The faulty nodes will get lower discourse rights in the voting process if any malicious behaviour is detected, with their reputation decreased (Lei et al. 2018). For more details, see Bishop (1995).

The weight decomposition will be set by default. 10,000 neural structures will be generated for all queries. There will be five neural networks that will have the best characteristics (based on the application of the least squares method—if there is no improvement, the calculation can be completed earlier). Furthermore, a set of results will be prepared for all samples (training, testing, validation). We obtain an overview of preserved artificial neural networks, weights of individual neurons in preserved networks, correlation coefficients (i.e. performance) of subsets of all preserved networks, statistical characteristics of balanced time series, and basic statistical characteristics of the original time series. Networks will also be saved in XML format. Moreover, graphs of balanced time series and graphs of predictions according to individual preserved networks will be created. Last but not least, there will be an analysis of data—data statistics in the form of a minimum, a maximum, average values, and standard deviation.

References

Bishop CM (1995) Neural networks for pattern recognition. Oxford University Press, New York

Cover T (1965) Geometrical and statistical properties of systems of linear inequalities with applications in pattern recognition. IEEE Trans Electron Comput 14:326–334

Lei K, Zhang Q, Xu L, Qi Z (2018) Reputation-based Byzantine Fault-Tolerance for consortium blockchain. In: 2018 IEEE 24th International Conference on Parallel and Distributed Systems (ICPADS)

Rosenblatt F (1957) The perceptron — a perceiving and recognizing automaton. Report 85-460-1. Cornell Aeronautical Laboratory

Rumelhart D, Hinton G, Williams R (1986) Learning representations by back-propagating errors. Nature 323:533–536

Yuan G, Lu X (2011) An active set limited memory BFGS algorithm for bound constrained optimization. Appl Math Model 35(7):3561–3573

Chapter 6
Data Evaluation: Results

The value of exports, imports, and trade balance was calculated and predicted on the basis of the date, using 1, 3, 6, and 12 steps, i.e. using the time series delay. The individual steps are always mentioned in the title of the subchapter, i.e. for individual variants.

6.1 Balance 1a

The first part presents the results of calculation and prediction of trade balance, using 1 step, i.e. one input neuron. Table 6.1 shows data statistics for the trade balance of Russia and the Czech Republic for the individual data sets which were divided according to information from the methodology, i.e. 70% of data into the training set, 15% of data into the test set, and 15% into the validation set. Statistical characteristics include minimum and maximum value, mean, and standard deviation.

From the table, it is obvious that for the observed period, the average value of the trade balance was USD 39,020.54 thousand.

According to the methodology, a total of 10,000 neural structures were generated, five of which showing the best results (according to the least squares method) were preserved and are shown in Table 6.2.

The table above shows that in this case, only RBF networks were preserved—in two cases, they were networks with 23 neurons in the hidden layer, in another case, we are speaking about networks with 28 neurons, then there is one network with 27 neurons and finally, one with 26 neurons in the hidden layer. All networks used the same RBFT-type training algorithm as well as activation functions in the hidden and output layers, namely the Gaussian and Identity functions, respectively. The networks show a relatively good performance, which will be described in more detail below. At the same time, we clearly see the error rate in the training, testing, and validation data set.

J. Horák et al., *Development of World Trade in the Context of the COVID-19 Pandemic*, Contributions to Economics,
https://doi.org/10.1007/978-3-031-27257-8_6

Table 6.1 Data statistics_E1_balance 1a

Samples	Month
Minimum (train)	34,028.00
Maximum (train)	44,043.00
Mean (train)	39,086.88
Standard deviation (train)	2895.43
Minimum (test)	34,000.00
Maximum (test)	44,012.00
Mean (test)	38,608.14
Standard deviation (test)	2928.16
Minimum (validation)	34,181.00
Maximum (validation)	43,921.00
Mean (validation)	39,117.47
Standard deviation (validation)	4455.34
Minimum (overall)	34,000.00
Maximum (overall)	44,043.00
Mean (overall)	39,020.54
Standard deviation (overall)	2912.73

Source: Own research

Table 6.3 shows the values of the weights of individual preserved neural structures. Due to its size, the table is shortened for clarity.

In the table, we can see how different are the values of the weights of the individual preserved networks.

Above, the relatively good performance of the networks was mentioned. This performance is presented in the form of correlation coefficients in Table 6.4. The correlation coefficients are therefore equal to the values for individual networks in the columns "Training perf.", "Test perf.", and "Validation perf." in Table 6.4.

It is evident that the performance of networks reaches relatively positive values. We are ideally looking for values as close as possible to 1.0. From this point of view, the highest performance is declared in the validation data set, when it reaches a value of around 0.9. In the other two data sets, values ranging from approximately 0.75 to 0.81 can be seen. From this data, we can already estimate that the best network from this set could be the fourth preserved RBF 1-23-1 network. To verify this deduction, we must take into consideration other results and outputs as well.

Table 6.5 shows the basic predictive statistics of individual preserved networks according to three defined data sets (test, training, validation). Basic statistics include minimum and maximum predictions, minimum and maximum residuals, and minimum and maximum standard residuals. Residuals speak of the difference between the observed and predicted value of the observed quantity. The smaller this difference, the better the predictive power. Large residual values, on the other hand, indicate a poor ability of the model to explain the target variable using explanatory variables. At the same time, any of their "systematic behaviour", even in small absolute values, is an indicator of a bad model, especially a poor choice of explanatory variables or their poor specification. It should therefore have an approximately

Table 6.2 Summary of active networks_E1_balance 1a

Index	Net. name	Training perf.	Test perf.	Validation perf.	Training error	Test error	Validation error	Training algorithm	Error function	Hidden activation	Output activation
1	RBF 1-26-1	0.759389	0.767809	0.893791	1755.868	2490.504	694.7803	RBFT	SOS	Gaussian	Identity
2	RBF 1-28-1	0.764204	0.811736	0.894890	1725.750	2212.311	676.8840	RBFT	SOS	Gaussian	Identity
3	RBF 1-27-1	0.760115	0.778833	0.902534	1751.294	2492.011	643.9099	RBFT	SOS	Gaussian	Identity
4	RBF 1-23-1	0.777244	0.797265	0.893855	1642.067	2356.637	726.3014	RBFT	SOS	Gaussian	Identity
5	RBF 1-23-1	0.755147	0.763554	0.900763	1782.521	2547.341	649.5622	RBFT	SOS	Gaussian	Identity

Source: Own research

Table 6.3 Network weights_E1_balance 1a

Weight ID	Connections	Weight values	Connections	Weight values	Connections	Weight values	Connections	Weight values	Connections	Weight values
	RBF 1-26-1	RBF 1-26-1	RBF 1_28-1	RBF 1-28-1	RBF 1-27-1	RBF 1-27-1	RBF 1-23-1	RBF 1-23-1	RBF 1-23-1	RBF 1-23-1
1	Month-1 --> hidden neuron 1	0.291762	Month-1 → hidden neuron 1	0.307039	Month-1 → hidden neuron 1	0.106540	Month-1 → hidden neuron 1	0.106540	Month-1 → hidden neuron 1	0.155067
2	Month-1 → hidden neuron 2	0.072891	Month-1 → hidden neuron 2	0.614079	Month-1 → hidden neuron 2	0.437644	Month-1 → hidden neuron 2	0.352671	Month-1 → hidden neuron 2	0.340389
3	Month-1 → hidden neuron 3	0.392112	Month-1 → hidden neuron 3	0.310135	Month-1 → hidden neuron 3	0.927009	Month-1 → hidden neuron 3	0.325412	Month-1 → hidden neuron 3	0.486271
4	Month-1 → hidden neuron 4	0.854119	Month-1 → hidden neuron 4	0.975637	Month-1 → hidden neuron 4	0.136895	Month-1 → hidden neuron 4	0.291762	Month-1 → hidden neuron 4	0.373839
5	Month-1 → hidden neuron 5	0.537993	Month-1 → hidden neuron 5	0.288967	Month-1 → hidden neuron 5	0.048627	Month-1 → hidden neuron 5	0.230954	Month-1 → hidden neuron 5	0.996905
6	Month-1 → hidden neuron 6	0.942287	Month-1 → hidden neuron 6	0.747778	Month-1 → hidden neuron 6	0.802297	Month-1 → hidden neuron 6	0.638342	Month-1 → hidden neuron 6	0.957364
7	Month-1 → hidden neuron 7	0.939191	Month-1 → hidden neuron 7	0.896655	Month-1 → hidden neuron 7	0.975637	Month-1 → hidden neuron 7	0.492461	Month-1 → hidden neuron 7	0.738592
8	Month-1 → hidden neuron 8	0.626061	Month-1 → hidden neuron 8	0.525811	Month-1 → hidden neuron 8	0.659511	Month-1 → hidden neuron 8	0.692961	Month-1 → hidden neuron 8	0.091263

9	Month-1 → hidden neuron 9	0.914828	Month-1 → hidden neuron 9	0.045632	Month-1 → hidden neuron 9	0.258412	Month-1 → hidden neuron 9	0.383025	Month-1 → hidden neuron 9	0.054818
10	Month-1 → hidden neuron 10	0.376835	Month-1 → hidden neuron 10	0.273689	Month-1 → hidden neuron 10	0.386021	Month-1 → hidden neuron 10	0.127808	Month-1 → hidden neuron 10	0.568447
…	…	…	…	…	…	…	…	…	…	…
81			Hidden neuron 25 → balance Russia/Czechia	–0.002506	Hidden neuron 27 → balance Russia/Czechia	–0.002072				
82			Hidden neuron 26 → balance Russia/Czechia	–0.000007	Hidden bias → balance Russia/Czechia	0.424939				
83			Hidden neuron 27 → balance Russia/Czechia	0.011001						
84			Hidden neuron 28 → balance Russia/Czechia	0.000282						
85			Hidden bias → balance Russia/Czechia	0.503824						

Source: Own research

Table 6.4 Correlation coefficients_E1_balance 1a

	Balance Russia/Czechia	Balance Russia/Czechia	Balance Russia/Czechia
1.RBF 1-26-1	0.759389	0.767809	0.893791
2.RBF 1-28-1	0.764204	0.811736	0.894890
3.RBF 1-27-1	0.760115	0.778833	0.902534
4.RBF 1-23-1	0.777244	0.797265	0.893855
5.RBF 1-23-1	0.755147	0.763554	0.900763

Source: Own research

Table 6.5 Predictions statistics_E1_balance 1a

	Target: Balance Russia/Czechia				
Statistics	1.RBF 1-26-1	2.RBF 1-28-1	3.RBF 1-27-1	4.RBF 1-23-1	5.RBF 1-23-1
Minimum prediction (train)	−109.421	−81.545	−96.663	−84.125	−82.739
Maximum prediction (train)	263.330	257.920	276.012	267.010	274.137
Minimum prediction (test)	−94.841	−69.661	1.045	−8.023	−42.758
Maximum prediction (test)	264.023	253.799	264.454	266.546	274.256
Minimum prediction (validation)	−32.157	−79.722	−82.467	−86.144	−87.891
Maximum prediction (validation)	258.293	257.338	257.684	254.000	251.657
Minimum residual (train)	−253.189	−194.916	−252.999	−216.433	−236.039
Maximum residual (train)	224.617	194.322	212.819	230.603	226.099
Minimum residual (test)	−314.490	−276.963	−317.873	−281.937	−300.034
Maximum residual (test)	106.068	133.655	145.216	89.119	161.267
Minimum residual (validation)	−108.224	−114.840	−111.131	−119.619	−103.390
Maximum residual (validation)	98.828	90.889	85.305	94.159	101.931
Minimum standard residual (train)	−6.042	−4.692	−6.046	−5.341	−5.591
Maximum standard residual (train)	5.360	4.678	5.085	5.691	5.355
Minimum standard residual (test)	−6.302	−5.888	−6.368	−5.808	−5.945
Maximum standard residual (test)	2.125	2.842	2.909	1.836	3.195
Minimum standard residual (validation)	−4.106	−4.414	−4.379	−4.439	−4.057
Maximum standard residual (validation)	3.749	3.493	3.362	3.494	3.999

Source: Own research

symmetrical distribution around the zero mean and a constant variance delimited from above.

It is clear from the table that the largest residuals are observed in the training data set which also contains the most data. However, even higher residuals are recorded

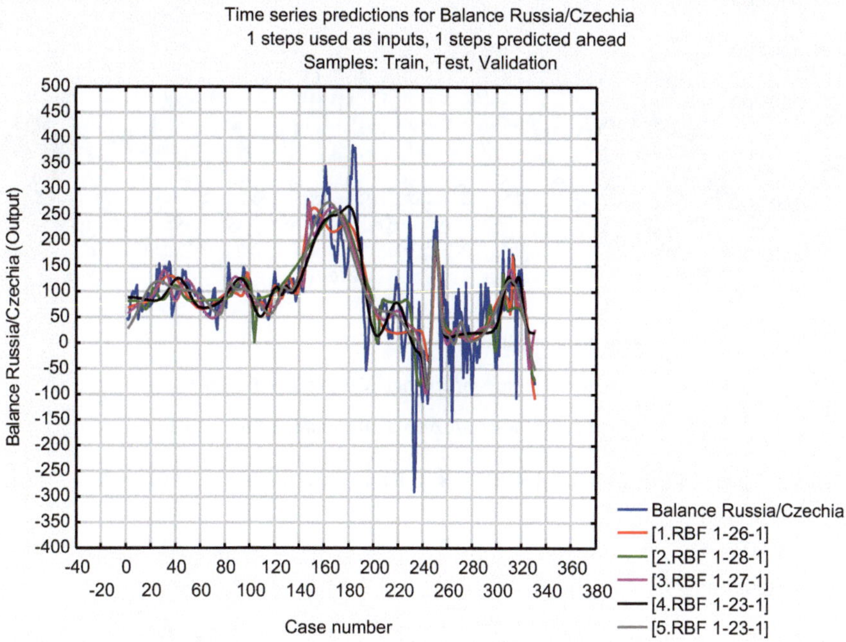

Fig. 6.1 Time series predictions_E1_balance 1a. Source: Own research

for the values of minimal residuals in the test data set. The minimum and maximum standard residuals are very close to the ideal value of 0 and indicate a relatively successful prediction.

Figure 6.1 presents balanced time series. The blue curve indicates the actual development of the Russia/Czechia trade balance, while the colourful curves indicate the individual generated and stored neural networks, or the predictions of the mentioned trade balance according to the individual neural structures.

The figure presents the fact that the preserved neural structures can roughly copy the real development of the trade balance. However, they cannot capture local maxima and minima. This will be better apparent from the figures of the individual conserved neural structures in relation to the actual evolution and value of the residuals. Figure 6.2 deals with the neural structure 1.RBF 1-26-1. The blue curve again indicates the actual development of the Russia/Czechia trade balance, the red curve indicates the output, i.e. the prediction according to the given neural structure, and the green curve presents the value of residuals.

The figure only confirms the above-stated—the given neural network can only roughly copy the value of the Russia/Czechia trade balance. However, it cannot capture the local minima and maxima. Therefore, it is rather unsuitable for use in practice, it can bring only a very approximate value of the trade balance.

Figure 6.3 presents the same issue, this time from the point of view of the second preserved neural structure 2.RBF 1-28-1.

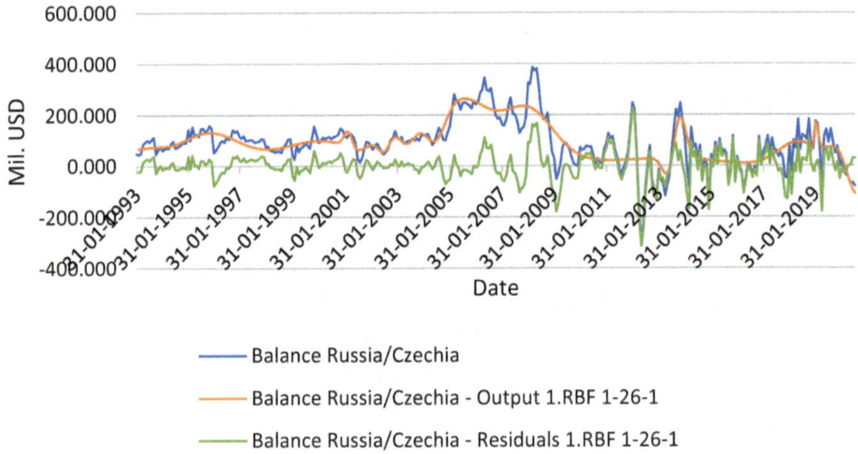

Fig. 6.2 Time series prediction—1. RBF 1-26-1_E1_balance 1a. Source: Own research

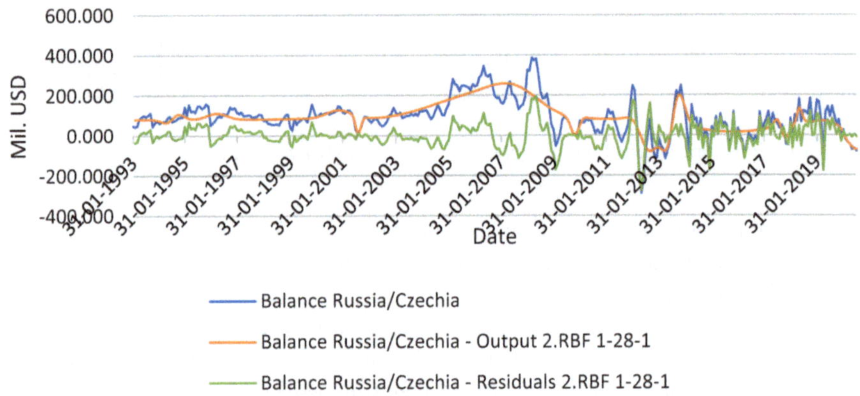

Fig. 6.3 Time series prediction—2. RBF 1-28-1_E1_balance 1a. Source: Own research

It is clear from the course of the individual curves that it is a neural network with a similar predictive ability as in the case of the above-mentioned first preserved structure. It has a similar performance, i.e. similar properties—it can roughly copy the development of the trade balance, but it cannot capture local minima and maxima. Thus, even this network does not seem to be applicable in practice.

The same is true for the third preserved network 3.RBF 1-27-1 which is presented in Fig. 6.4.

In a similar manner, the fourth conserved neural structure 4.RBF 1-23-1 shown in Fig. 6.5 is presented.

The worst of the five preserved networks is the last one, i.e. the fifth neural structure 5.RBF 1-23-1 which has a slightly lower prediction accuracy than the previous networks (see Fig. 6.6).

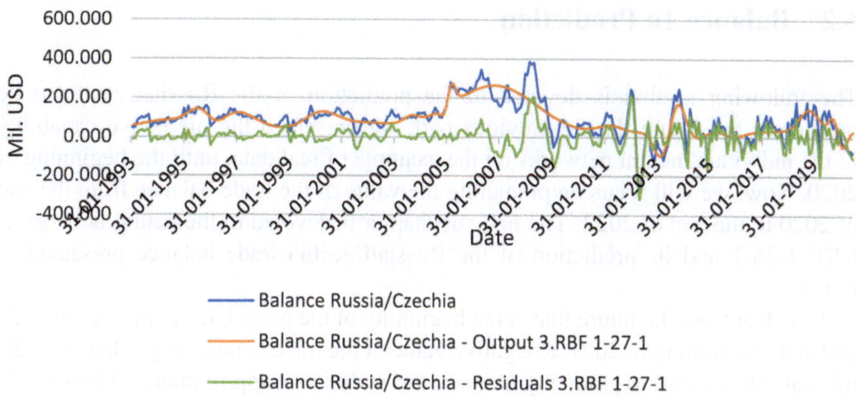

Fig. 6.4 Time series prediction—3. RBF 1-27-1_E1_balance 1a. Source: Own research

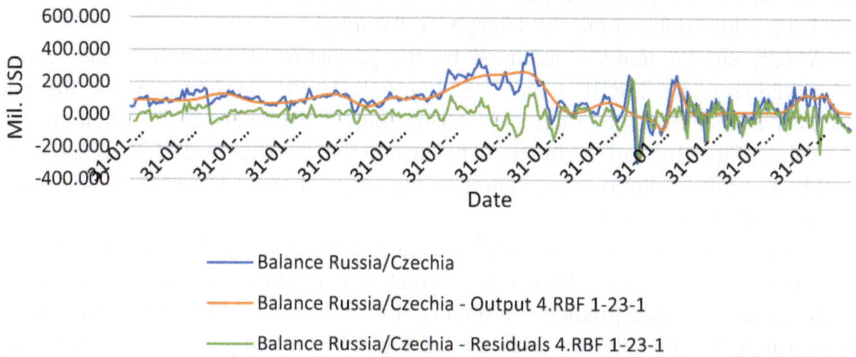

Fig. 6.5 Time series prediction—4. RBF 1-23-1_E1_balance 1a. Source: Own research

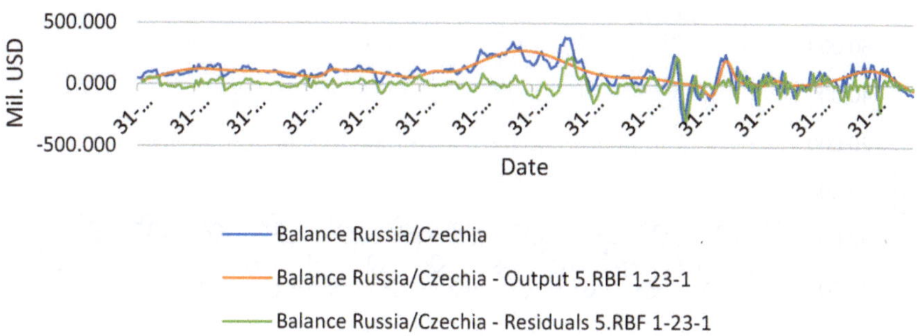

Fig. 6.6 Time series prediction—5. RBF 1-23-1_E1_balance 1a. Source: Own research

6.2 Balance 1a Prediction

The following section is devoted to the prediction of the Russia/Czechia trade balance in the future. In the previous part, we presented the predictive capability of the individual neural networks on the example of real data, until the beginning of 2020. Now, we will focus on predicting the value of the trade balance from the end of 2020 to the end of 2022. The first subchapter is devoted to the neural network 1. RBF 1-26-1 and its prediction of the Russia/Czechia trade balance presented in Fig. 6.7.

It is clear from the figure that at the beginning of the period, i.e. at the end of 2020 and at the beginning of 2021, a negative value of the trade balance is predicted, while this value is forecast to gradually increase and stabilize at approximately USD 47–48 million at the end of 2021. It also shows the phenomenon of steady value in the case of the long-term prediction which is generally not considered accurate—in the second half of the predicted period, the value remains almost unchanged and the prediction does not assume any changes in the trend.

A very similar trend is assumed by the prediction selected over the second preserved structure 2. RBF 1-28-1 (see Fig. 6.8). Unlike the first network, this one predicts a negative value of the trade balance only at the end of 2020, assuming that the value of the Russia/Czechia trade balance in the whole period of 2021 and 2022 will be in positive numbers oscillating in the range of about USD 80 million in the second half of the period.

The growing trend of the Russia/Czechia trade balance is also confirmed by the third preserved structure 3. RBF 1-27-1 which also assumes growth at the beginning of the predicted period predicting a stabilization of the value at USD 32.8040 million approximately from February 2021 on (see Fig. 6.9). At first glance, compared to the previous two figures, a much more specific targeting for a given value of around USD 32.80 million can be seen. According to the third preserved network, the trade

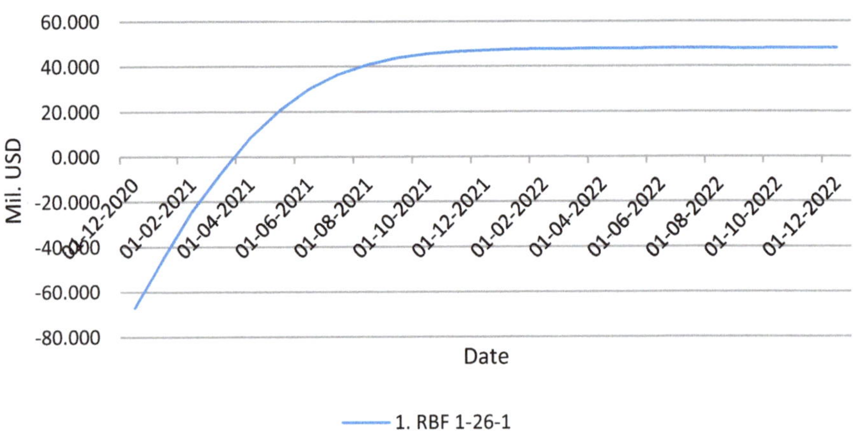

Fig. 6.7 Balance prediction—1. RBF 1-26-1_E1_balance 1a. Source: Own research

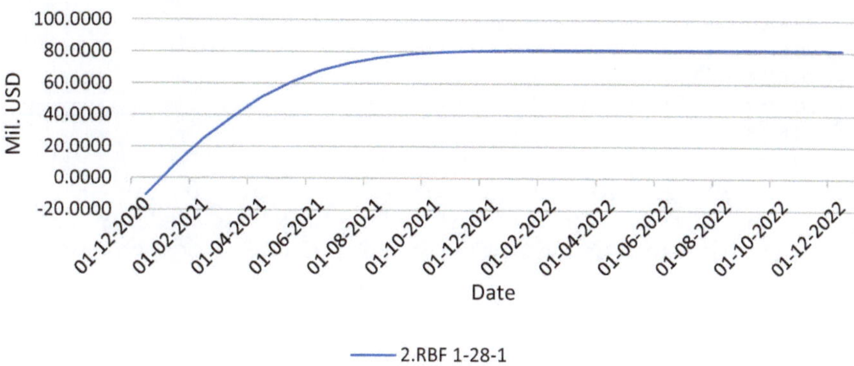

Fig. 6.8 Balance prediction—2. RBF 1-28-1_E1_balance 1a. Source: Own research

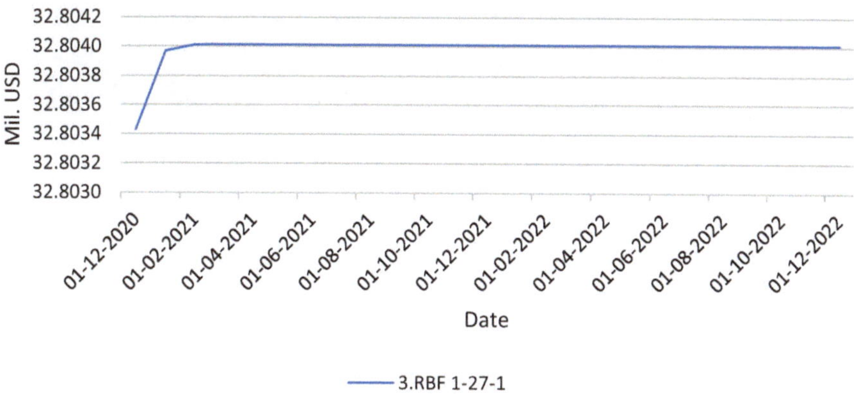

Fig. 6.9 Balance prediction—3. RBF 1-27-1_E1_balance 1a. Source: Own research

balance should stay at this value for more than 2 years, it does not assume a negative value of the trade balance or any larger or smaller fluctuations.

In a similar way, the Russia/Czechia trade balance is also predicted by the fourth conserved network 4. RBF 1-23-1 shown in Fig. 6.10. This network predicts a slight decline in the trade balance at the beginning of the period, while from April 2021, a stabilization at USD 206,758 million is predicted. Again, the same phenomenon that was declared for the previous network occurred there as well.

A completely different view of the Russia/Czechia trade balance forecast is offered by the fifth retained network 5. RBF 1-23-1 assuming a negative trade balance value in the whole period, which is initially a value of approximately USD −80 million, by the end of 2022 then approximately USD −10 million. The neural network therefore predicts a gradual increase (see Fig. 6.11).

Based on the above-presented facts, it is clear that all networks can roughly predict the actual development of the Russia/Czechia trade balance, but they cannot capture the local minima and maxima. Therefore, they are rather unusable in

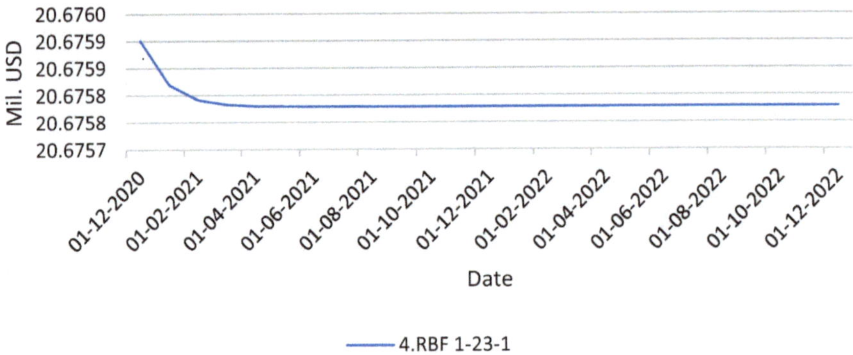

Fig. 6.10 Balance prediction—4. RBF 1-23-1_E1_balance 1a. Source: Own research

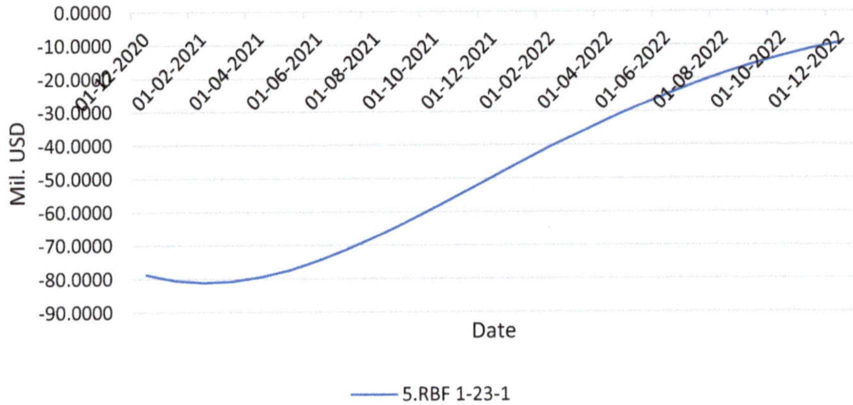

Fig. 6.11 Balance prediction—5. RBF 1-23-1_E1_balance 1a. Source: Own research

practice. As for future forecasts, the networks predict the value of the trade balance relatively differently, three of which tend to the initial negative value of the trade balance which should reach positive numbers during the predicted period. The two preserved and presented networks predict a rather stable value of the trade balance in positive numbers. The predictions seem rather meaningless, especially for a longer period. Here, prediction networks can no longer cope well. To evaluate the real success of these networks will of course be the subject of further research which will compare the real development of the Russia/Czechia trade balance and the predicted development according to these preserved networks.

6.3 Balance 3a

According to the methodology, a total of 10,000 neural structures were generated in this case as well, five of which showing the best results (according to the least squares method) were preserved and are shown in Table 6.6.

It is clear from the table that the best results were obtained only by the MLP-type networks, with four to eight neurons in the hidden layer. All preserved networks were generated using the BFGS training algorithm. In the hidden layer, three of them use the hyperbolic tangent function and the remaining two use the logistic function. The same three networks use the exponential output function, the others the logistic one, and the last, fifth preserved network the hyperbolic tangent function. At the same time, the relatively high performance of the given networks is noticeable in all data groups. The highest performance is achieved in the test data set.

Based on this information, we cannot accurately determine the most suitable neural structure, so we continue with further analysis. Its principle is identical to the one that has already been mentioned, so only its shortened version will be presented due to its extent that would otherwise exceed many hundreds of pages.

The weights of individual preserved neural structures were analysed, correlation coefficients as well as basic prediction statistics of individual preserved networks according to three defined data sets were examined in more detail. Based on this information, we can state that the performance of all preserved networks is approximately the same, especially the standard residuals are very low and close to the ideal value. The minimum and maximum predictions and residuals are very similar for individual data sets in the case of all preserved networks, which means a relatively successful result.

Figure 6.12 presents balanced time series. The blue curve again indicates the actual development of the Russia/Czechia trade balance, while otherwise the coloured curves indicate the individual generated and stored neural networks, or the predictions of the mentioned trade balance according to the individual neural structures.

The given figure expresses a very similar situation as in the previous version (balance 1a), i.e. the fact that the preserved networks can balance the time series of the Russia/Czechia trade balance only roughly and cannot capture the local minimums and maximums. This, of course, was confirmed by the individual figures of the balanced time series. The best preserved network in this case appears to be the fourth preserved network 4. MLP 3-7-1, which is presented in Fig. 6.13.

However, it can also be deduced from the course of this network that especially the not very large fluctuations in the real value of the Russia/Czechia trade balance cannot be balanced and predicted by the given network. In practice, therefore, these preserved networks will not be entirely suitable. However, their performance could be enhanced by further learning.

As in the previous case, figures of Russia/Czechia trade balance forecasts were drawn for this variant, for the period from the end of 2020 to the end of 2022. The first retained network 1. MLP 3-8-1 predicted a negative trade balance for the whole

Table 6.6 Summary of active networks_E1_balance 3a

Index	Net. name	Training perf.	Test perf.	Validation perf.	Training error	Test error	Validation error	Training algorithm	Error function	Hidden activation	Output activation
1	MLP 3-8-1	0.803928	0.873299	0.763466	1468.332	1478.009	1434.354	BFGS 223	SOS	Tanh	Exponential
2	MLP 3-4-1	0.754668	0.859839	0.764163	1782.043	1868.921	1417.662	BFGS 91	SOS	Tanh	Exponential
3	MLP 3-5-1	0.757259	0.828786	0.811405	1765.919	2212.303	1169.172	BFGS 250	SOS	Logistic	Logistic
4	MLP 3-7-1	0.779150	0.837315	0.796574	1634.143	2029.537	1302.705	BFGS 189	SOS	Tanh	Exponential
5	MLP 3-4-1	0.744269	0.825185	0.829268	1850.250	2226.349	1061.241	BFGS 105	SOS	Logistic	Tanh

Source: Own research

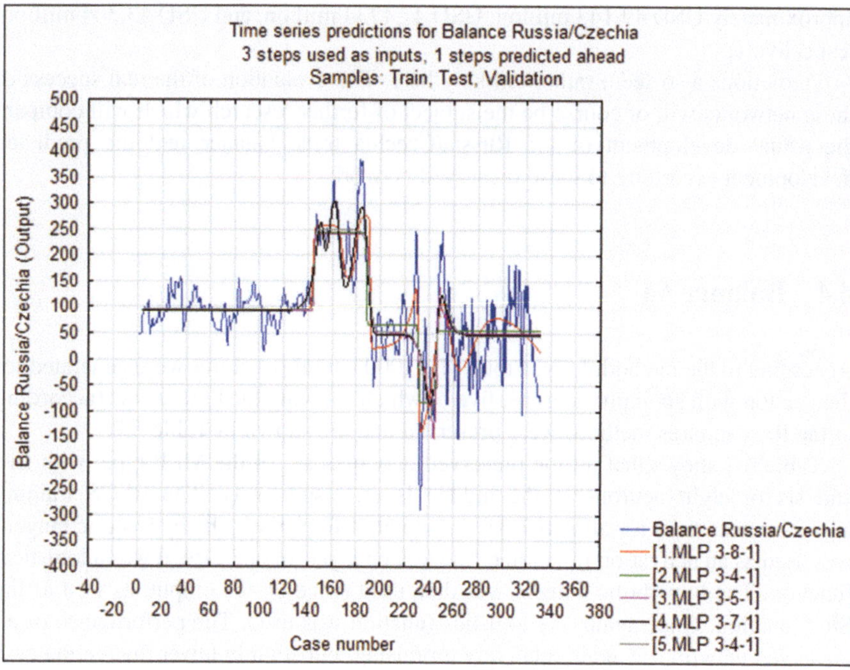

Fig. 6.12 Time series predictions_E1_balance 3a. Source: Own research

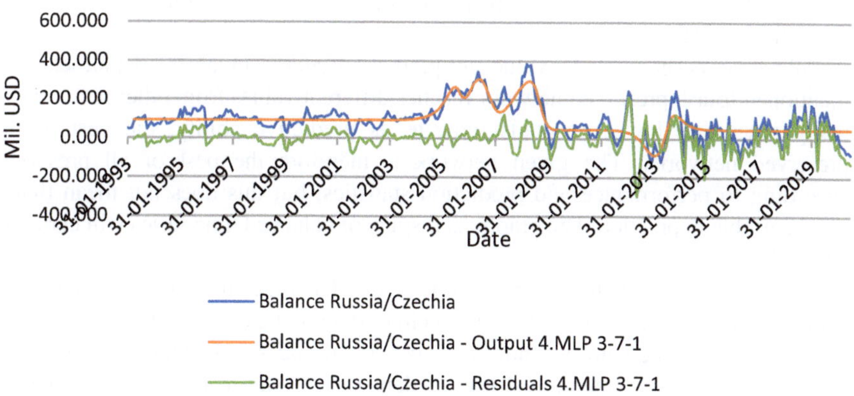

Fig. 6.13 Time series prediction—4. MLP 3-7-1_E1_balance 3a. Source: Own research

period where the final value reached USD −100 million. The second maintained network 2. MLP 3-4-1 predicted a constant value of approximately USD 53–54 million for the entire period. The other three retained networks agreed on relatively constant values of the trade balance which should decline only slightly during the forecast period, with some stabilization at the end of the period. All three networks also predict a similar value of the Russia/Czechia trade balance, namely approximately USD 49.143 million, USD 47.4734 million, and USD 43.304 million, respectively.

Predictions also seem rather unlikely here. The evaluation of the real success of these networks will of course be the subject of further research which will compare the actual development of the Russia/Czechia trade balance and the predicted development according to these preserved networks.

6.4 Balance 6a

According to the methodology, a total of 10,000 neural structures were generated for the version with six input neurons, five of which showing the best results (according to the least squares method) were preserved and are shown in Table 6.7.

Table 6.7 shows that all the preserved networks are of the MLP type, with five and six or eight neurons in the hidden layer, respectively. The BFGS training algorithm was used for all networks. In a total of four cases, the hyperbolic tangent was used as an activation function of the hidden layer. In one case, it was a logistical function. The hyperbolic tangent was then used twice on the output, as well as the Sine function. Once again, the logistics function was used. The performance of all preserved networks is again relatively promising, but slightly lower than in the case of previous variants. In all data sets, the fourth network 4. MLP 6-8-1 achieved the best performance in this case. To confirm its functionality, we will proceed to the evaluation of the weights of the given networks, closer correlation coefficients, and predictive statistics.

All networks show similar values for predictions and residuals in all data sets. The mentioned fourth preserved network reaches different values from other networks in many cases and lower residuals indicate its predictive ability, the best of the preserved networks. The given network is therefore the best of all preserved according to performance and prediction statistics, but this does not mean that it will be usable in practice. The graphical display of balanced time series will certainly also help.

Figure 6.14 presents the balanced time series. The blue curve again indicates the actual development of the Russia/Czechia trade balance, while otherwise the colourful curves indicate the individual generated and stored neural networks, or the predictions of the mentioned trade balance according to the individual neural structures.

The generated figure shows that none of the preserved networks can accurately balance the time series of the Russia/Czechia trade balance for the observed period. They can only respond to larger deviations in the time series, but they still cannot cover the local minima or maxima at all, or even other smaller deviations in the time series. In this respect, the fourth conserved network 4. MLP 6-8-1 is indeed the best, but, as it can be seen in Fig. 6.15, still very far from the required accuracy and reality.

Subsequently, it is necessary to conduct the analysis of the predictive ability of individual preserved neural structures. The value of the Russia/Czechia trade balance

Table 6.7 Summary of active networks_E1_balance 6a

Index	Net. name	Training perf.	Test perf.	Validation perf.	Training error	Test error	Validation error	Training algorithm	Error function	Hidden activation	Output activation
1	MLP 6-8-1	0.705805	0.741605	0.748883	2077.212	2733.757	1499.872	BFGS 237	SOS	Tanh	Sine
2	MLP 6-5-1	0.749560	0.766856	0.742953	1818.975	2483.413	1548.124	BFGS 94	SOS	Tanh	Tanh
3	MLP 6-5-1	0.731936	0.764883	0.735370	1921.678	2601.402	1587.848	BFGS 284	SOS	Logistic	Sine
4	MLP 6-8-1	0.767525	0.835947	0.798831	1704.231	2050.918	1270.207	BFGS 193	SOS	Tanh	Logistic
5	MLP 6-6-1	0.712869	0.748046	0.773504	2036.545	2681.908	1367.354	BFGS 106	SOS	Tanh	Tanh

Source: Own research

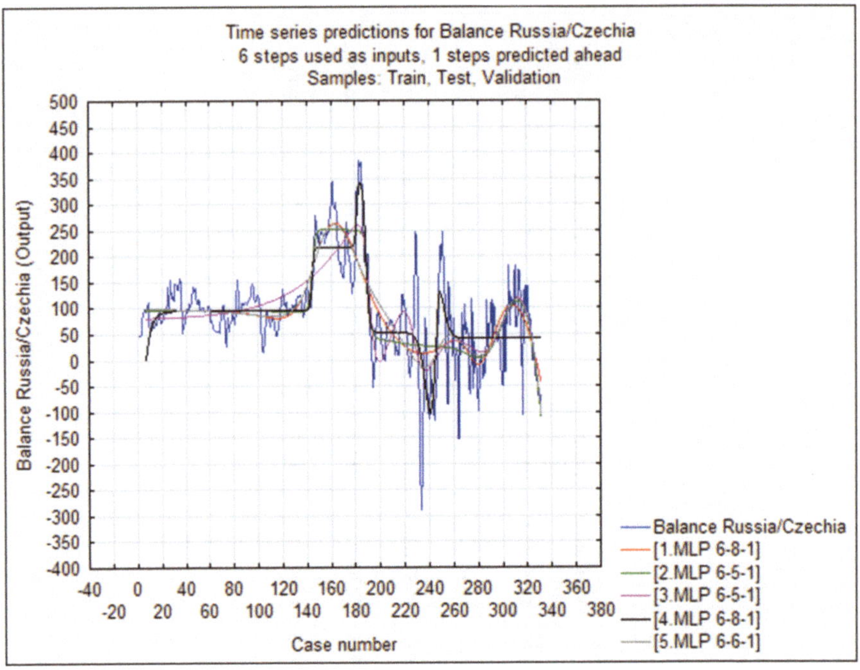

Fig. 6.14 Time series predictions_E1_balance 6a. Source: Own research

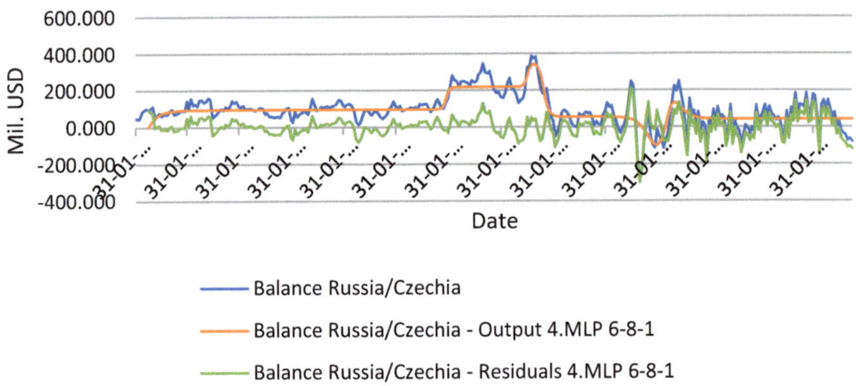

Fig. 6.15 Time series prediction—4. MLP 6-8-1_E1_balance 6a. Source: Own research

was again predicted for the period from the end of 2020 to the end of 2022. As for the first neural structure 1. MLP 6-8-1, it predicts a rather steeply falling negative value of the trade balance (at the beginning of the period at the value around USD USD −100 million USD, at the end of the period then USD −425 million). The second network 2. MLP 6-5-1 predicts a similar course, but at the beginning it predicts the value of the trade balance at USD −250 million, while at the end of the period even

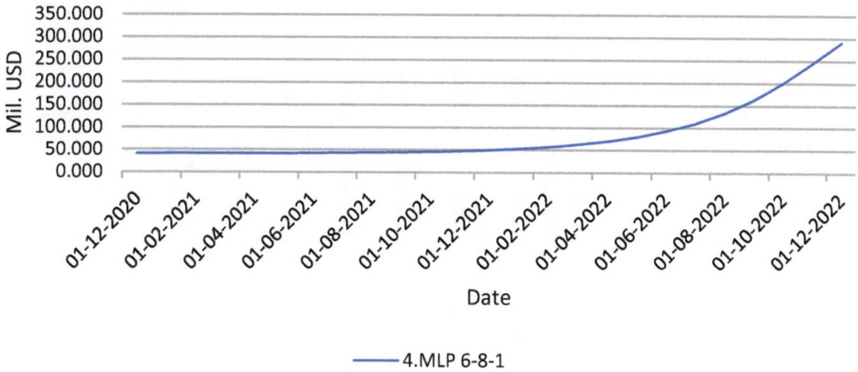

Fig. 6.16 Balance prediction—4. MLP 6-8-1_E1_balance 6a. Source: Own research

about USD −750 million. The third network 3. MLP 6-5-1 also predicts the value of the Russia/Czechia trade balance very similarly, while at the end of the observed period, we reach a value of approximately USD −825 million. As for the fourth preserved structure 4. MLP 6-8-1 that has already been mentioned several times, it really stands out in the context of these preserved networks and predicts a relatively stable positive trade balance value approaching USD 50 million from the beginning, while at the beginning of 2022, this value will further grow quite significantly and will reach the final value of about USD 300 million in the next 12 months (see Fig. 6.16).

As for the fifth network 5. MLP 6-6-1, its prediction corresponds to the course of predictions of the first three above-mentioned preserved networks. Thus, it also predicts a negative value of the trade balance starting at about USD −250 million and ending in 2022 at almost USD −700 million.

The results of this variant show that again, none of the preserved networks will be completely usable in practice. The 4. MLP 6-8-1 network seemed to be the most suitable from the beginning. This is also proved by the prediction made by this network which, however, as well as the adjustment of the real time series of the Russia/Czechia trade balance, is very general and not very specific, and therefore also essentially unusable in practice (at least without further learning and improvement).

6.5 Balance 12a

According to the methodology, a total of 10,000 neural structures were generated in this case, i.e. in the version with 12 input neurons, five of which showing the best results (according to the least squares method) were preserved and are shown in Table 6.8.

Table 6.8 Summary of active networks_E1_balance 12a

Index	Net. name	Training perf.	Test perf.	Validation perf.	Training error	Test error	Validation error	Training algorithm	Error function	Hidden activation	Output activation
1	MLP 12-6-1	0.728917	0.760985	0.772490	1936.780	2622.076	1387.913	BFGS 142	SOS	Tanh	Sine
2	MLP 12-6-1	0.707002	0.745603	0.743912	2067.333	2715.116	1518.762	BFGS 163	SOS	Tanh	Tanh
3	MLP 12-4-1	0.693316	0.756870	0.771486	2146.202	2686.385	1385.953	BFGS 103	SOS	Logistic	Sine
4	MLP 12-5-1	0.739087	0.852789	0.786091	1876.224	2067.697	1296.767	BFGS 95	SOS	Logistic	Tanh
5	MLP 12-6-1	0.754990	0.860082	0.747324	1779.713	1873.428	1512.670	BFGS 195	SOS	Tanh	Logistic

Source: Own research

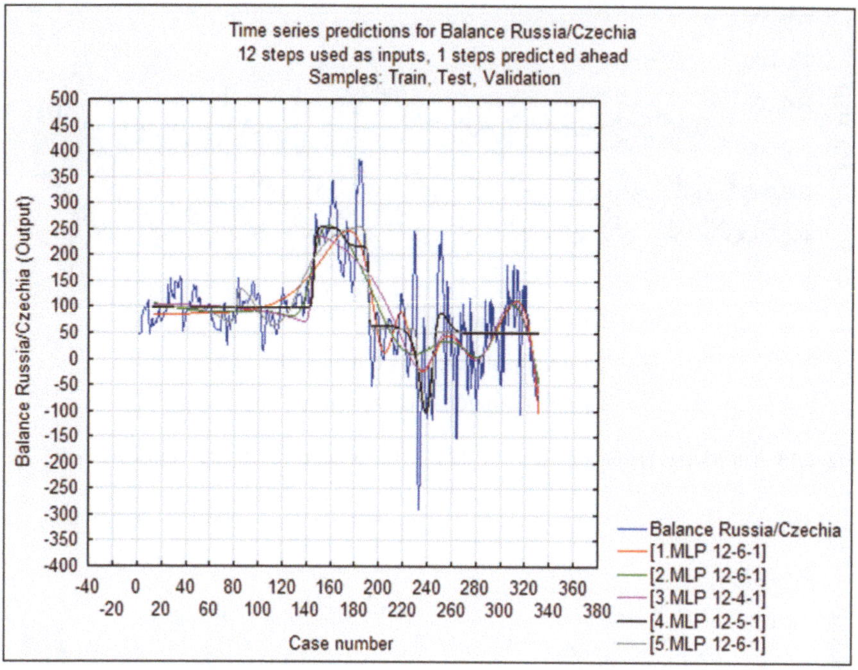

Fig. 6.17 Time series predictions_E1_balance 12a. Source: Own research

The table shows all five preserved networks which in this case are all MLP types, with four, five, and six neurons in the hidden layer, respectively. The BFGS algorithm was used to train all networks. The functions used to activate the hidden and output layers alternated between logistic, hyperbolic tangent and sine. As for the performance of individual networks, it is relatively high, with the fifth network 5. MLP 12-6-1, or the fourth preserved network 4. MLP 12-5-1. In most cases, network performance in the test and validation data set achieves better parameters than in the training data set.

In this case, it is once again necessary to proceed to further analyses that will reveal the capabilities and actual performance of the individual preserved networks. As for the prediction statistics, they are very similar for all networks—similar values in individual data sets, relatively positive values of maximum and minimum standard residuals in all data sets. As in the previous cases, it is appropriate to compare the predictions of individual networks with the actual time series of the Russia/Czechia trade balance. This comparison is offered by Fig. 6.17, where at first glance, we can see the state observed in the previous versions as well, i.e. the low ability of networks to predict local minima and maxima, the ability to only very roughly copy the actual values of the trade balance, etc.

Not even the individual figures of balanced time series changed the view of the low predictive power. All networks can copy the real development of the trade balance really only very roughly. It is also very difficult to determine which of the

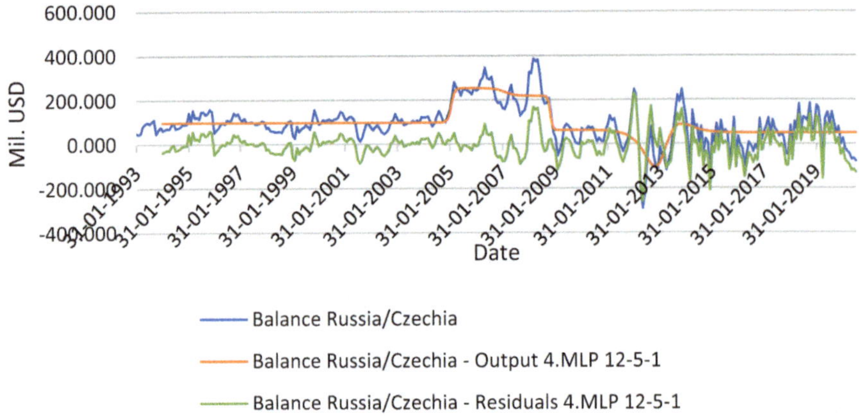

Fig. 6.18 Time series prediction—4. MLP 12-5-1_E1_balance 12a. Source: Own research

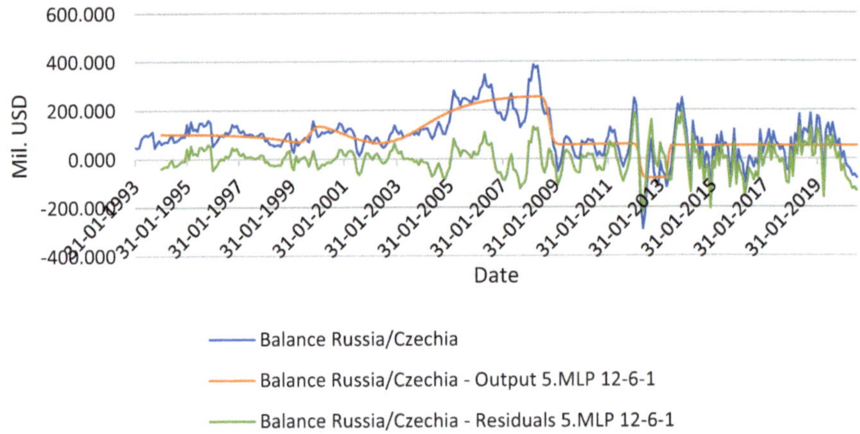

Fig. 6.19 Time series prediction—5. MLP 12-6-1_E1_balance 12a. Source: Own research

networks is the most successful in this case. For comparison, we present the two networks mentioned above, namely the fourth network 4. MLP 12-5-1 (Fig. 6.18) and the fifth network 5. MLP 12-6-1 (Fig. 6.19).

It is clear from the figures that the network cannot copy the actual development of the trade balance, any extreme fluctuations only very sparingly. The same is presented in another presented network.

To create the whole image, the networks were again used to predict the trade balance from the end of 2020 to the end of 2022. The predictions also confirm a similar trend of the first three preserved networks and a similar trend of the other two. Network 1. MLP 12-6-1 predicts a negative value of the trade balance at all times (from about USD −250 million to about USD −590 million). Very similarly, the second network 2. MLP 12-6-1 (from about USD −110 million to about USD −430

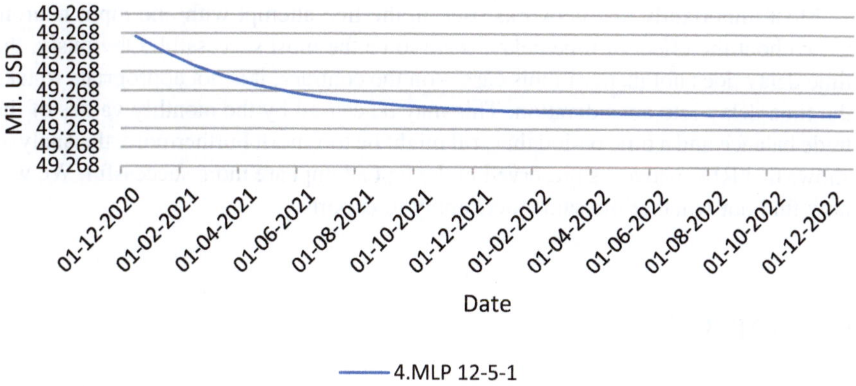

Fig. 6.20 Balance prediction—4. MLP 12-5-1_E1_balance 12a. Source: Own research

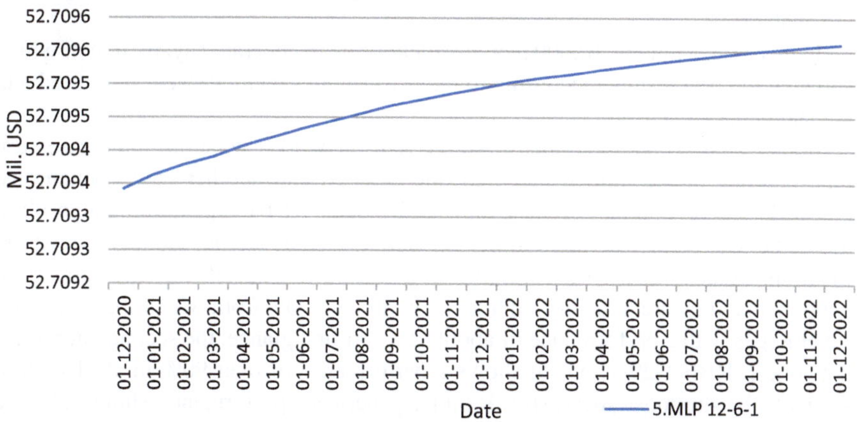

Fig. 6.21 Balance prediction—5. MLP 12-6-1_E1_balance 12a. Source: Own research

million) and the third network 3. MLP 12-4-1 (from about USD −140 million to approx. USD −570 million). In contrast, the fourth network 4. MLP 12-5-1 predicts a relatively constant value of the Russia/Czechia trade balance (approximately USD 49.268 million)—see Fig. 6.20.

The same applies also for the 5. MLP 12-6-1 network which predicts a slightly increasing value of approximately USD 52.7094 million up to USD 52.7096 million—see Fig. 6.21.

Not even the preserved networks in the variant with 12 input neurons are applicable in practice for the prediction of the Russia/Czechia trade balance. Thus, they can only roughly estimate the development of the trade balance, but they cannot capture the local minima and maxima, while the predicted values can be said unrealistic (of course, once again, further research and verification according to the actual reality will be important).

Most importantly, the networks used in the first attempt with one input neuron, i.e. without the effect of time delay, seem to be the most successful. Obviously, the time delay does not matter in this case—on the contrary, it is not appropriate to take the time delay into consideration. This may be caused by the monthly values of the trade balance and a time period that still might be too short. Furthermore, the analysis shows that RBF networks preserved in the first attempt are more successful. We will now find out whether the same facts apply to exports.

6.6 Export 1a

The second observed matter, according to the established methodology, is the export between Russia and Czechia, again in different variants with different number of input neurons due to work with time series delays, which can fundamentally affect the analysis.

In this case, a total of 10,000 neural structures were generated again, five of which showing the best results (according to the least squares method) were preserved and are shown in Table 6.9.

It is clear from the table that these are RBF networks, which in three cases use nine neurons in the hidden layer, in one case 26 and another case 23 neurons. Networks are very similar because they use the same RBFT-type training algorithm, the same Gaussian activation function, and the same output-identity activation function. In terms of the network performance, or more specifically the correlation coefficients, they are at a very high level, in all data sets, from which the validation set emerges with a performance of about 95%. At first glance, the second successful network 2. RBF 1-29-1, which shows a performance of over 90% in all data sets, seems to be the most successful. Promising network performance should also be confirmed by Table 6.10 which deals with predictive statistics in the individual data sets.

As for residuals, they should ideally be as low as possible and ideally similar in all data sets. We see that this is indeed the case, especially for the standard residuals, and the promising performance of the networks is therefore based on predictive statistics.

Figure 6.22 shows the prediction of time series, respectively, the alignment of the actual time series by means of the preserved neural structures.

It is clear from the figure that the networks predict quite successfully the gross development of exports, while they have problems with the local minima and maxima. However, it is already clear from this figure that the networks are more successful in this case than in the case of the previous variants and time series of the trade balance. For a closer evaluation, we must provide figures of aligned time series for each preserved network separately. First, there is the alignment of the time series according to 1. RBF 1-29-1 in Fig. 6.23.

The figure shows the ability of the neural network to roughly copy the development of the actual export values. It can only respond to larger changes in the annual

Table 6.9 Summary of active networks_E1_export 1a

Index	Net. name	Training perf.	Test perf.	Validation perf.	Training error	Test error	Validation error	Trai. Alg.	Error function	Hidden activation	Output activation
1	RBF 1-29-1	0.896082	0.870243	0.954748	2063.603	2242.973	993.156	RBFT	SOS	Gaussian	Identity
2	RBF 1-29-1	0.941117	0.904961	0.948926	1197.558	1856.331	1228.496	RBFT	SOS	Gaussian	Identity
3	RBF 1-26-1	0.885767	0.857278	0.950068	2256.083	2355.868	1119.084	RBFT	SOS	Gaussian	Identity
4	RBF 1-23-1	0.890454	0.862730	0.954402	2168.935	2324.944	1056.574	RBFT	SOS	Gaussian	Identity
5	RBF 1-29-1	0.823083	0.923501	0.949917	3501.170	1296.772	1058.422	RBFT	SOS	Gaussian	Identity

Source: Own research

Table 6.10 Predictions statistics_E1_export 1a

Statistics	Target: Export 1.RBF 1-29-1	2.RBF 1-29-1	3.RBF 1-26-1	4.RBF 1-23-1	5.RBF 1-29-1
Minimum prediction (train)	31.296	82.511	95.575	88.614	79.401
Maximum prediction (train)	635.689	708.556	616.119	677.590	685.910
Minimum prediction (test)	81.851	85.710	110.690	90.019	93.987
Maximum prediction (test)	531.245	654.495	536.871	581.307	552.776
Minimum prediction (validation)	102.437	84.062	107.504	105.568	81.681
Maximum prediction (validation)	645.674	628.387	622.063	659.941	687.266
Minimum residual (train)	−221.360	−204.903	−235.704	−249.797	−279.949
Maximum residual (train)	227.608	166.021	243.824	236.440	393.144
Minimum residual (test)	−245.079	−241.029	−219.633	−240.528	−127.684
Maximum residual (test)	166.249	97.202	187.733	138.141	107.931
Minimum residual (validation)	−117.609	−99.861	−101.487	−101.397	−95.711
Maximum residual (validation)	130.406	172.058	154.017	116.139	136.545
Minimum standard residual (train)	−4.873	−5.921	−4.962	−5.364	−4.731
Maximum standard residual (train)	5.010	4.798	5.133	5.077	6.644
Minimum standard residual (test)	−5.175	−5.594	−4.525	−4.988	−3.546
Maximum standard residual (test)	3.510	2.256	3.868	2.865	2.997
Minimum standard residual (validation)	−3.732	−2.849	−3.034	−3.119	−2.942
Maximum standard residual (validation)	4.138	4.909	4.604	3.573	4.197

Source: Own research

dimensions, not, for example, to small changes in the value of exports during a shorter period.

According to the correlation coefficients, a very promising network 2. RBF 1-29-1 is presented in Fig. 6.24.

The success of the neural network is also demonstrated by the time series prediction figure. We see here probably the best network so far which already very successfully predicts the real development of Russia/Czechia exports even in the local minima or maxima. For example, it copies the local extreme very well in the period 2008–2009, i.e. during the great economic crisis. However, the network is still not flawless and deviations and residuals are noticeable in many cases.

In the following, the performance of the network 3. RBF 1-26-1 is presented (see Fig. 6.25).

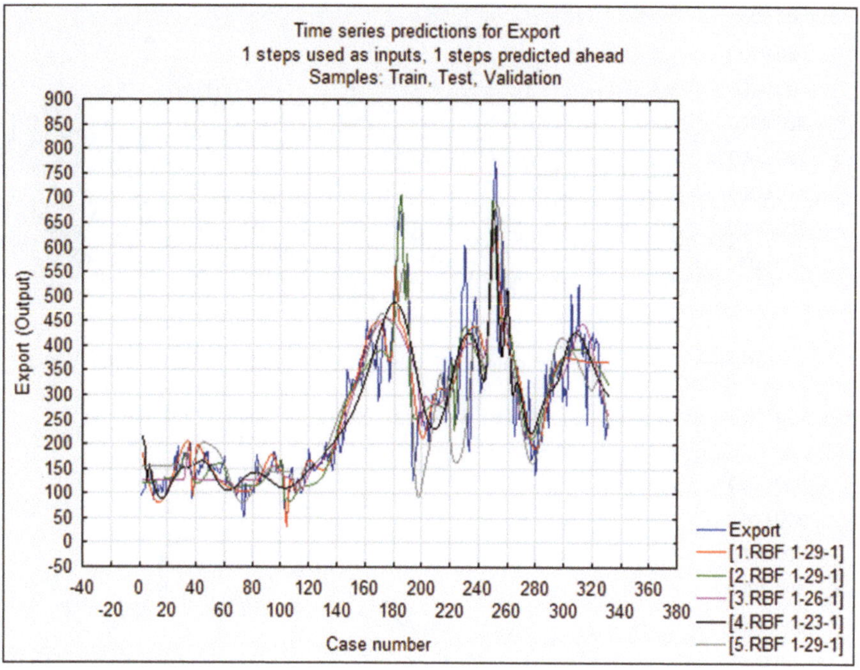

Fig. 6.22 Time series predictions_E1_export 1a. Source: Own research

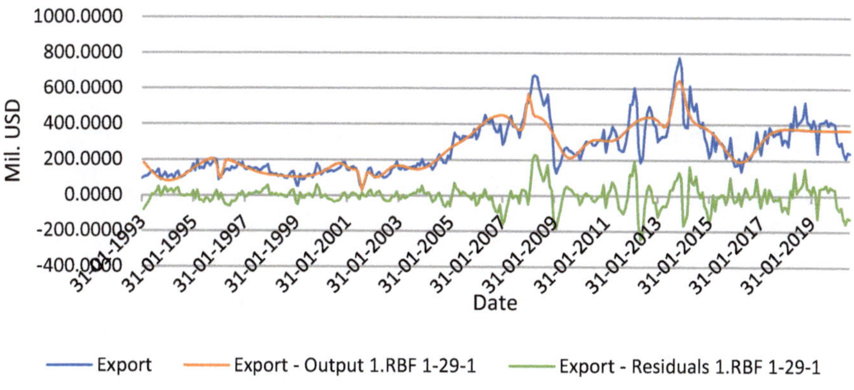

Fig. 6.23 Time series prediction—1. RBF 1-29-1_E1_export 1a. Source: Own research

Again, greater differences between the actual development of exports and the balanced time series can be observed. Moreover, we can witness larger residuals and a not entirely convincing network performance.

Figure 6.26 illustrates the prediction of the time series according to the network 4. RBF 1-23-1.

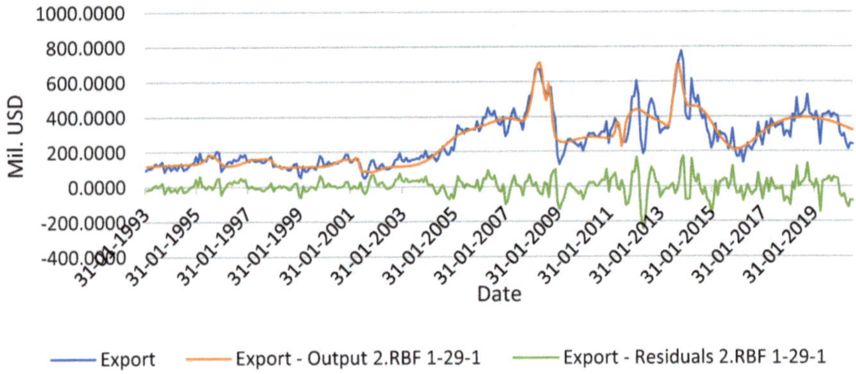

Fig. 6.24 Time series prediction—2. RBF 1-29-1_E1_export 1a. Source: Own research

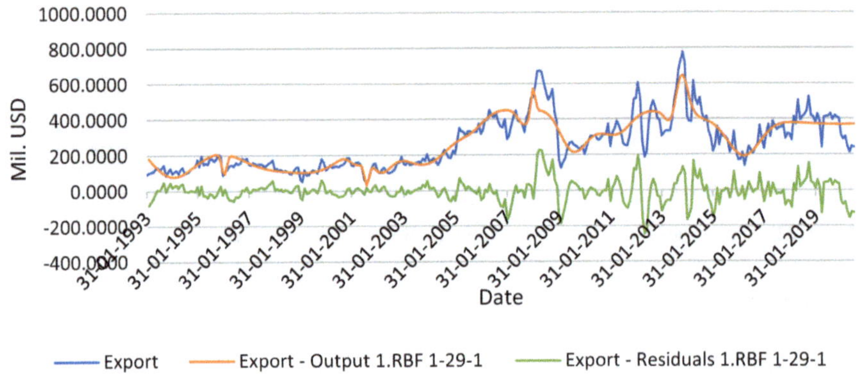

Fig. 6.25 Time series prediction—3. RBF 1-26-1_E1_export 1a. Source: Own research

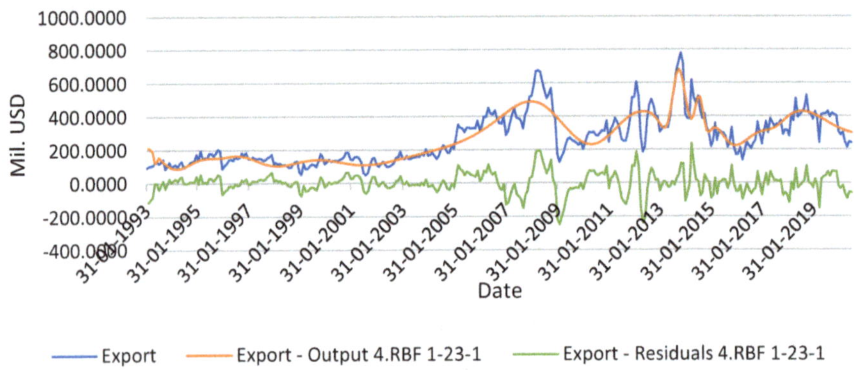

Fig. 6.26 Time series prediction—4. RBF 1-23-1_E1_export 1a. Source: Own research

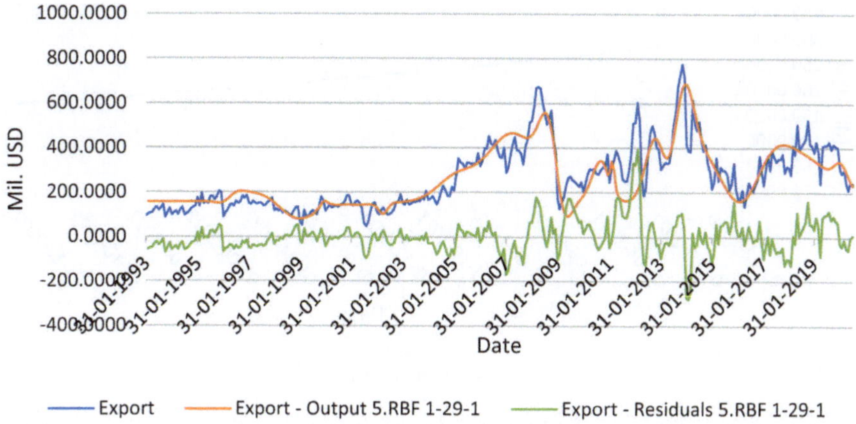

Fig. 6.27 Time series prediction—5. RBF 1-29-1_E1_export 1a. Source: Own research

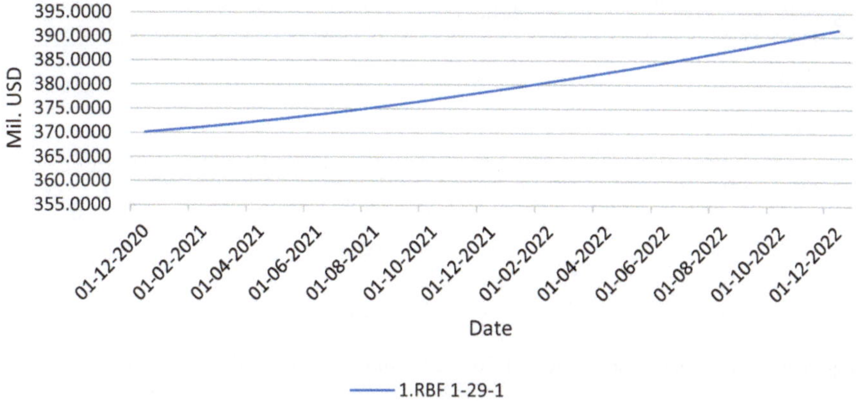

Fig. 6.28 Export prediction—1. RBF 1-29-1_E1_export 1a. Source: Own research

Its development is very similar to the previous neural structure meaning that the network copies the actual development of exports only very roughly and the residuals are quite large.

To present the full image, Fig. 6.27 is presented, showing the adjustment of the time series of exports according to the network 5. RBF 1-29-1.

From the shape of the green curve of the residuals, it is clear that this network has probably the lowest predictive power, while the residuals are in many cases enormous.

As in the previous cases, there are now figures of predictions according to the individual preserved networks, for the period from the end of 2020 to the end of 2022. First, the predictions according to 1. RBF 1-29-1 are presented (see Fig. 6.28).

It is obvious that the first neural structure predicts the value of exports for a given period at the level of about USD 370 million for the beginning of the period and

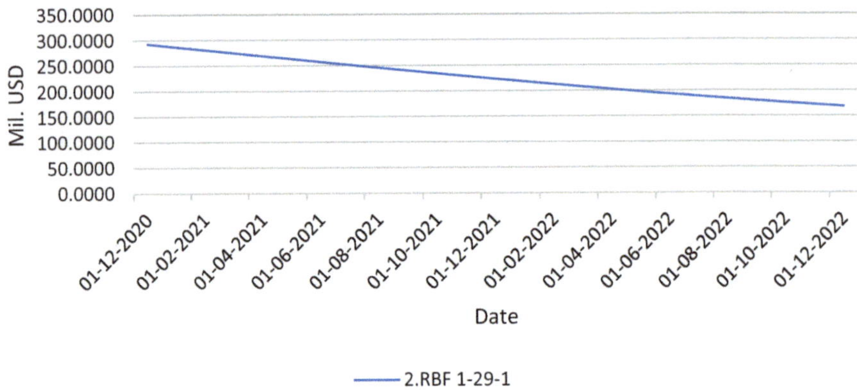

Fig. 6.29 Export prediction—2. RBF 1-29-1_E1_export 1a. Source: Own research

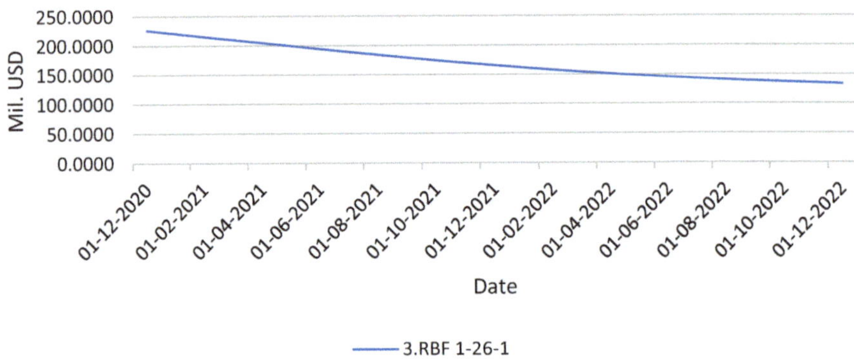

Fig. 6.30 Export prediction—3. RBF 1-26-1_E1_export 1a. Source: Own research

about USD 393 million for the end of the period. Thus, a slightly rising tendency of the Russia/Czechia export is forecast.

Out of all the results so far, the network 2. RBF 1-29-1 is the most successful one, whose prediction of export value is the subject of Fig. 6.29.

We see that this network predicts the opposite direction of the development of the value of Russia/Czechia exports than the first preserved neural structure. According to the second network, exports should reach the value of approximately USD 300 million at the beginning of the predicted period and then, it should gradually decline to about USD 170 million at the end of 2022.

Figure 6.30 illustrating the prediction of the network 3. RBF 1-26-1 also declares a decline in the value of exports, from about USD 225 million at the end of 2020 to about USD 135 million at the end of 2022.

A slight decrease in the value of exports is also predicted by the network 4. RBF 1-23-1. According to this structure, the value of the Russia/Czechia exports will

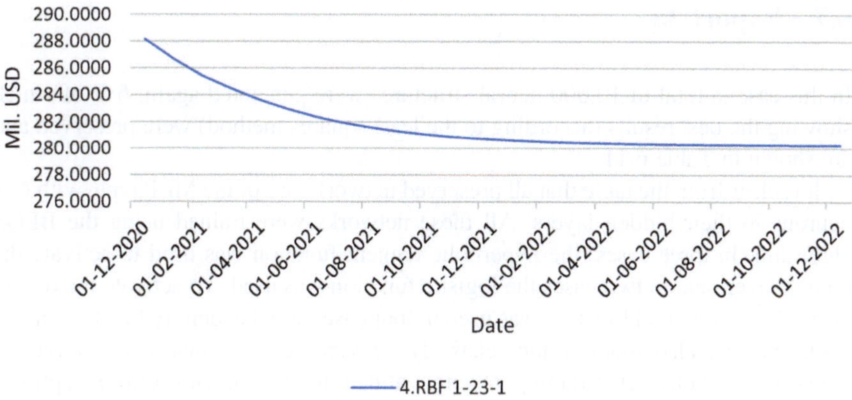

Fig. 6.31 Export prediction—4. RBF 1-23-1_E1_export 1a. Source: Own research

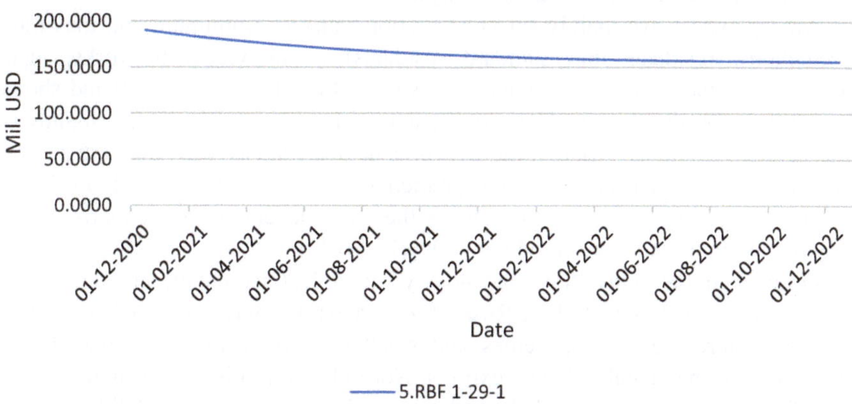

Fig. 6.32 Export prediction—5. RBF 1-29-1_E1_export 1a. Source: Own research

reach around USD 288 million at the end of 2020, while the values should stabilize at the value of more than USD 280 million at the beginning of 2022 (see Fig. 6.31).

The last of the preserved networks in this variant, 5. RBF 1-29-1, also predicts a gradual decline in the value of the Russia/Czechia exports over the entire period by about USD 30 million (see Fig. 6.32).

In this part of the research, the network 2. RBF1-29-1 proved to be the most successful by showing relatively low values of residual and high correlation coefficients in all data sets. After further modifications (further learning and setting of parameters), this neural network can be potentially suitable for the Russia/Czechia export prediction. In this form, however, it is not very applicable in practice, as well as other generated and preserved structures.

6.7 Export 3a

In this case, a total of 10,000 neural structures were generated again, five of which showing the best results (according to the least squares method) were preserved and are shown in Table 6.11.

It is clear from the table that all preserved networks are of the MLP type, with 6–8 neurons in their hidden layers. All these networks were trained using the BFGS algorithm. In three cases, the hyperbolic tangent function was used to activate the hidden layer, and in two cases the logistic function was used. To activate the output layer, the exponential function was used in four cases and the identity function in one case. We can also monitor the relatively convincing performance of individual networks in all data sets (training, testing, validation), which, with some exceptions, exceeds 90%. The networks are very similar in terms of performance; the fifth most successful network 5. MLP 3-7-1 seems to be the most successful here. However, this fact is to be verified by further analyses.

Among others, we mainly select prediction statistics (minimum and maximum predictions, residuals and standard residuals) of individual networks, again according to the data sets. Residual values should ideally be close to 0 and should be constant for all data sets. Here we see that such a presumption is met mainly by the standard residuals. None of the networks deviates in any way, they are all very similar, even when it comes to the predictive statistics. Again, the figure of the balanced time series will be important, i.e. the actual development of exports and the highlighted individual preserved networks (Fig. 6.33).

Once again, the figure shows the already known fact that the preserved networks copy the real development of the Russia/Czechia exports only very roughly and they cannot capture the local extremes and smaller, or in many cases even larger, deviations of the actual value of exports. Not only from this particular figure, but also from the figures of the balanced time series according to individual neural structures, it can be concluded that all preserved networks are very similar in their performance and ability to balance the actual time series of Russia/Czechia exports. There are no big differences here, the networks roughly copy the real development of exports, but, as it was already mentioned, they cannot capture the local minima and maxima. Nevertheless, they managed to copy the development of the curve relatively accurately during the great economic crisis in 2008–2009.

Very similar characteristics of the given networks are confirmed by the prediction figures. The development of Russia/Czechia exports was again predicted for the period from the end of 2020 to the end of 2022. All networks predict a positive value of exports. The first of them, 1. MLP 3-8-1, assumes the value of exports at the beginning of the period at about USD 370.35 million. At the end of 2022, the value should fall at about USD 363 million, i.e. there is a gradually declining value of exports. Network 2. MLP 3-8-1 predicts the same direction of development of the export curve starting at the beginning of the period at around USD 270 million and ending at around USD 205 million at the end of the observed period. The other two networks predict a slight and gradual increase in the value of the exports at around

Table 6.11 Summary of active networks_E1_export 3a

Index	Net. name	Training perf.	Test perf.	Validation perf.	Training error	Test error	Validation error	Training algorithm	Error function	Hidden activation	Output activation
1	MLP 3-8-1	0.913532	0.903104	0.918358	1713.142	1762.938	1818.968	BFGS 265	SOS	Tanh	Identity
2	MLP 3-8-1	0.919497	0.917803	0.898341	1599.012	1571.261	2270.223	BFGS 314	SOS	Logistic	Exponential
3	MLP 3-6-1	0.909089	0.905232	0.898515	1796.168	1667.143	2186.507	BFGS 284	SOS	Tanh	Exponential
4	MLP 3-8-1	0.912651	0.899137	0.927478	1729.007	1795.918	1630.041	BFGS 274	SOS	Logistic	Exponential
5	MLP 3-7-1	0.920588	0.908958	0.922538	1579.406	1573.148	1789.128	BFGS 246	SOS	Tanh	Exponential

Source: Own research

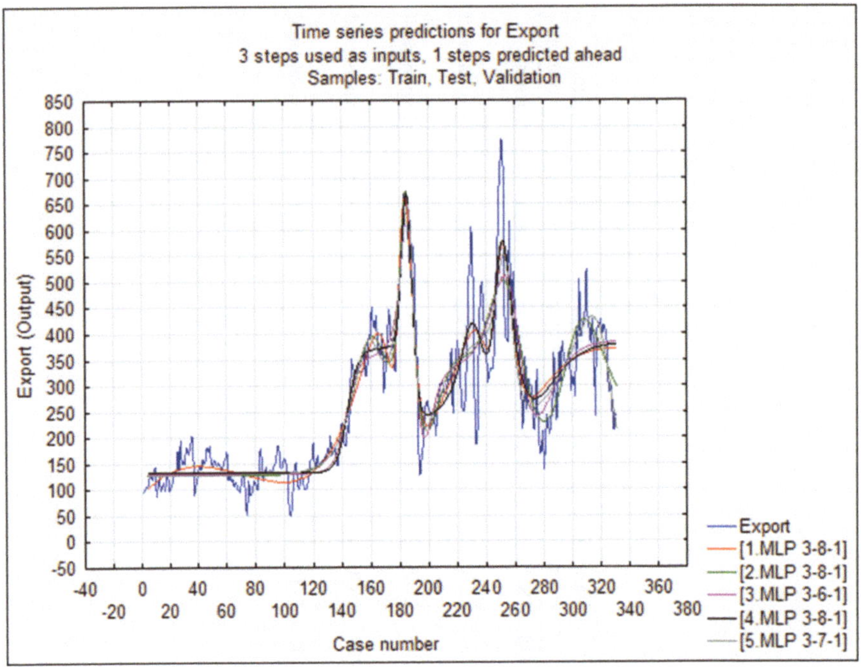

Fig. 6.33 Time series predictions_E1_export 3a. Source: Own research

USD 383–384 million and USD 381–383 million, respectively. The fifth preserved network 5. MLP 3-7-1 returns to the model of a declining tendency of the export curve, predicting a value of approximately USD 145 million at the beginning of the period which is expected to stabilize at approximately USD 90 million at the beginning of 2022.

All networks are therefore relatively successful in their performance and predictive statistics, but they are not sufficient for practical use. They can only roughly copy the actual development of the Russia/Czechia exports, so even their predictions for the next period may not be completely accurate. As in the previous cases, further research and verification of predictions according to new data would be necessary.

6.8 Export 6a

In this case, a total of 10,000 neural structures were generated again, five of which showing the best results (according to the least squares method) were preserved and are shown in Table 6.12.

For the third variant in case of the first experiment and the Russia/Czechia export, the best networks show a relatively solid performance in all data sets. Out of all the data sets, the validation set achieved the very best performance. According to the

Table 6.12 Summary of active networks_E1_export 6a

Index	Net. name	Training perf.	Test perf.	Validation perf.	Training error	Test error	Validation error	Training algorithm	Error function	Hidden activation	Output activation
1	MLP 6-6-1	0.906036	0.898311	0.922222	1823.355	1652.833	1706.395	BFGS 9999	SOS	Tanh	Tanh
2	MLP 6-8-1	0.911848	0.915293	0.926744	1718.909	1500.536	1715.151	BFGS 180	SOS	Logistic	Identity
3	MLP 6-5-1	0.882946	0.872489	0.919924	2245.513	2101.626	1791.482	BFGS 170	SOS	Logistic	Exponential
4	MLP 6-8-1	0.899057	0.890397	0.918087	1952.159	1778.123	1803.623	BFGS 199	SOS	Tanh	Logistic
5	MLP 6-8-1	0.917413	0.908367	0.925500	1612.040	1664.322	1680.224	BFGS 403	SOS	Tanh	Exponential

Source: Own research

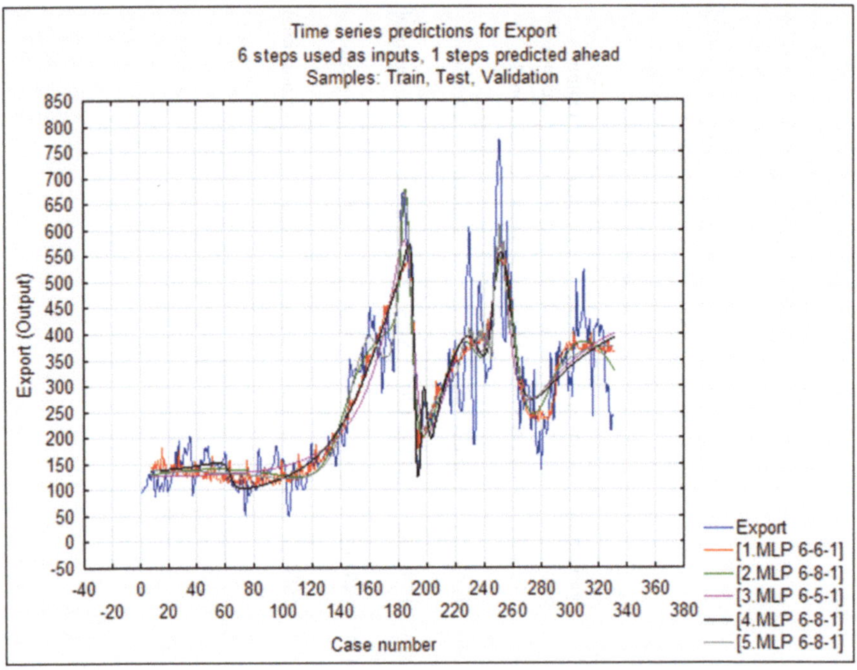

Fig. 6.34 Time series predictions_E1_export 6a. Source: Own research

performance, the most successful is the 2. MLP 6-8-1 network which shows over 91% performance in all data sets. These are MLP-type networks with 5, 6, and 8 neurons in the hidden layer, respectively. The same training algorithm was used for all the structures, namely the BFGS algorithm. In three cases, the hyperbolic tangent function was used to activate the hidden layer, in two cases the logistic function. Regarding the activation of the output layer, the variation of the functions used is wide. In two cases, the exponential function was used, followed by the hyperbolic tangent, identity, and logistic functions.

In order to determine the accuracy and predictive ability of the given neural structures, the prediction statistics of individual networks and individual data sets were again examined. Once again, the relatively high quality of the preserved networks is confirmed, especially in the case of standard residuals. Residual values are very similar not only in all data sets, but also in all networks. This is also confirmed by the graphical presentation in Fig. 6.34 showing the balanced time series of the actual development of exports according to the individual preserved networks.

It is obvious that, once again, the networks can roughly copy the real development of the Russia/Czechia exports, however, they cannot react to the local minimums and maximums. The network 1. MLP 6-6-1 seems to be interesting, whose curve is irregular compared to the others and pulsates in a special way throughout the period. Figure 6.35 is shown for better illustration.

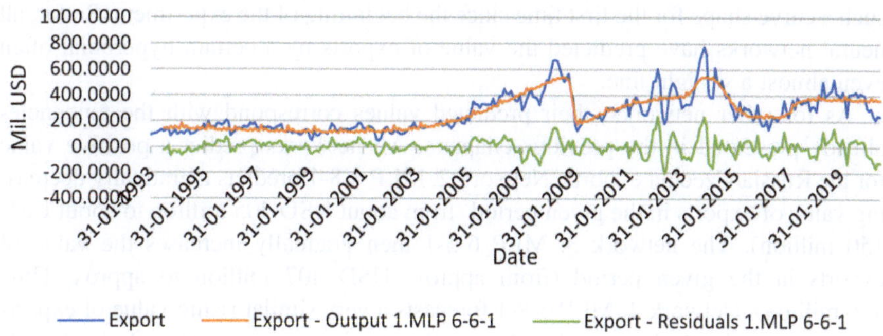

Fig. 6.35 Time series prediction—1. MLP 6-6-1_E1_export 6a. Source: Own research

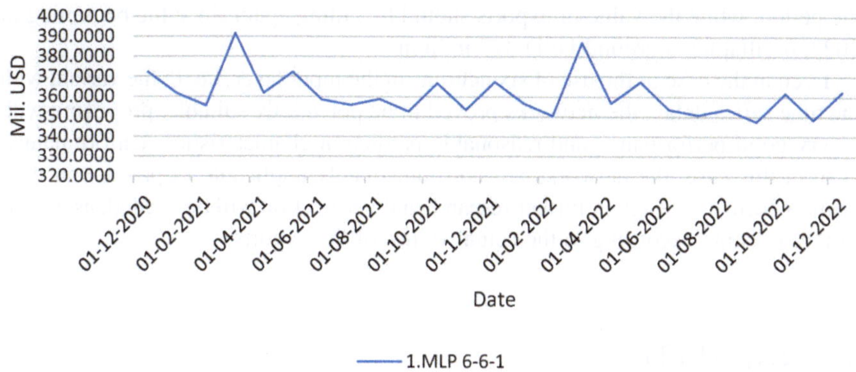

Fig. 6.36 Export prediction—1. MLP 6-6-1_E1_export 6a. Source: Own research

It can be observed that this network tries to react to the local minima but is not very successful—this is confirmed by the green curve of residuals.

Other networks were again able to balance the time series of exports relatively well during the great economic crisis in 2008–2009, but otherwise, they copy the real development only very roughly. Even the best network according to the performance, 2. MLP 6-8-1, does not show better results than other networks from this point of view.

Furthermore, the Russia/Czechia exports are again predicted for the period from the end of 2020 to the end of 2022 according to individual networks. An interesting development tendency is predicted by the first preserved network 1. MLP 6-6-1, the course of which is shown in Fig. 6.36.

The figure shows the prediction of the value of exports which is divided into roughly annual cycles. It can be seen that the curve repeats its pattern after about a year, with the only difference being that the peaks of the local highs and lows are shifted lower by about USD 4–5 million each year. Thus, this network predicts a gradually increasing and decreasing value of exports ranging from about USD 392 million to about USD 348 million in the given observed period. We encounter such a curve shape for the first time since the beginning of the experiment. So far, all neural networks have predicted the value of exports by a certain hyperbola, often even almost a straight line.

As for other networks, their predicted values correspond with the tendencies already presented in the previous chapters. All networks predict a positive value for the Russia/Czechia exports. Network 2. MLP 6-8-1 predicts a gradually decreasing value of exports in the given period (from about USD 305 million to about USD 150 million). The network 3. MLP 6-5-1 then gradually increases the value of exports in the given period (from approx. USD 407 million to approx. USD 426 million). Network 4. MLP 6-8-1 forecasts a very similar rising value of exports starting at a slightly lower value than in the previous case, namely at about USD 398 million, and ending at about USD 421 million in 2022. Network 5. MLP 6-8-1 proves to be more moderate and predicts a slightly rising value from the beginning of the period, while the value of exports should be falling again since the beginning of 2022, oscillating at around USD 377 million.

Even in the case of the use of six neurons in the input layer, i.e. in the variant with the time series delay, the networks proved to be potentially suitable, proposing with a very good performance and reasonable prediction characteristics. Unfortunately, even in this case, the networks are not immediately applicable in practice in their primary form. Once again, further research and verification will be needed, as well as further learning according to the actual values of the exports.

6.9 Export 12a

Even in the case of export, a variant with 12 neurons in the input layer is added, i.e. the variant with the highest time series delay. In this case, a total of 10,000 neural structures were generated again, five of which showing the best results (according to the least squares method) were preserved and are shown in Table 6.13.

Even in this case, all stored networks belong to the MLP type and include six, seven, or eight neurons in the hidden layer. Again, the BFGS training algorithm is used, in four cases to activate the hidden layer of the hyperbolic tangent function and in one case the logistic function. To activate the output layer, the exponential function was used in four cases, and the sine function in one case. We see that the performance of all networks measured by correlation coefficients is very favourable, reaching more than 90% in all cases and all data sets. The differences between the networks are again minimal, but it can be argued that depending on the performance, the 5. MLP 12-7-1 network could be the most successful one.

According to the prediction statistics, it can be concluded that the networks will again be able to predict the development of exports only roughly. The residual values do not reach bad ranges, but the overall performance is still far from the ideal. For a better understanding of the situation, a figure of balanced time series according to the individual preserved networks is presented (see Fig. 6.37).

Table 6.13 Summary of active networks_E1_export 12a

Index	Net. name	Training perf.	Test perf.	Validation perf.	Training error	Test error	Validation error	Training algorithm	Error function	Hidden activation	Output activation
1	MLP 12-8-1	0.916436	0.904894	0.916922	1594.569	1560.536	1803.500	BFGS 555	SOS	Tanh	Exponential
2	MLP 12-6-1	0.911075	0.901776	0.934343	1693.025	1614.699	1372.081	BFGS 264	SOS	Tanh	Exponential
3	MLP 12-7-1	0.933766	0.915588	0.913571	1272.854	1484.450	1948.238	BFGS 332	SOS	Logistic	Exponential
4	MLP 12-6-1	0.918609	0.906806	0.938990	1558.577	1616.288	1416.353	BFGS 277	SOS	Tanh	Sine
5	MLP 12-7-1	0.925281	0.926067	0.937174	1431.686	1339.913	1612.226	BFGS 235	SOS	Tanh	Exponential

Source: Own research

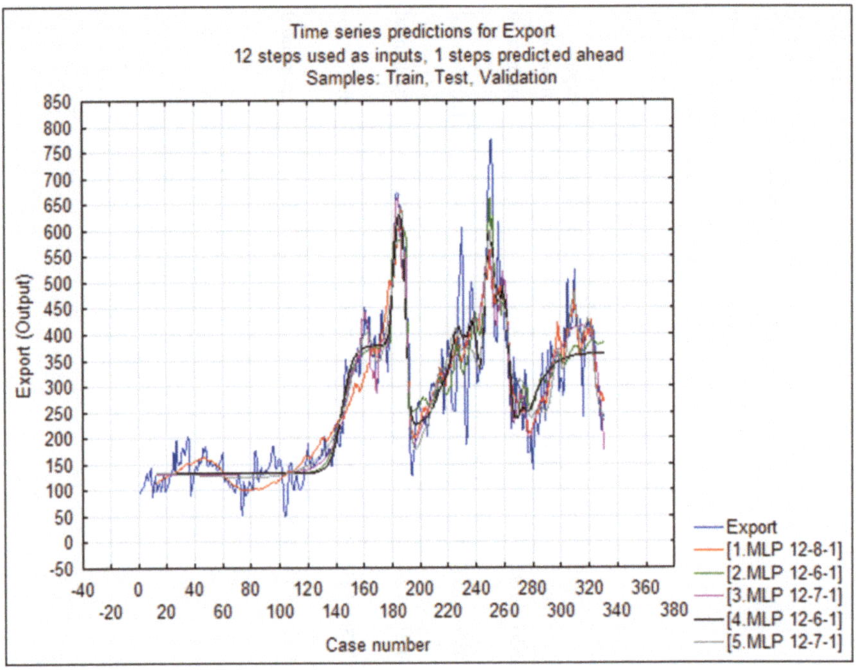

Fig. 6.37 Time series predictions_E1_export 12a. Source: Own research

The figure only confirms the assumption that neural networks will predict the true value of exports only very roughly and cannot capture the local minima and maxima. The first preserved network 1. MLP 12-8-1 and the fifth network 5. MLP 12-7-1 can probably balance the time series of exports sufficiently, especially in the second half of the observed period. The actual development of Russia/Czechia exports during the Great Depression 2008–2009 is illustrated very accurately by the network 3. MLP 12-7-1. Nevertheless, residual levels are relatively high.

Regarding the predictions for the period from the end of 2020 to the end of 2022, the predictions of the first two preserved networks are interesting, as their curves are not in the form of a simple line or hyperbola, but can predict certain local extremes—the minima and maxima. These figures are certainly interesting; the first of them, Fig. 6.38, representing the structure 1. MLP 12-8-1 declares a rather declining trend in the value of exports starting at about USD 230 million and ending at around USD 85 million at the end of 2022.

The prediction curve according to the network 2. MLP 12-6-1 in Fig. 6.39 also has an interesting shape indicating the fact that the network could be potentially successful in predicting local extremes.

Other networks have already predicted the value of exports again in the form of a hyperbola, when the 3. MLP 12-7-1 network predicted a declining value of exports with a subsequent stabilization in mid-2021 at approximately USD 48 million. The 4. MLP 12-6-1 network, on the other hand, predicts a slightly increasing value of

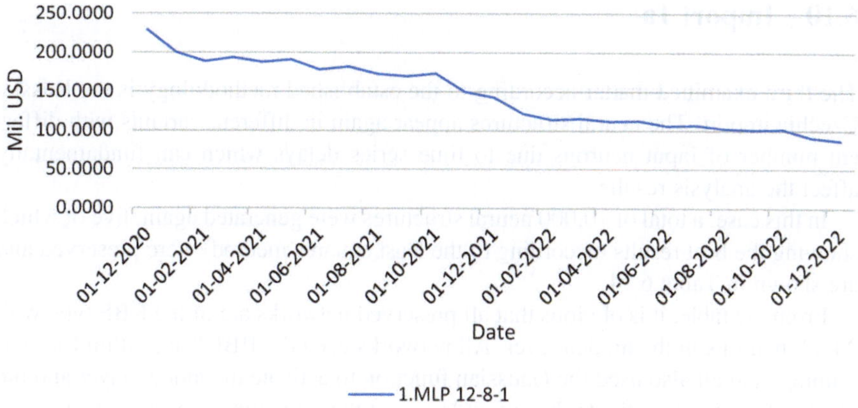

Fig. 6.38 Export prediction—1. MLP 12-8-1_E1_export 12a. Source: Own research

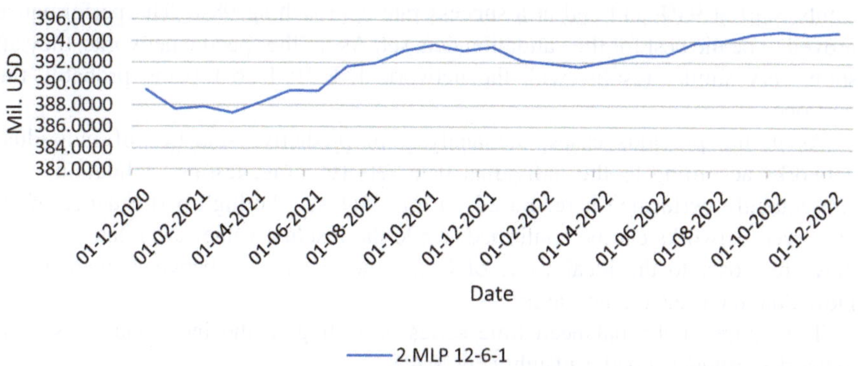

Fig. 6.39 Export prediction—2. MLP 12-6-1_E1_export 12a. Source: Own research

exports, however, it still oscillates at the value around USD 262 million throughout the period. The network 5. MLP 12-7-1 returns to the declining trend of the export curve which begins at the beginning of the predicted period at approximately USD 165 million and ends at approximately USD 57–58 million at the end of 2022.

From the above-stated facts, the conclusions that have already been declared in the previous parts of the experiment apply here as well. The neural networks stored here are again potentially usable for predicting the value of Russia/Czechia exports.

6.10 Import 1a

The third examined matter according to the established methodology is the Russia/Czechia import. The neural structures appear again in different variants with different number of input neurons due to time series delays which can fundamentally affect the analysis results.

In this case, a total of 10,000 neural structures were generated again, five of which showing the best results (according to the least squares method) were preserved and are shown in Table 6.14.

From the table, it is obvious that all preserved networks are of the RBF type with 24–28 neurons in the hidden layer. All networks used the RBFT algorithm for their training, and all also used the Gaussian function to activate the hidden layer and the identity function to activate the output layer. At the same time, we can notice a very high performance of all networks in all data sets (even the highest performance of all the previous variants was spotted here). The performances, i.e. correlation coefficients, start at 94% and end at a success rate approaching 98%. The performance proved to be the best for the validation data set. As for the specific networks, they all show very similar results, with the network 4. RBF 1-26-1 being probably the best one.

As in the previous cases, the analysis of predictive statistics of individual networks according to the individual data sets (training, testing, validation) was subsequently performed here. Based on this analysis, the high performance of all preserved networks can be confirmed, while the residual values are relatively low, they are closer to the ideal value of 0 and the differences between them in the individual data sets are not large.

The figure of the balanced time series according to the individual preserved networks provides a better insight (Fig. 6.40).

The figure shows that the networks, although having a very high performance, can predict the value of the Russia/Czechia imports again rather roughly. At the beginning of the period, the networks are able to predict the value of imports relatively accurately, but this is obviously due to the relatively stable development of the value of imports, which did not show any significant fluctuations in this period. This fact is also confirmed by figures of predictions and residuals of the individual preserved networks. This can be observed, for example, on the most successful network 4. RBF 1-26-1. Low residual values can be seen here until about the time before the great economic crisis in 2008–2009. Then, as import values have changed significantly, the network has a greater problem monitoring these fluctuations, so the residual values are also more prominent (see Fig. 6.41).

The figures of the Russia/Czechia import forecasts for the period from the end of 2020 to the end of 2022 also declare great similarity of the individual networks. It is rather rare that all structures agree on the declining trend of the value of imports, always in positive numbers. However, each network assumes a different pace of the decline in different values. Network 1. RBF 1-28-1 assumes a value of imports at the end of 2020 at about USD 285 million and then at about USD 215 million at the end

Table 6.14 Summary of active networks_E1_import 1a

Index	Net. name	Training perf.	Test perf.	Validation perf.	Training error	Test error	Validation error	Training algorithm	Error function	Hidden activation	Output activation
1	RBF 1-28-1	0.962066	0.959043	0.975050	744.912	666.1642	579.0949	RBFT	SOS	Gaussian	Identity
2	RBF 1-26-1	0.965316	0.954073	0.977655	686.041	751.8491	493.1110	RBFT	SOS	Gaussian	Identity
3	RBF 1-24-1	0.956747	0.941547	0.974756	846.772	958.7437	559.4534	RBFT	SOS	Gaussian	Identity
4	RBF 1-26-1	0.970406	0.965379	0.979374	585.843	594.5133	472.0669	RBFT	SOS	Gaussian	Identity
5	RBF 1-25-1	0.944686	0.952816	0.979723	1084.816	767.7326	464.6908	RBFT	SOS	Gaussian	Identity

Source: Own research

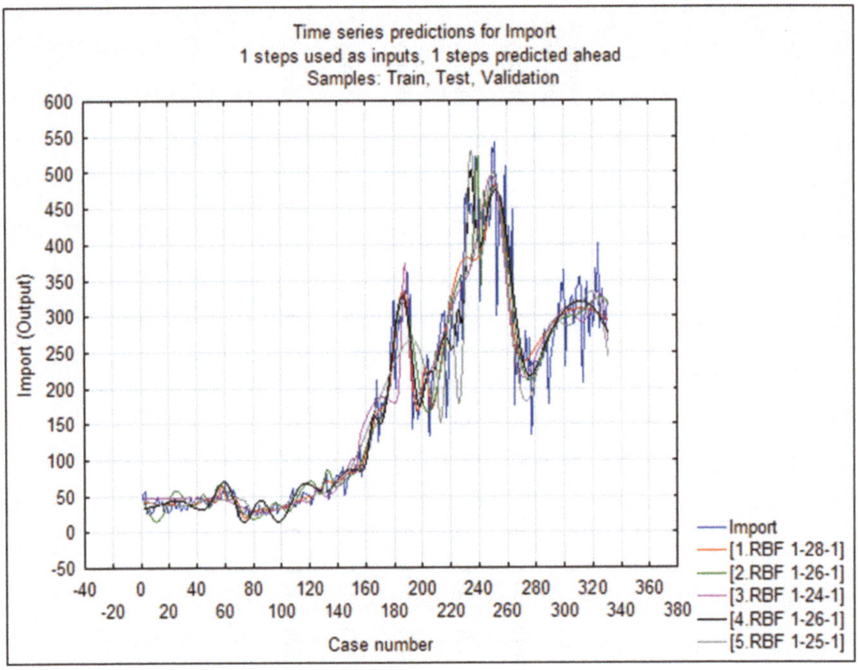

Fig. 6.40 Time series predictions_E1_import 1a. Source: Own research

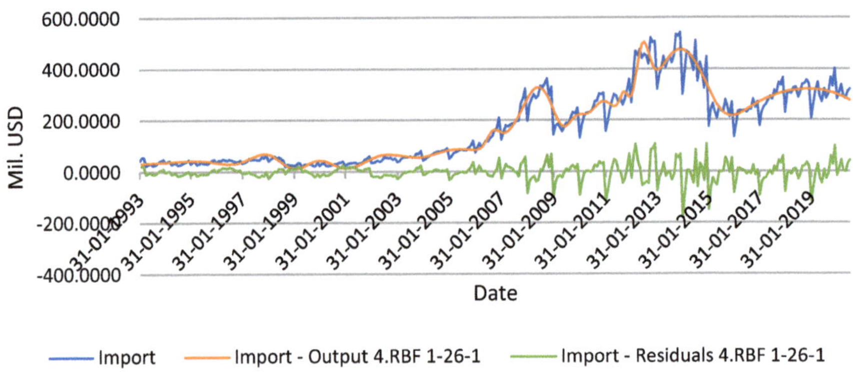

Fig. 6.41 Time series prediction—4. RBF 1-26-1_E1_import 1a. Source: Own research

of 2022. Network 2. RBF 1-26-1 predicts very similar values, only with a steeper curve and the final value at USD 100 million. Network 3. RBF 1-24-1 has been moving in slightly different numbers since the beginning and predicts a decline in the value of imports during the predicted period from about USD 168 million to about USD 47 million. The decrease from the initial approx. USD 254 million to approx. USD 135 million is predicted by the 4. RBF 1-26-1 network; the decrease from approx. USD 180 million to approximately USD 55 million then by the 5. RBF 1-25-1 network.

All preserved networks showed a very promising performance but the residuals were still too high to be used in practice to accurately predict the development of the value of the Russia/Czechia imports.

6.11 Import 3a

In this case, a total of 10,000 neural structures were generated again, five of which showing the best results (according to the least squares method) were preserved and are shown in Table 6.15.

In the case of this variant with a time series delay equalling 3, only MLP-type networks with 4–7 neurons in the hidden layer were preserved. The training algorithm used was the same type of BFGS, while the hyperbolic tangent (4x) and the logistic function (1x) were used as activation functions in the hidden layers. To activate the output layer, two cases of exponential and identity functions were used, in one case it was a hyperbolic tangent. The performance of all networks in all data sets is again very promising, most often reaching values around 96–97%. Depending on the performance, the second or first preserved structure could be the most successful one. However, the differences are really minimal, so we will proceed to further analyses that will verify the predictive ability of these neural structures.

The prediction statistics again show relatively favourable numbers, especially the values of standard residuals approaching the required value of 0. The graphical representation of the balanced time series of the value of Russia/Czechia imports according to the individual preserved MLP networks will provide a better illustration (Fig. 6.42).

It is evident from the figure that the networks are again able to roughly copy the actual development of imports, but they cannot capture the local minima and maxima at all. Even from the individual figures of the balanced time series, it is not possible to determine which neural network is most suitable for this case. Residual values are still relatively high.

If we look at the specific predictions of import values for the period from the end of 2020 to the end of 2022, we can state that most networks assume a growing trend in the value of imports. Network 1. MLP 3-7-1 assumes a slight increase in value in the given predicted period from about USD 321 million to the final value about USD 324.5 million in 2022. Network 2. MLP 3-4-1 also predicts a slight increase in the value of imports from about USD 318 million to about USD 319.2 million, i.e. very similar values to the ones declared by the first preserved network. The third network 3. MLP 3-4-1 predicting values from approx. USD 330 million to approx. USD 339 million does not deviate far either. The predictions of the other two preserved networks are more interesting. Network 4. MLP 3-7-1 represented in Fig. 6.43 predicts a similar trend as it is shown for exports in the case of the variant with a

Table 6.15 Summary of active networks_E1_import 3a

Index	Net. name	Training perf.	Test perf.	Validation perf.	Training error	Test error	Validation error	Training algorithm	Error function	Hidden activation	Output activation
1	MLP 3-7-1	0.971545	0.960179	0.973931	557.0981	648.8512	590.6560	BFGS 300	SOS	Tanh	Exponential
2	MLP 3-4-1	0.972114	0.962186	0.972882	546.1297	617.5990	600.5600	BFGS 179	SOS	Tanh	Tanh
3	MLP 3-4-1	0.969818	0.960733	0.973589	590.4413	643.1422	588.9792	BFGS 245	SOS	Logistic	Identity
4	MLP 3-7-1	0.971438	0.957636	0.974499	559.1657	688.7209	566.0289	BFGS 299	SOS	Tanh	Exponential
5	MLP 3-5-1	0.969893	0.957018	0.973480	589.0092	702.6236	593.8111	BFGS 353	SOS	Tanh	Identity

Source: Own research

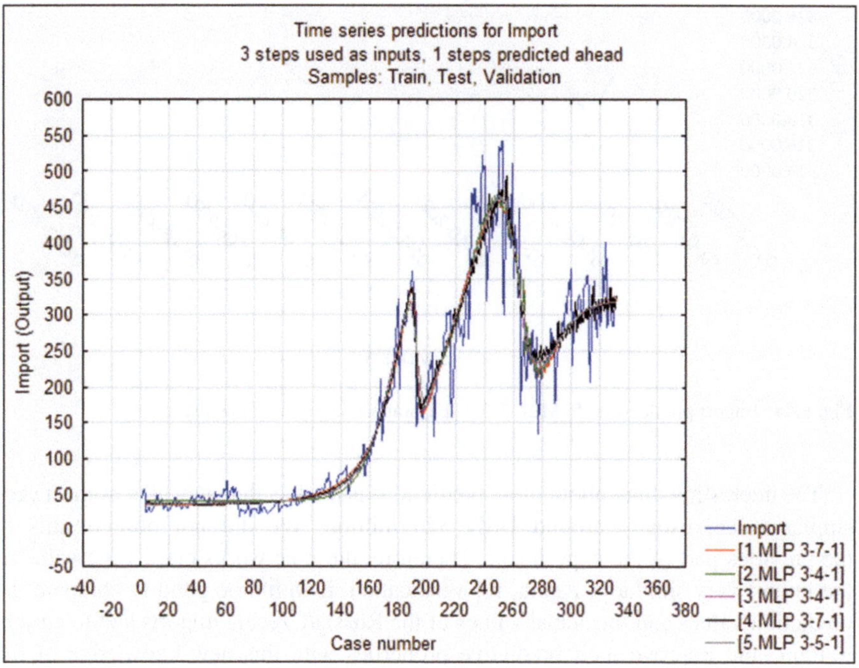

Fig. 6.42 Time series predictions_E1_import 3a. Source: Own research

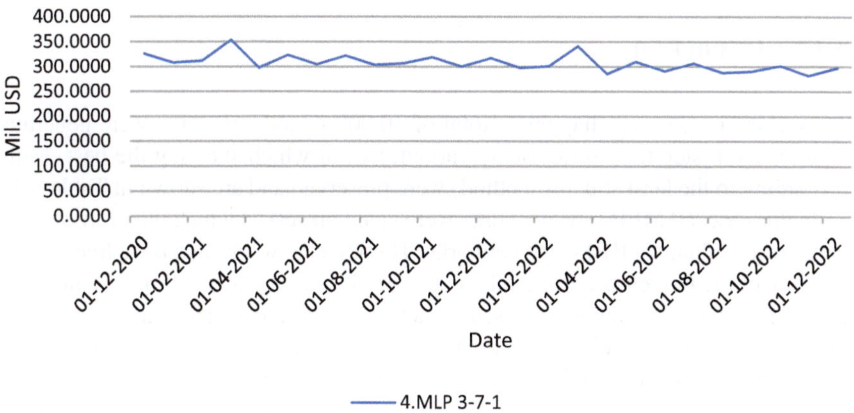

Fig. 6.43 Import prediction—4. MLP 3-7-1_E1_import 3a. Source: Own research

time delay of 6 steps and specifically by the network 1. MLP 6-6-1. This means that the prediction is assumed to have a certain rhythm lasting about 1 year. In this case, therefore, with a decreasing tendency for the import value.

The prediction according to the 5. MLP 3-5-1 network is very similar, but it counts on a slight increase in the value of the Russia/Czechia imports (see Fig. 6.44).

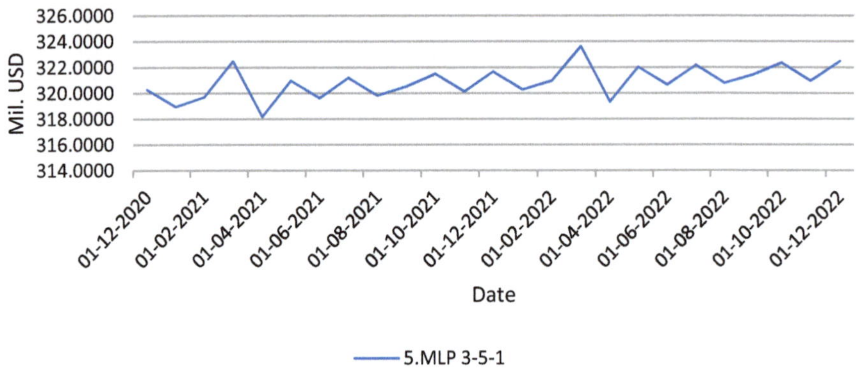

Fig. 6.44 Import prediction—5. MLP 3-5-1_E1_import 3a. Source: Own research

The interesting thing about these predictions is the fact that they all assume a very similar value, usually around USD 320 million. We did not observe this in the previous part of the experiment. Therefore, these networks predict the value of the import very similarly. Again, for verification, it would be good to compare the prediction values and the actual values of the Russia/Czechia imports and to enrich, re-train, and improve their predictive properties with this new knowledge of the network.

6.12 Import 6a

As well as in other subchapters, a total of 10,000 neural structures were generated here for the 6-step time series delay variant, five of which showing the best results (according to the least squares method) were preserved and are shown in Table 6.16.

In this case, all MLP-type networks were again preserved which therefore showed better results than the RBF-type networks. These are networks that have five to eight neurons in the hidden layer and all use the BFGS training algorithm. In four cases, the logistic tangent function is used to activate the hidden layer, in one case the logistic function. Regarding the activation of the output layer, the identity function is used in three cases and the hyperbolic tangent and sine functions in one case. Here, too, we can observe a very good performance, i.e. high correlation coefficients of individual networks in all data sets. Depending on the performance, the 5. MLP 6-5-1 network could be the most successful one; nevertheless, the differences are minimal. Slightly higher performance is achieved in the validation data sample.

As far as the prediction statistics are concerned, even in this case they are relatively consistent, the residual values are not very large, but they still differ from the required value. The graphical representation of the results is once again presented by the Fig. 6.45 illustrating the balanced time series of the Russia/Czechia imports by all the preserved networks.

Table 6.16 Summary of active networks_E1_import 6a

Index	Net. name	Training perf.	Test perf.	Validation perf.	Training error	Test error	Validation error	Training algorithm	Error function	Hidden activation	Output activation
1	MLP 6-8-1	0.970846	0.957695	0.973458	558.5552	701.5710	588.6586	BFGS 176	SOS	Tanh	Tanh
2	MLP 6-7-1	0.968921	0.955571	0.973448	594.9978	730.3464	598.1419	BFGS 125	SOS	Logistic	Identity
3	MLP 6-7-1	0.969661	0.956961	0.972854	580.8015	706.3606	603.5247	BFGS 244	SOS	Tanh	Identity
4	MLP 6-8-1	0.968466	0.960975	0.972777	603.6779	637.4874	604.8242	BFGS 226	SOS	Tanh	Sine
5	MLP 6-5-1	0.973536	0.963538	0.973162	507.1051	602.3944	594.4276	BFGS 166	SOS	Tanh	Identity

Source: Own research

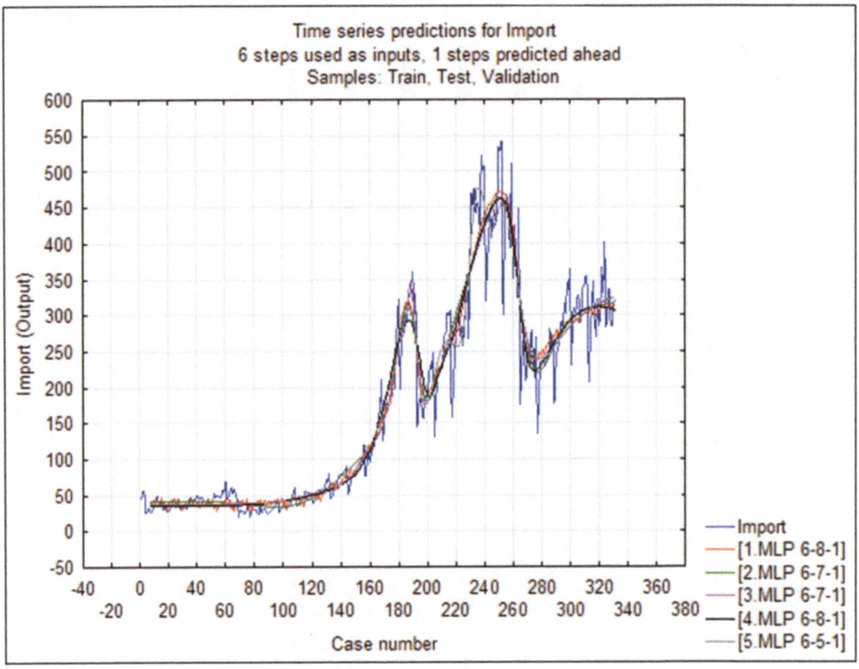

Fig. 6.45 Time series predictions_E1_import 6a. Source: Own research

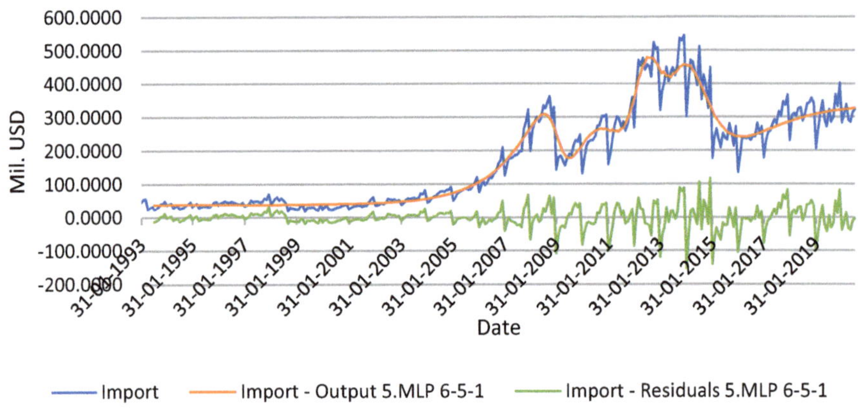

Fig. 6.46 Time series prediction—5. MLP 6-5-1_E1_import 6a. Source: Own research

The figure shows the facts that can be observed in the previous variants as well, i.e. the networks copy the actual development of the value of imports only very roughly. The neural networks cannot detect larger deviations from the normal state. This is also confirmed by figures of the balanced time series and the residuals for the individual networks. This can also be seen in Fig. 6.46 which again shows the actual

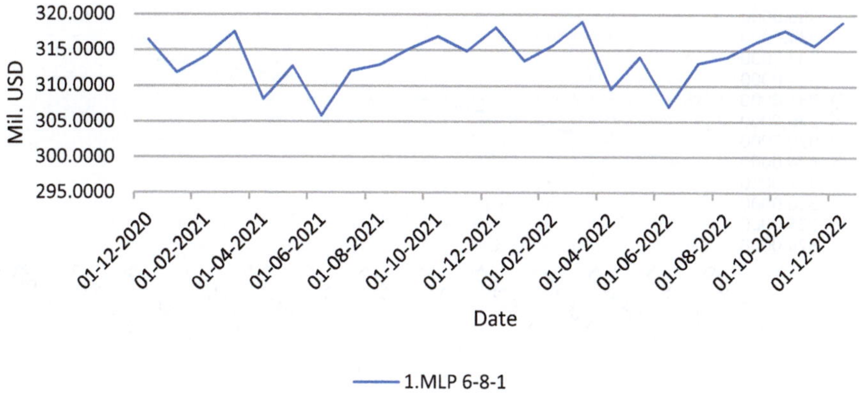

Fig. 6.47 Import prediction—1. MLP 6-5-1_E1_import 6a. Source: Own research

development of imports represented by the blue curve, the prediction of the 5. MLP 6-5-1 network (which achieved the highest performance) by the red curve and finally, the residuals by the green curve. It is the residual values that deviate quite significantly from the required value of 0 in some periods.

Regarding the predictions for the period from the end of 2020 to the end of 2022, all networks predict a positive value of the Russia/Czechia imports again, while, as it was the case also for the variant with a time series delay of 3 steps, all networks predict a similar value of around USD 300–320 million for the observed period. Very interesting is the prediction of the network 1. MLP 6-8-1 which can be seen in Fig. 6.47. We see that the shape of the prediction curve repeats again with the repetition period of about 1 year. According to this network, the value of imports will fluctuate between approx. USD 306 million and USD 319 million in the examined period.

According to the 2.MLP 6-7-1 network, the value of imports in the predicted period will rise slightly from about USD 317.6 million to about USD 319.6 million at the end of 2022. Very similarly, the value of imports is predicted by the 3. MLP 6-7-1 with an initial value of about USD 328 million and the value of about USD 339 million at the end of 2022. The opposite trend of the import value is predicted by the network 4. MLP 6-8-1. This network assumes the value of approx. USD 301.5 million at the beginning of the predicted period and the value of approx. USD 264 million at the end of the predicted period. As for the last network 5. MLP 6-5-1, according to Fig. 6.48, it returns to the growing trend of the value of imports. According to this network, the value of imports should reach approx. USD 327.6 million at the end of 2020 and approx. USD 333.7 million at the end of 2022.

The conclusion from the variant with a time series delay of six steps is actually the same as in the previous variants. Thus, the networks can only follow the actual development of imports roughly, the residue values are still quite far from the ideal value. For use in practice, it will be necessary to verify the predictions with the actual values of the Russia/Czechia imports and then to re-train the networks.

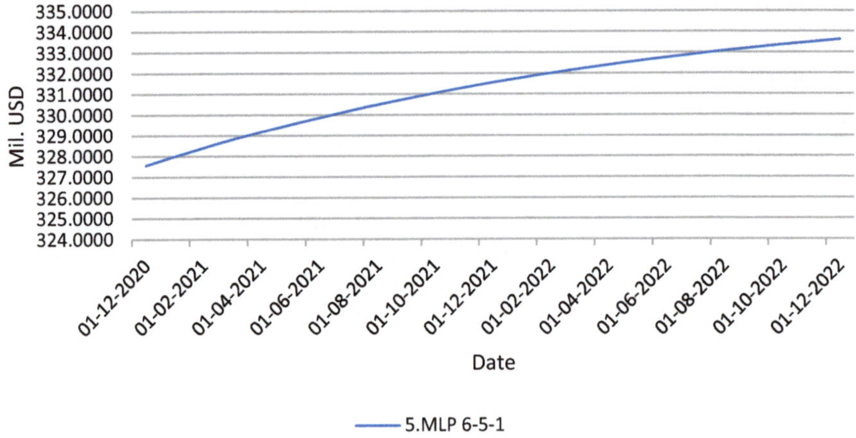

Fig. 6.48 Import prediction—5. MLP 6-5-1_E1_import 6a. Source: Own research

6.13 Import 12a

A total of 10,000 neural structures were also generated for the 12-step time delay variant, five of which showing the best results (according to the least squares method) were preserved and are shown in Table 6.17.

Also in the last variant of the import, only MLP-type networks were preserved, with 5–8 neurons in the hidden layer. Here, too, the BFGS algorithm was used for network training. The function used to activate the hidden layer, namely the hyperbolic tangent, is identical. Only the function used in the activation of the output layer differs slightly—in three cases, it is the exponential function, in two cases it is the identity function. If we take into account all the previous variants of the trade balance, exports, and imports, here we get the highest network performance of around 97–98%. The performance is high mainly for the training and validation data set. According to its performance, the 1. MLP 12-6-1 network seems to be the most successful but the differences between the networks are negligible. Network prediction statistics, i.e. the minimum and maximum predictions, residuals and standard residuals, could provide a better insight, see Table 6.18.

It is clear from Table 6.18 that the values of residuals are lower than in the previous variants, if we calculate the trade balance, exports, and imports, they are closer to the required value of 0. Thus, there is a very high network performance. Here, too, the first conserved network 1. MLP 12-6-1 is the most successful in terms of residual values (the residual values are closer to 0 than in the case of the other networks). Of course, these advantages should also be reflected in the graphical representation of the balanced time series of the Russia/Czechia imports according to these preserved networks (see Fig. 6.49).

It really is the case indeed. These networks are much closer to the actual development of imports. The figure shows that the curves of the networks intersect

Table 6.17 Summary of active networks_E1_import 12a

Index	Net. name	Training perf.	Test perf.	Validation perf.	Training error	Test error	Validation error	Training algorithm	Error function	Hidden activation	Output activation
1	MLP 12-6-1	0.980977	0.982067	0.985550	352.4705	303.6639	291.0363	BFGS 9999	SOS	Tanh	Exponential
2	MLP 12-5-1	0.978123	0.972898	0.985810	406.5479	430.0156	298.8540	BFGS 10000	SOS	Tanh	Identity
3	MLP 12-7-1	0.982846	0.976696	0.987202	333.3509	401.8440	262.6097	BFGS 3417	SOS	Tanh	Exponential
4	MLP 12-7-1	0.982347	0.976121	0.987995	326.4963	378.6731	245.9436	BFGS 451	SOS	Tanh	Identity
5	MLP 12-8-1	0.983130	0.971281	0.986364	312.0189	456.8130	273.0844	BFGS 327	SOS	Tanh	Exponential

Source: Own research

Table 6.18 Predictions statistics_E1_import 12a

Statistics	Target: Import 1.MLP 12-6-1	2.MLP 12-5-1	3.MLP 12-7-1	4.MLP 12-7-1	5.MLP 12-8-1
Minimum prediction (train)	36.0712	30.797	20.1614	5.8844	30.5034
Maximum prediction (train)	519.6620	515.321	534.6104	504.1348	512.4842
Minimum prediction (test)	36.3338	32.587	20.2402	8.4510	31.4743
Maximum prediction (test)	458.5005	479.668	441.6229	474.5183	468.3591
Minimum prediction (validation)	38.1559	34.106	20.3541	16.3157	31.9980
Maximum prediction (validation)	547.5076	510.148	563.2430	522.6480	550.7892
Minimum residual (train)	−73.2781	−100.399	−77.6997	−87.2125	−83.9665
Maximum residual (train)	103.7528	130.207	108.2960	111.1780	104.4882
Minimum residual (test)	−61.3099	−74.149	−60.6665	−53.3376	−54.3527
Maximum residual (test)	61.7083	116.571	71.2409	112.0022	110.2966
Minimum residual (validation)	−81.6061	−57.660	−51.3832	−54.7968	−48.5574
Maximum residual (validation)	46.5492	99.315	91.3266	98.5028	85.6661
Minimum standard residual (train)	−3.9031	−4.979	−4.2557	−4.8266	−4.7535
Maximum standard residual (train)	5.5264	6.458	5.9315	6.1529	5.9153
Minimum standard residual (test)	−3.5183	−3.576	−3.0264	−2.7409	−2.5430
Maximum standard residual (test)	3.5412	5.621	3.5539	5.7557	5.1605
Minimum standard residual (validation)	−4.7835	−3.335	−3.1708	−3.4941	−2.9384
Maximum standard residual (validation)	2.7286	5.745	5.6356	6.2810	5.1839

Source: Own research

and they follow the blue curve of the actual development of imports. For a better picture, figures of balanced time series with residual values for all preserved networks will now be presented. Figure 6.50 shows the prediction and residuals according to the network 1. MLP 12-6-1.

We see that the network is able to copy the actual development of the value of imports relatively accurately, especially in the second half of the period under review. The residuals are therefore significantly lower than in all the previous variants. The 2.MLP 12-5-1 network in Fig. 6.51 is also performing very well.

Figure 6.52 shows the balanced time series and residuals according to the network 3. MLP 12-7-1. Here, once more, a relatively successful prediction and relatively low residuals are noticeable.

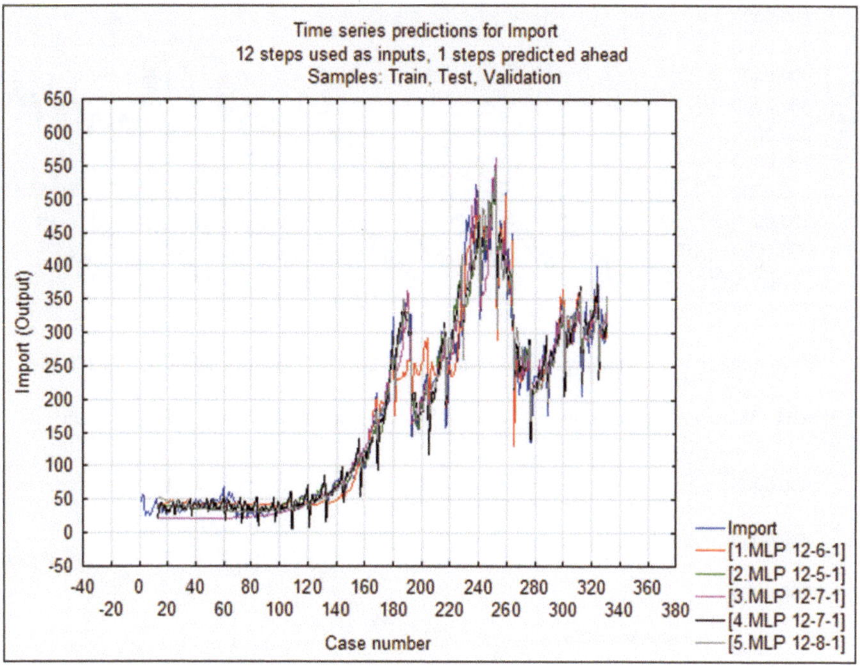

Fig. 6.49 Time series predictions_E1_import 12a. Source: Own research

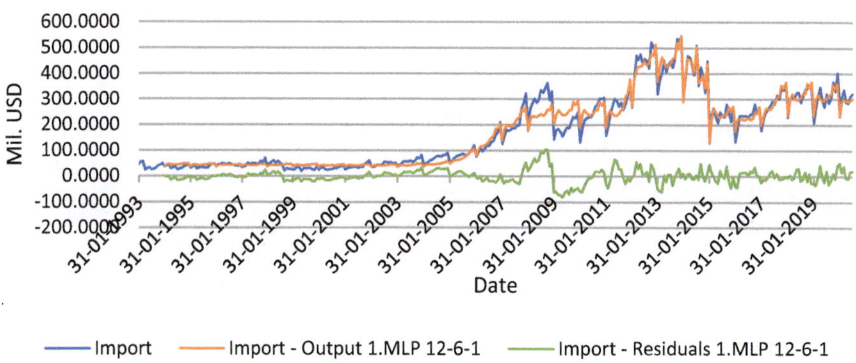

Fig. 6.50 Time series prediction—1. MLP 12-6-1_E1_import 12a. Source: Own research

The same applies for the balanced time series according to the network 4. MLP 12-7-1 as well (see Fig. 6.53).

The 5. MLP 12-8-1 network also does a very good job at balancing the time series, the result of which can be seen in Fig. 6.54.

These very positive characteristics of the preserved networks should also be reflected in the predictions for the period from the end of 2020 to the end of 2022. According to all networks, the value of imports will be positive in the predicted

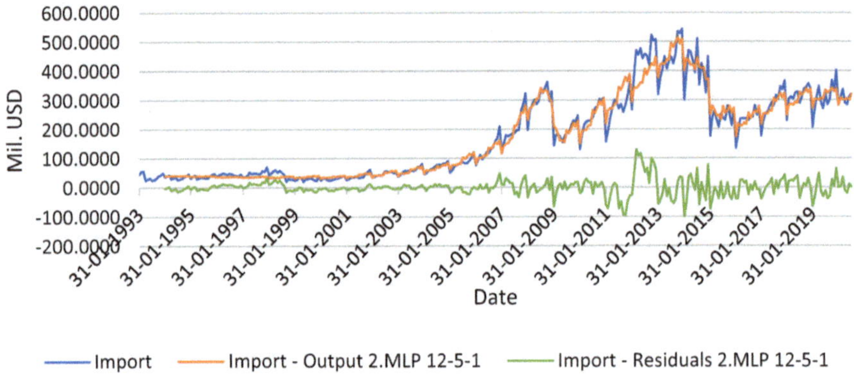

Fig. 6.51 Time series prediction—2. MLP 12-5-1_E1_import 12a. Source: Own research

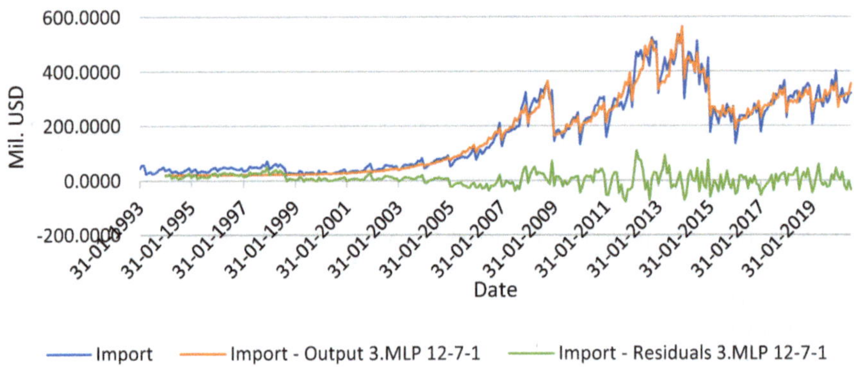

Fig. 6.52 Time series prediction—3. MLP 12-7-1_E1_import 12a. Source: Own research

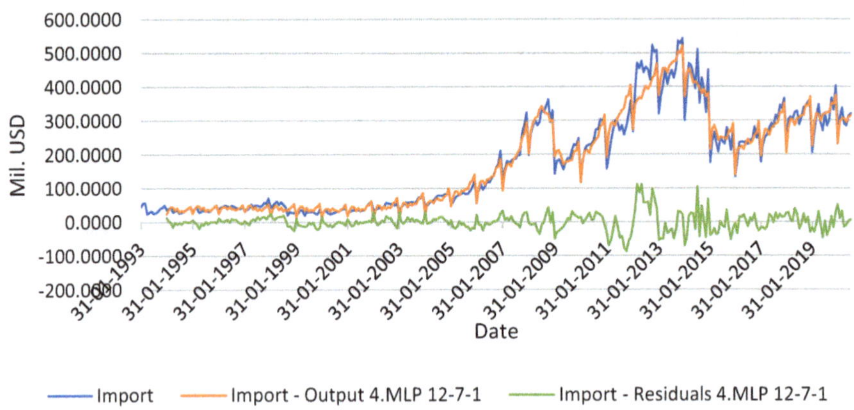

Fig. 6.53 Time series prediction—4. MLP 12-7-1_E1_import 12a. Source: Own research

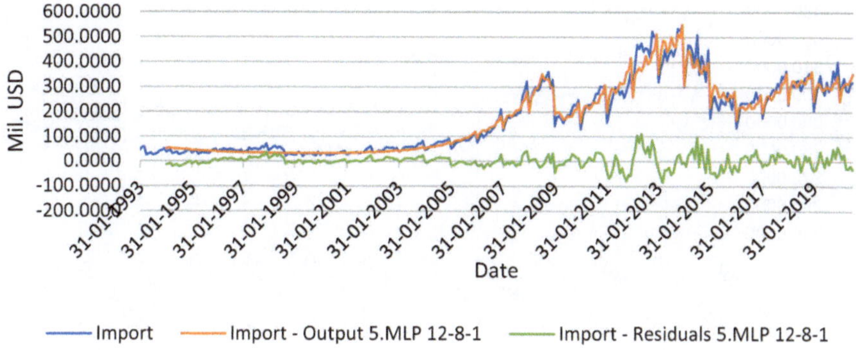

Fig. 6.54 Time series prediction—5. MLP 12-8-1_E1_import 12a. Source: Own research

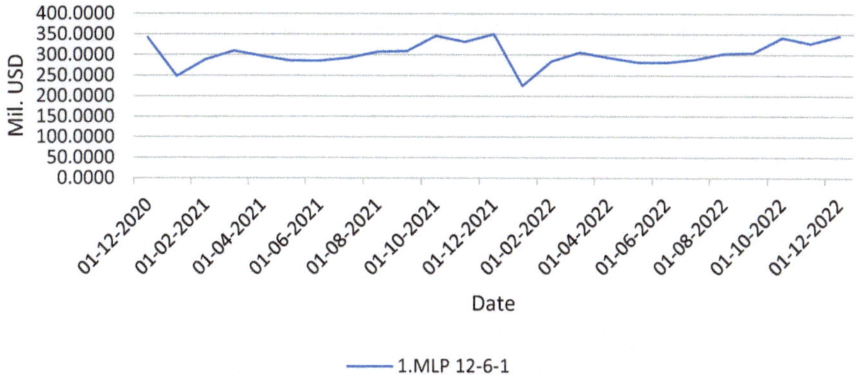

Fig. 6.55 Import prediction—1. MLP 12-6-1_E1_import 12a. Source: Own research

period, relatively well above 0. It can also be noted that all networks identically predict a sharp decline in the value of imports at the beginning of 2022, so that the value rises again in the coming months. In some cases, after this decline, the value of imports reaches a maximum in this predicted period, in other cases, the value stabilizes at a similar value as before this decline. The first of this series is a figure of import prediction according to the 1. MLP 12-6-1 (see Fig. 6.55).

This network predicts the value of imports in the predicted period in the range of approx. USD 230 million to USD 350 million. The maximum value is predicted before the fall at the end of 2021. The next figure, Fig. 6.56, shows the prediction of imports according to the network 2. MLP 12-5-1.

This network predicts a narrower range of import value movements, from about USD 274 million declared in the slump at the beginning of 2022 to about USD 320 million at the beginning of the predicted period. Figure 6.57 with a prediction of imports according to the 3. MLP 12-7-1 offers a larger range.

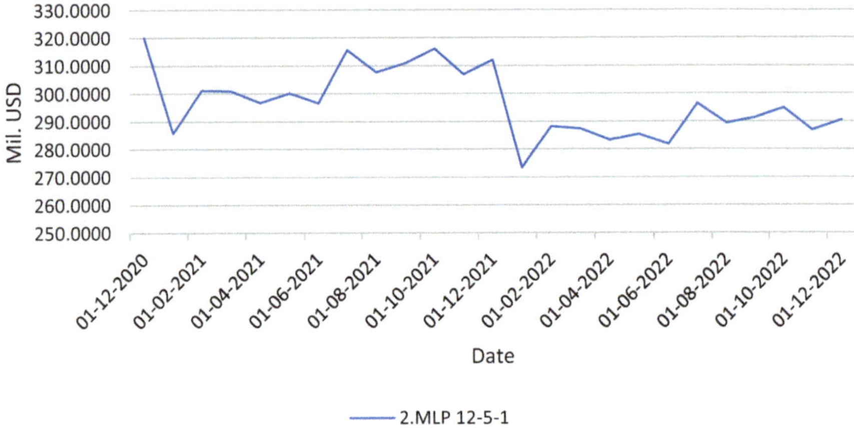

Fig. 6.56 Import prediction—2. MLP 12-5-1_E1_import 12a. Source: Own research

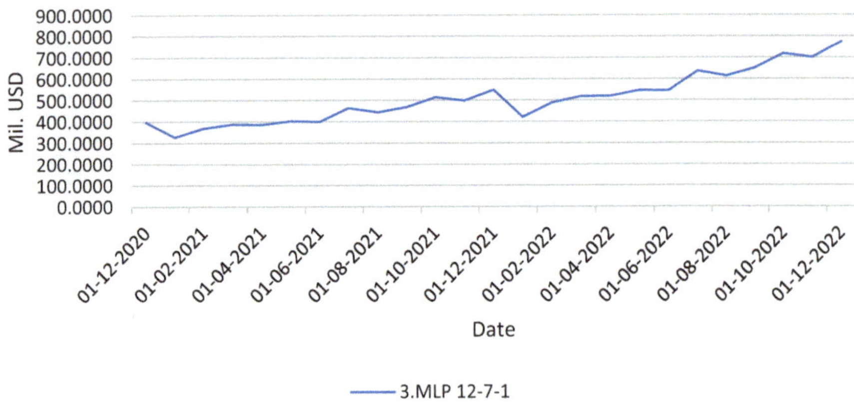

Fig. 6.57 Import prediction—3. MLP 12-7-1_E1_import 12a. Source: Own research

The figure above shows the declared decline in the value of imports again which should grow in the long run, from USD 400 million to approx. USD 780 million. The predictions made by the network 4. MLP 12-7-1 can be seen in Fig. 6.58.

Here, the network is again limited to a smaller range of import values in the predicted period, there is again a very clear decline in value at the beginning of 2022 by about USD 130 million and another larger decrease at the beginning of 2021 by approx. USD 100 million. The value of imports is otherwise stable at around USD 300 million. The prediction according to the last preserved network 5. MLP 12-8-1 is also presented in Fig. 6.59.

This network also predicts a relatively significant decline in the value of imports at the beginning of 2022 (by up to about USD 180 million). Otherwise, however, it assumes a mostly stable and significant growth from about USD 400 million at the

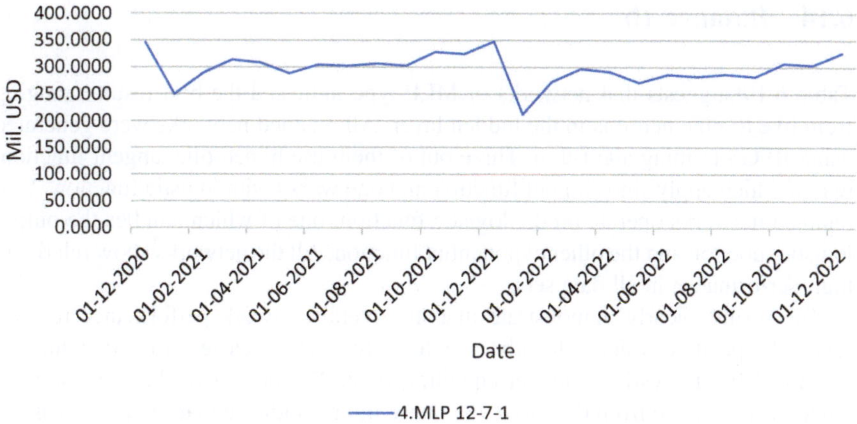

Fig. 6.58 Import prediction—4. MLP 12-7-1_E1_import 12a. Source: Own research

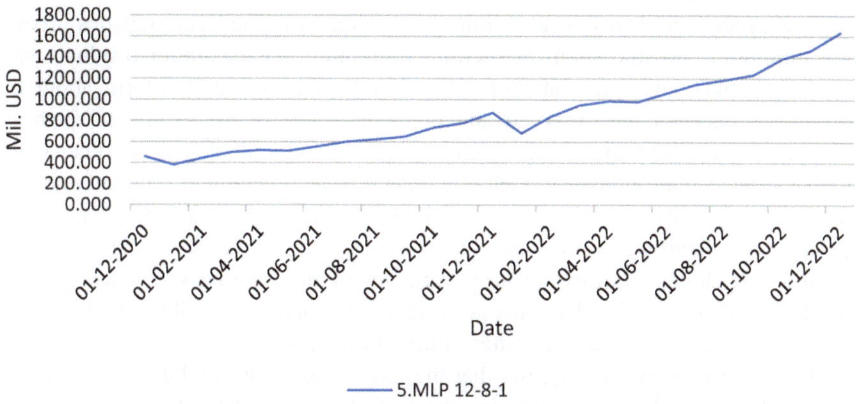

Fig. 6.59 Import prediction—5. MLP 12-8-1_E1_import 12a. Source: Own research

beginning of the predicted period to USD 1630 million, which is by far the highest predicted value of the Russia/Czechia imports.

The networks generated and preserved as part of the import tracking and 12-step delay variants are arguably the most successful networks in this entire experiment, including export and trade balance tracking. The given networks have a very high performance, relatively low values of residuals, which guarantee a relatively accurate balancing of the time series of the Russia/Czechia imports. The success of the networks is also reflected in the predictions, when the networks all predict a significant decline in the value of imports at the beginning of 2022. Depending on the shapes and directions of the curves, these predictions are more realistic. These preserved networks therefore have a great potential for use in practice. The verification of their abilities in further analyses and research will be essential.

6.14 Balance 1b

Table 6.19 suggests that networks of MLP type indicated the best results, ranging from five to nine neurons in the hidden layer. All retained networks were generated using BFGS training algorithm. Three out of them use hyperbolic tangent function, two of which apply sinus output function and one works with logistic function. Two retained networks operate on the logistic function, one of which handles the output logistic function and the other exponential function. All the networks show relatively high performance in all data sets.

The results clearly demonstrate that the overall network performance reaches relatively positive values. Ideally, we look for values closest to 1.0, which is generated by the testing data set equalling 0.82. The other two data sets suggest values with a range from 0.70 to 0.78. These figures indicate that MLP 3-5-1 is the best network from this data set. The following results and outputs will assess this inference.

Table 6.20 suggests basic prediction statistics of the retained networks according to three predefined data sets (test, train, and validation). The basic statistics involve the minimum and maximum prediction, minimum and maximum residuals, and minimum and maximum standardized residuals. The residuals inform about the difference between the observed and predicted value of the examined quantity. The subtler the difference is, the better the prediction will be. On the other hand, high residual values indicate model's frequent misidentification to expound upon the target quantity using explanatory variables. At the same time, any "systematic behaviour", albeit in low absolute values, indicates a poor model, mostly resulting from a bad choice from explanatory variables or their wrong specifications. The residuals should thereby demonstrate roughly symmetrical distribution around the mean zero value and constant scatter limited from above.

The tabular overview suggests that the largest residuals can be observed in the testing data set, which also contains the hugest mass of data. The minimum and maximum standardized residuals are very close to the ideal value 0, indicating a relatively accurate prediction.

Minimum and maximum standardized residuals are very close to the ideal value 0, indicating a relatively accurate prediction.

Table 6.21 illustrates data statistics of the balance of trade between Russia and Czechia in individual data sets classified according to the methodological information—70% in the training data set, 15% in the testing data set, and 15% in the validation data set. The statistical characteristics involve minimum and maximum value, mean and standard deviation.

The tabular depiction demonstrates that the mean value of the balance of trade was USD 39,020.54 (monthly) and USD 2006.296 (annual) (Fig. 6.60).

Although the given neural network provides a rough imitation of Russia/Czech balance of trade, it does not fit to estimate local maximums and minimums. For that reason, the structure is rather unsuitable for practice use.

Table 6.19 Summary of active networks_E2_balance 1b

Index	Net. name	Training perf.	Test perf.	Validation perf.	Training error	Test error	Validation error	Training algorithm	Error function	Hidden activation	Output activation
1	MLP 3-7-1	0.703772	0.784835	0.760327	2093.847	2439.417	1436.962	BFGS 192	SOS	Tanh	Sine
2	MLP 3-8-1	0.712644	0.761095	0.752564	2041.650	2544.261	1481.198	BFGS 133	SOS	Logistic	Logistic
3	MLP 3-6-1	0.715874	0.777309	0.775102	2032.397	2386.426	1376.479	BFGS 126	SOS	Logistic	Exponential
4	MLP 3-9-1	0.749138	0.770926	0.747890	1820.028	2462.780	1517.457	BFGS 82	SOS	Tanh	Logistic
5	MLP 3-5-1	0.737293	0.819844	0.745387	1893.431	2165.976	1534.745	BFGS 87	SOS	Tanh	Sine

Source: Authors

Table 6.20 Predictions statistics_E2_balance 1b

Statistics	Target: Balance Russia/Czechia 1.MLP 3-7-1	2.MLP 3-8-1	3.MLP 3-6-1	4.MLP 3-9-1	5.MLP 3-5-1
Minimum prediction (train)	−35.128	−28.569	−41.989	−77.371	−158.046
Maximum prediction (train)	261.980	293.669	266.004	251.319	249.910
Minimum prediction (test)	−29.790	−28.373	−46.315	−65.239	−106.823
Maximum prediction (test)	261.572	286.884	267.497	251.437	245.818
Minimum prediction (validation)	−23.884	−18.657	−49.183	−22.994	−62.488
Maximum prediction (validation)	244.918	276.785	253.977	246.396	245.146
Minimum residual (train)	−246.182	−243.498	−224.224	−257.179	−205.490
Maximum residual (train)	239.797	211.006	228.305	207.171	195.264
Minimum residual (test)	−298.527	−303.481	−283.727	−318.575	−183.137
Maximum residual (test)	125.453	139.091	129.961	114.506	97.571
Minimum residual (validation)	−115.730	−122.376	−107.566	−141.727	−151.505
Maximum residual (validation)	186.888	203.867	174.759	212.341	195.723
Minimum standard residual (train)	−5.380	−5.389	−4.974	−6.028	−4.722
Maximum standard residual (train)	5.240	4.670	5.064	4.856	4.487
Minimum standard residual (test)	−6.044	−6.017	−5.808	−6.419	−3.935
Maximum standard residual (test)	2.540	2.758	2.660	2.307	2.096
Minimum standard residual (validation)	−3.053	−3.180	−2.899	−3.638	−3.867
Maximum standard residual (validation)	4.930	5.297	4.710	5.451	4.996

Source: Authors

Figure 6.61 illustrates the same circumstance; this time the second retained neural structure 2. MLP 3-8-1 is to be dealt with.

The movement of individual curves suggests a neural network with a similar predictive ability as it was in the event of the first retained structure. The second structure delivers similar performance with similar characteristics—provides only a rough tracking of the balance of trade trend, but cannot detect local maximums and minimums, which again indicates unsuitability for practical application.

The third retained neural network 3. MLP 3-6-1 applies analogical approach presented in Fig. 6.62.

The same applies to the fourth retained neural structure 4. MLP 3-9-1 depicted in Fig. 6.63.

The last, fifth neural structure MLP 3-5-1 shows the worst characteristics, i.e. much lower prediction accuracy than the previous networks (see Fig. 6.64).

Table 6.21 Data statistics_E2_balance 1b

Samples	Month	Year	Month in a year	Balance Russia/ Czechia
Minimum (train)	34,028.00	1993.000	1.00000	−228.240
Maximum (train)	44,043.00	2020.000	12.00000	386.070
Mean (train)	39,086.88	2006.485	6.36052	90.858
Standard deviation (train)	2895.43	7.925	3.38462	91.276
Minimum (test)	34,000.00	1993.000	1.00000	−289.960
Maximum (test)	44,012.00	2020.000	12.00000	320.020
Mean (test)	38,608.14	2005.163	6.48980	93.577
Standard deviation (test)	2928.16	8.024	3.61203	110.350
Minimum (validation)	34,181.00	1993.000	1.00000	−117.670
Maximum (validation)	43,921.00	2020.000	12.00000	266.830
Mean (validation)	39,117.47	2006.531	6.81633	83.958
Standard deviation (validation)	4455.34	12.161	3.56672	35.140
Minimum (overall)	34,000.00	1993.000	1.00000	−289.960
Maximum (overall)	44,043.00	2020.000	12.00000	386.070
Mean (overall)	39,020.54	2006.296	6.44713	90.239
Standard deviation (overall)	2912.73	7.977	3.45176	92.971

Source: Authors

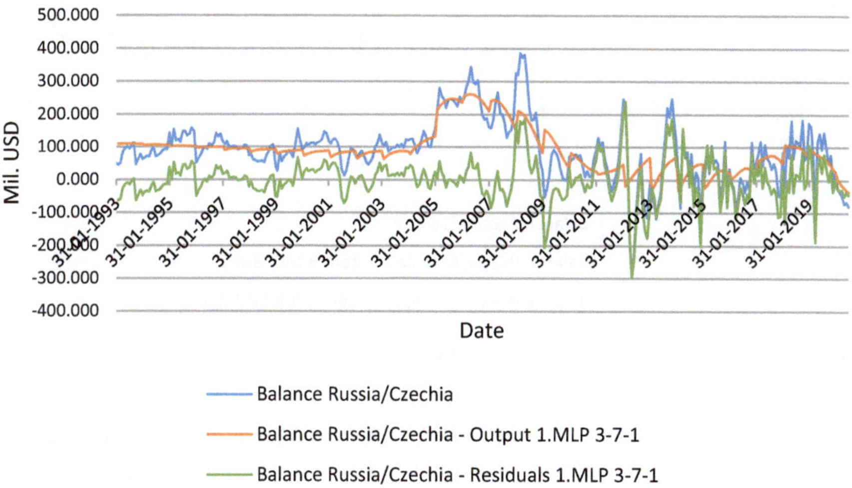

Fig. 6.60 Time series prediction—1. MLP 3-7-1_E2_balance 1b. Source: Authors

The diagram suggests that retained neural structures can roughly define the actual balance of trade development (Fig. 6.65). However, they cannot precisely estimate local minimums and maximums. This may be seen from graphs of individual neural structures in relation to the actual trend in residual values, as shown in Graph 1 depicting neural structure 1. MLP 3-7-1. The blue arrow indicates the actual

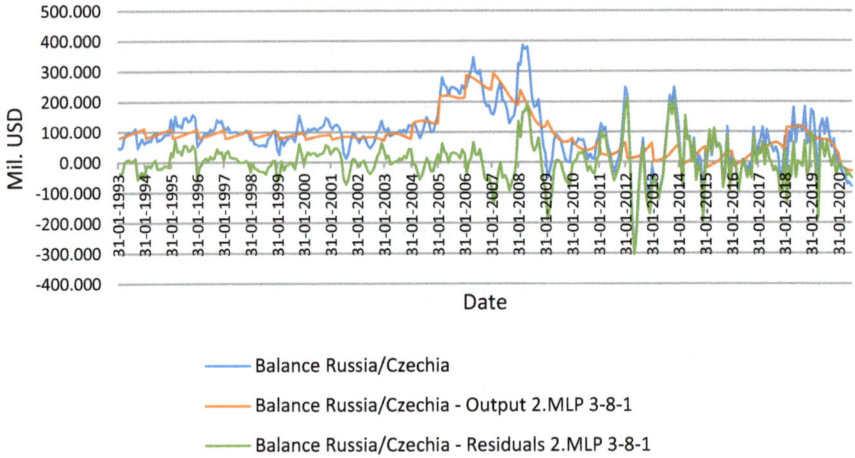

Fig. 6.61 Time series prediction—2. MLP 3-8-1_E2_balance 1b. Source: Authors

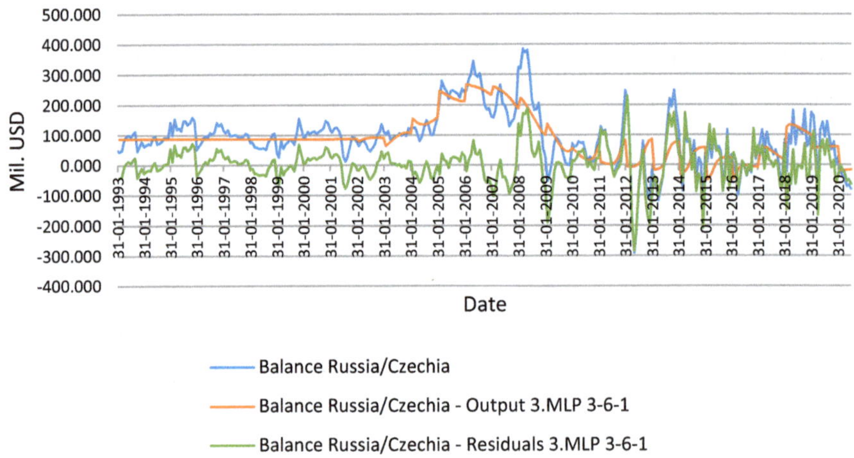

Fig. 6.62 Time series prediction—3. MLP 3-6-1_E2_balance 1b. Source: Authors

movement of the balance of trade between Russia/Czechia, the red arrow demonstrates an increase (predictions according to a specific neural structure), whereas the green curve represents residual values.

The following part focuses on predicting Russia/Czechia balance of trade to the future. The previous part laid out the prediction ability of separate neural networks, giving actual data until the beginning of 2020 as an example. Now we will concentrate on predicting the balance of trade value from the end of 2020 until the end of 2022. These predictions again contain five retained neural structures. The first one is neural network 1.MLP 3-7-1 predicting Russia/Czechia balance of trade suggested in Fig. 6.66.

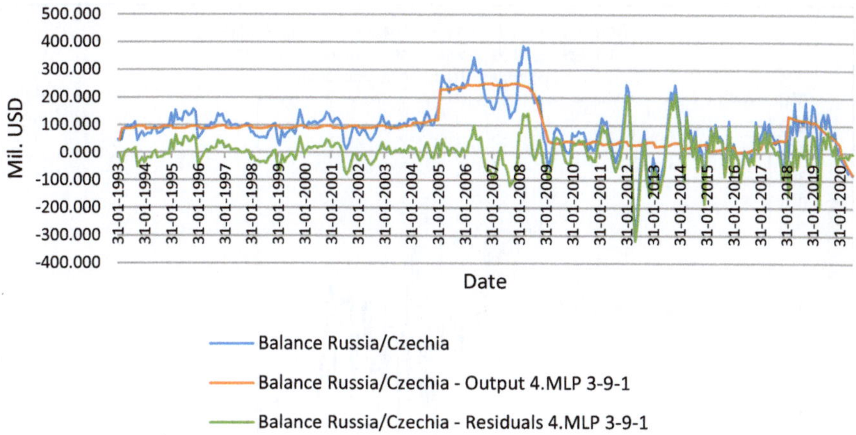

Fig. 6.63 Time series prediction—4. MLP 3-9-1_E2_balance 1b. Source: Authors

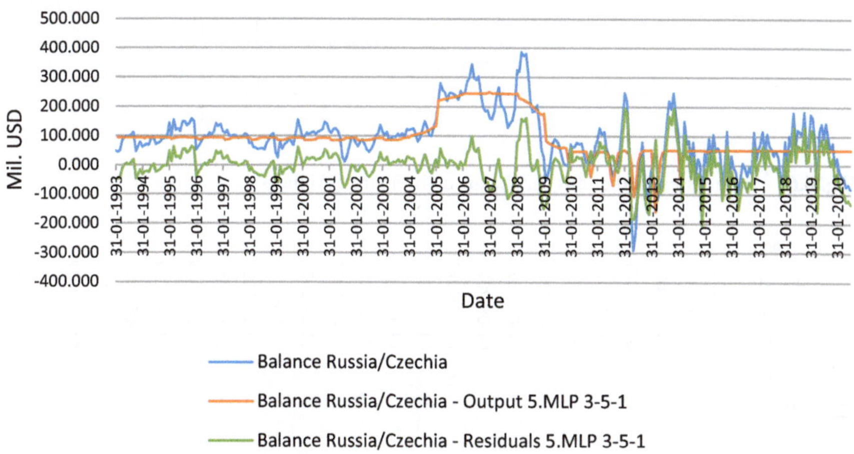

Fig. 6.64 Time series prediction—5. MLP 3-5-1_E2_balance 1b. Source: Authors

The graph shows a negative balance of trade value predicted from the end of 2020 until the end of 2022. We see a rather gentle descent to the negative balance of trade until the beginning of 2022, followed by a steep plunge from the end of January 2021 until the end of February 2021. The follow-up decline will then be settling in the previous steady measures. The balance of trade value is then predicted for a steady decrease peaking USD –400,000 mil. by the end of 2022.

The second retained structure 2. MLP 3-8-1 (see Fig. 6.67) indicates a very similar trend. As contrasted to the first network, this structure predicts a sharp decline of the negative balance of trade value for two periods, namely from January 2021 to the end of February 2021 and from January 2022 to the end of February 2022. The

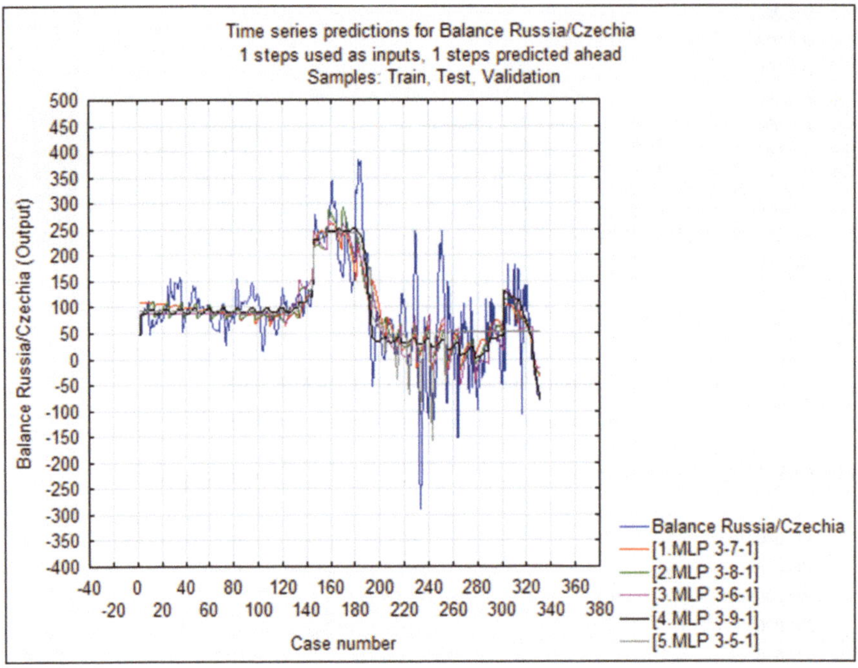

Fig. 6.65 Time series predictions_E2_balance 1b. Source: Authors

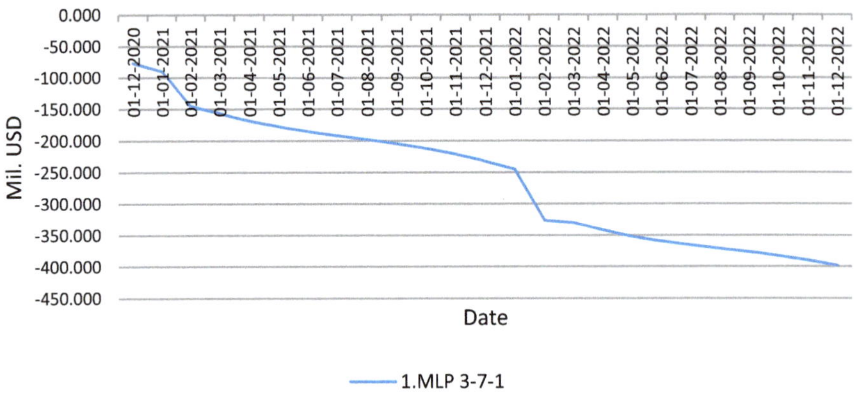

Fig. 6.66 Balance prediction—1. MLP 3-7-1_E2_balance 1b. Source: Authors

prediction implies that the balance of trade value between Russia/Czechia will be around USD −110,000 mil throughout 2021 and USD-160,000 mil. in 2022.

The downward trend of Russia/Czechia balance of trade is confirmed by the third retained structure 3. MLP 3-6-1. This network foresees a sharp drop at the beginning of the examined period, predicting a constant balance value of USD −58 mil. approximately from February 2021 (see Fig. 6.68). We will then be witnessing a

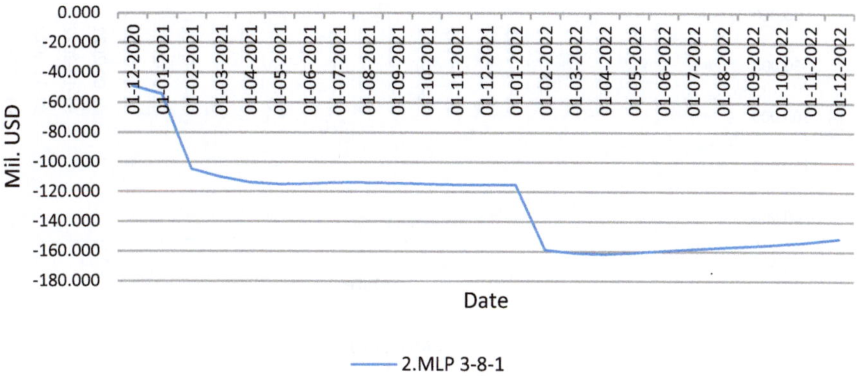

Fig. 6.67 Balance prediction—2. MLP 3-8-1_E2_balance 1b. Source: Authors

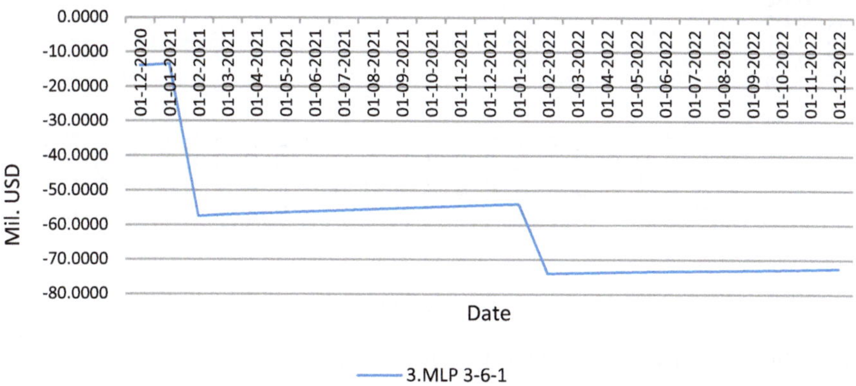

Fig. 6.68 Balance prediction—3. MLP 3-6-1_E2_balance 1b. Source: Authors

steep plunge to USD −74 mil. at the beginning of 2022, with a subsequent stabilization. The third retained network predicts violent annual fluctuations, with no likelihood of getting to black numbers.

The prediction of the fourth retained network 4. MLP 3-9-1, depicted in Fig. 6.69, of Russia/Czechia balance of trade comes up with different results. The structure foresees a marked decline of the balance of trade at the beginning of the monitored period, indicating stabilization on a value of USD −225 mil. as of August 2022.

As a result of an error occurred in values on y axis in Fig. 6.70, we refrain from any comments.

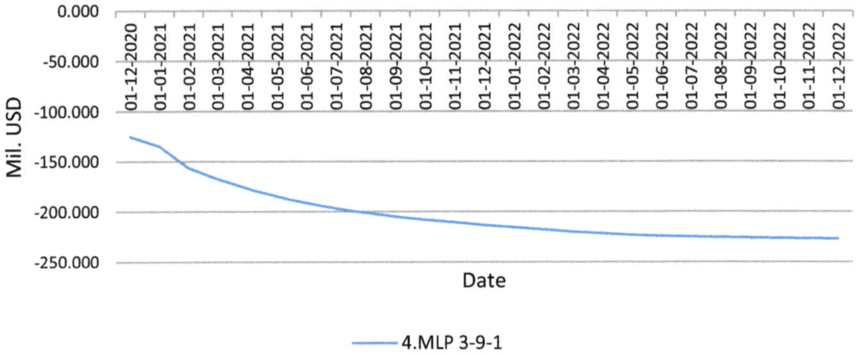

Fig. 6.69 Balance prediction—4. MLP 3-9-1_E2_balance 1b. Source: Authors

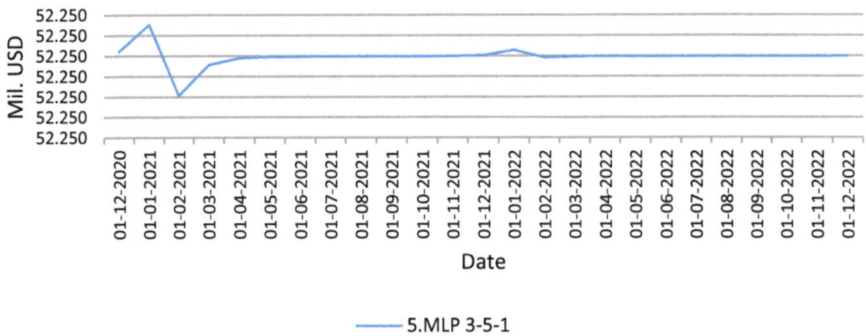

Fig. 6.70 Balance prediction—5. MLP 3-5-1_E2_balance 1b. Source: Authors

6.15 Balance 3b

We methodologically generated 10,000 neural structures, five of which with the best results (according to the least square method) were retained. They are illustrated in Table 6.22.

The tabular overview shows that MLP networks with a range from three to ten neurons in the hidden layer indicated the best results. All the retained networks were generated using training algorithm BFGS. Four of them employ the hyperbolic tangent function and one operates on logistic function in the hidden layer. Three out of the four aforementioned networks use tangent as an output function, while one works on the output-identity function. The last hidden network runs on the logistic function and output exponential function. At the same time, there is a relatively high performance apparent in the discussed networks in all data sets. The testing data set shows the highest performance.

So far, we have been discussing a relatively high network performance, which is represented by correlation coefficients in the table above. Correlation coefficients are

Table 6.22 Summary of active networks_E2_balance 3b

Index	Net. name	Training perf.	Test perf.	Validation perf.	Training error	Test error	Validation error	Training algorithm	Error function	Hidden activation	Output activation
1	MLP 9-5-1	0.678845	0.793165	0.722987	2238.564	2380.405	1634.991	BFGS 37	SOS	Tanh	Identity
2	MLP 9-10-1	0.785364	0.748665	0.731244	1586.444	2619.699	1696.907	BFGS 200	SOS	Tanh	Tanh
3	MLP 9-3-1	0.714835	0.762452	0.719608	2024.794	2636.866	1649.723	BFGS 90	SOS	Logistic	Exponential
4	MLP 9-4-1	0.703123	0.747963	0.719193	2093.735	2747.906	1665.302	BFGS 68	SOS	Tanh	Tanh
5	MLP 9-3-1	0.616157	0.689828	0.723297	2573.980	3304.613	1772.257	BFGS 103	SOS	Tanh	Tanh

Source: Authors

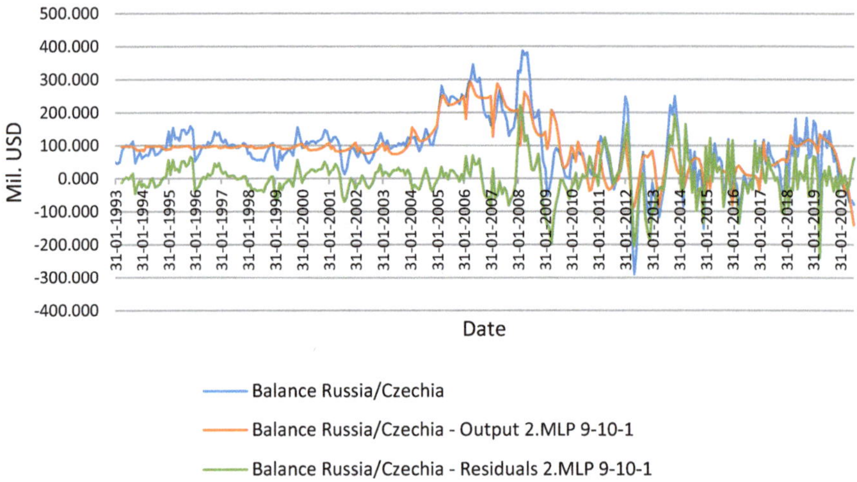

Fig. 6.71 Time series prediction—2. MLP 9-10-1_E2_balance 3b. Source: Authors

thereby equal to values of individual networks in columns 'Training perf.", "Test perf.", and "Validation perf." in Table Summary of active networks (Data_2).

The table proves that the network performance reaches relatively positive values, us seeking values closest to 1.0. The highest performance is the most apparent in the testing data set, amounting to about 0.79. The following two data sets include values in a range from approximately 0.61 to 0.78. These figures imply that the second retained network MLP 9-10-1 of this data set may be the best one. For empirical verification, we need to observe further results and outcomes.

Basic prediction statistics of individual retained networks according to three predefined data sets (test, train, validation) were stated. The basic statistics involve minimum and maximum prediction, minimum and maximum residuals, and minimum and maximum standardized residuals. Residuals expound upon the difference between the observed and predicted value of the examined quantity. The smaller the difference is, the more accurate the prediction will be. On the other hand, high residual values relate to model's frequent misidentification of the target quantity using explanatory variables. At the same time, any "systematic behaviour", albeit in low absolute values", indicates a bad model, mostly referring to a poor choice of explanatory variables or their wrong specifications. The residuals should thereby exhibit roughly symmetrical distribution around the mean zero value and constant scatter limited from above.

The largest residuals may be observed in the training data set, which, at the same time, contains most data, being slightly ahead of the testing data set. Yet, larger residuals are present in minimum residuals in the testing data set, while minimum and maximum standardized residuals are very close to the ideal value 0, indicating a relatively accurate prediction. The results indicate the balance of trade median being USD 39,020.54 within the monitored period.

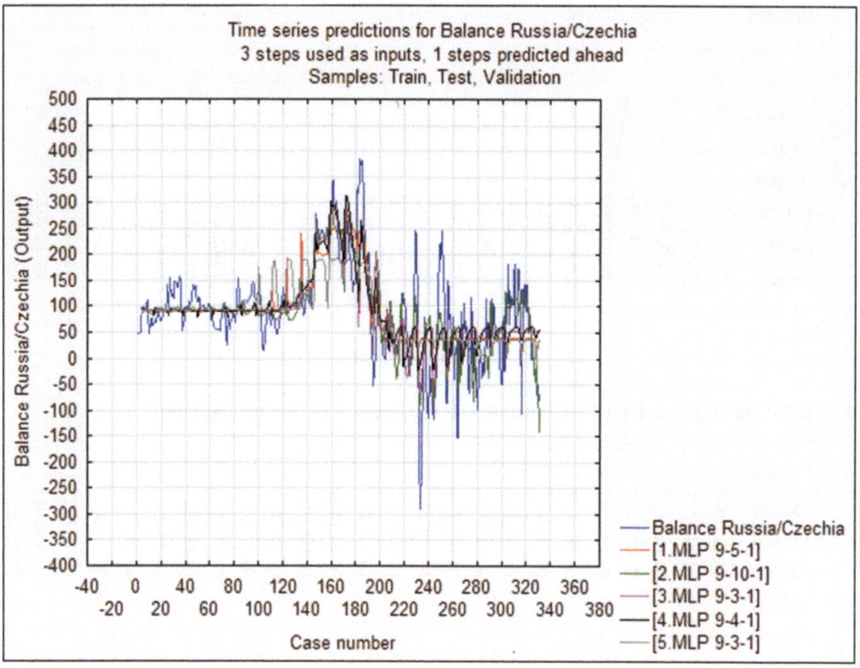

Fig. 6.72 Time series predictions_E2_balance 3b. Source: Authors

Figure 6.71 shows that the given neural network provides only a rough imitation of Russia/Czechia balance of trade value, but cannot precisely define local minimums and maximums. We do not thereby recommend using the network in practice, as it provides only a rough estimate of the balance of trade value.

The graphical illustration suggests that the retained neural structures provide only a rough imitation of the actual balance of trade movement, without a precisely defining local maximums and minimums (Fig. 6.72). This situation is clearly apparent from previous graphs of individual retained neural structures relating to the actual development and residual values.

The following part will focus on predicting Russia/Czechia balance of trade to the future. The previous part dealt with the prediction ability of separate neural networks, giving actual data until the beginning of 2020 as an example. Now we will predict the balance of trade value from the end of 2020 until the end of 2022. The specific predictions will again involve five retained neural structures, the first one being neural network 1. MLP 9-5-1 with its graphical prediction of Russia/Czechia balance of trade in Fig. 6.73.

The graphical illustration indicates a prediction of a dramatic fall of the balance of trade down to negative values—from USD 40 mil. down to ca USD −14 mil. from the beginning of March 2021 until the end of April 2021. However, we will be witnessing its return to the original value of USD 40 mil. at the beginning of May

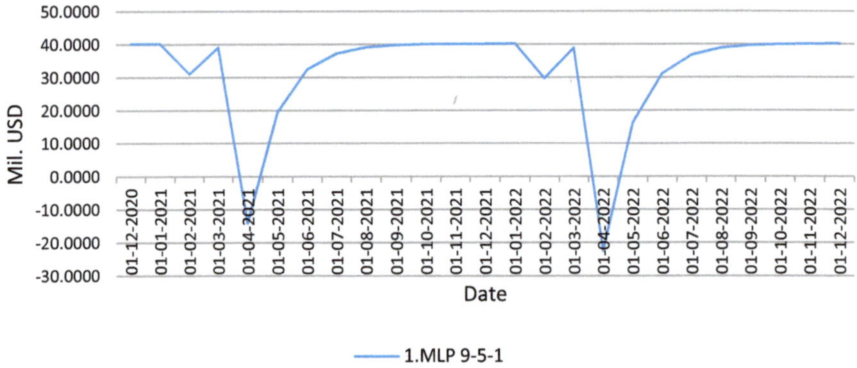

Fig. 6.73 Balance prediction—1. MLP 9-5-1_E2_balance 3b. Source: Authors

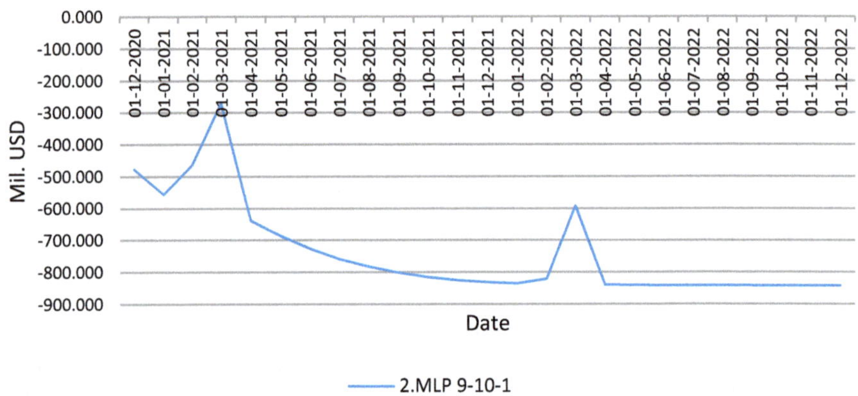

Fig. 6.74 Balance prediction—2. MLP 9-10-1_E2_balance 3b. Source: Authors

2021. The same drastic decline is foreseen from the end of March 2022 until the beginning of May 2022, namely down to USD −22 mil.

The almost identical trend, yet in opposite figures, is predicted by the second retained structure 2. MLP 9-10-1 in Fig. 6.74. The marked difference is no less than 20 fold value in balance of trade negative values, namely USD −850 mil.

3. MLP 9-3-1 predicts a slight decrease of the balance of trade from USD 52.125 mil. to 51.980 mil. from the beginning of March 2021 to the end of April 2021. However, the balance of trade returns to its original value at the beginning of May 2021. Even a gentler decline is foreseen from the end of March 2022 until the beginning of May 2022, in this case indicating only a half-decrease. The course was similar for other networks.

It is thereby evident that all the networks can roughly predict the actual Russia/ Czechia balance of trade movement and precisely detect local minimums and maximums, indicating great utility in practice. As far as future predictions go, the networks make rather inconsistent predictions of balance of trade values, three of them inclining to the positive value of the balance of trade, which is foreseen to fall to negative figures within the examined period. The next presented network predicts conflicting numbers—up to twice as high negative values. The predictions seem rather nonsensical, mostly for longer periods, indicating irrelevance for further predictions. The follow-up research will thereby focus on the actual success rate of these networks, analysed with respect to the predicted and actual development of Russia/Czechia balance of trade.

6.16 Balance 6b

Based upon the methodology, we generated 10,000 neural structures; five of them with the best results were retained (according to the least square methodology) and summarized in Table 6.23.

The table shows that MLP networks demonstrated the best results, with a range from four to seven neurons in the hidden layer. All retained structures were generated using train algorithm BFGS. Four of them apply the logistic function and one works on the hyperbolic tangent in the hidden layer. Two networks out of the four operate on the output hyperbolic tangent; the other two employ identity function and the last, fifth retained network, uses logistic function. All the networks show relatively high performance in all data sets, with the highest performance spotted in the training data set.

We have been talking about a relatively high network performance, presented by correlation coefficients in the tabular overview. The correlation coefficients equal values of individual networks in columns "Training perf.", "Test perf.", and "Validation perf." in Network Weights Table (Data_2).

The table suggests comparatively positive values throughout the network performance. We ideally look for variables that are closest to 1.0, which indicates the highest performance is the training data set, reaching 0.72. The other two data sets involve values in a range from 0.69 to 0.70. These figures imply that the fourth retained network MLP 18-4-1 could be the best. For empirical verification, we need to consider other results and outcomes.

The results show that the largest residuals may be observed in the testing data set, which, at the same time, contains most data. Yet, larger residuals are present in minimum residuals in the testing data set, while minimum and maximum standardized residuals are very close to the ideal value 0, indicating a relatively accurate prediction. The results suggest that the balance of trade mean value was USD 39,020.54 in the monitored period.

Figure 6.75 provides only a rough tracking of local minimums and maximums and is not thereby suitable for practical use.

Almost all networks suggesting that the given neural network cannot track Russia/Czechia balance of trade at all, with no capacity to identify local minimums and maximums whatsoever. The structure is not recommended for practical use either, as it brings only a rough balance of trade value.

Table 6.23 Summary of active networks_E2_balance 6b

Index	Net. name	Training perf.	Test perf.	Validation perf.	Training error	Test error	Validation error	Training algorithm	Error function	Hidden activation	Output activation
1	MLP 18-6-1	0.712096	0.679982	0.699212	2040.457	3236.415	1736.776	BFGS 67	SOS	Logistic	Tanh
2	MLP 18-4-1	0.694135	0.632658	0.702582	2145.400	3599.934	1719.593	BFGS 57	SOS	Logistic	Identity
3	MLP 18-7-1	0.690940	0.649472	0.698707	2163.173	3469.144	1745.276	BFGS 93	SOS	Logistic	Identity
4	MLP 18-4-1	0.706534	0.724361	0.698813	2073.498	3030.458	1750.089	BFGS 38	SOS	Tanh	Logistic
5	MLP 18-5-1	0.706493	0.682268	0.699830	2073.799	3222.245	1735.274	BFGS 65	SOS	Logistic	Tanh

Source: Authors

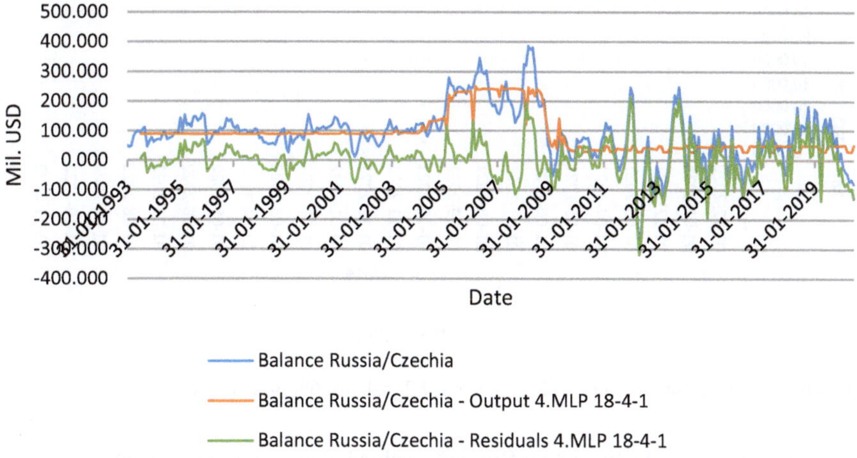

Fig. 6.75 Time series prediction—4. MLP 18-4-1_E2_balance 6b. Source: Authors

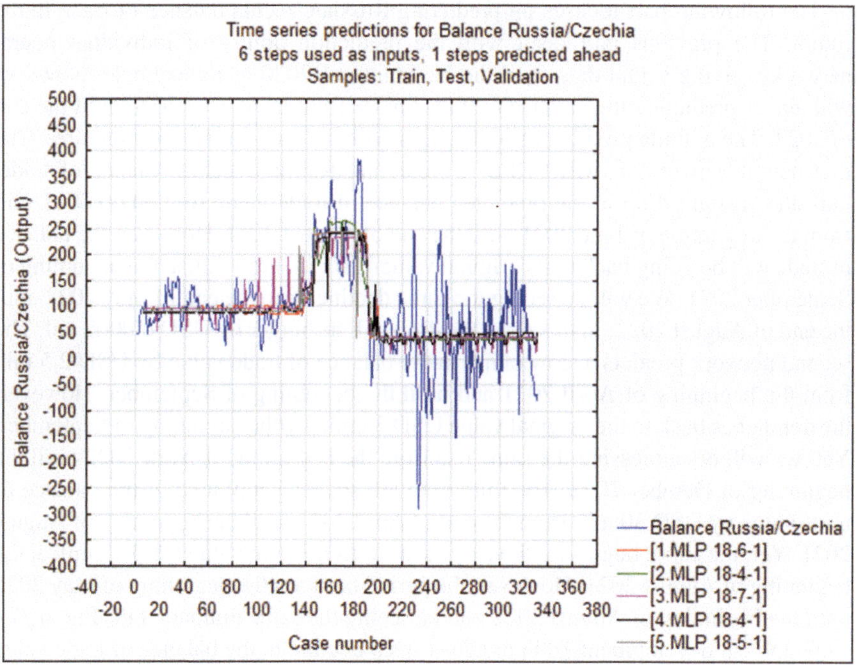

Fig. 6.76 Time series predictions_E2_balance 6b. Source: Authors

Figure 6.76 indicates that retained neural structures can only roughly detect the actual balance of trade development, with no ability to track local maximums and minimums. Graphical illustrations of individual neural structures will provide a clearer picture of this situation regarding the actual development and residual values.

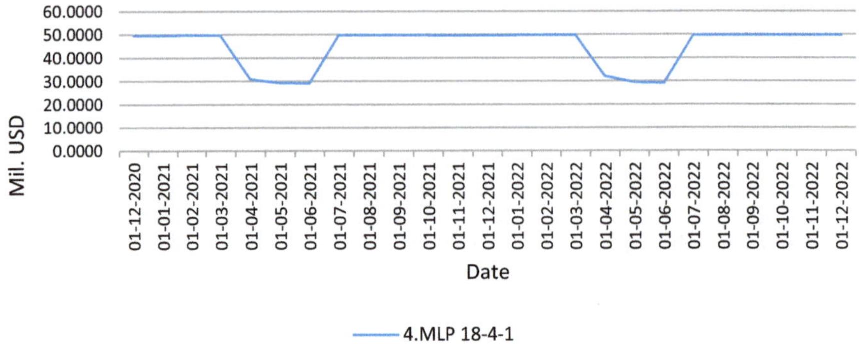

Fig. 6.77 Balance prediction—4. MLP 18-4-1_E2_balance 6b. Source: Authors

The blue arrow marks the actual Russia/Czechia balance of trade movement, the red arrow shows an increasing trend, predicted by the specific neural network, and the green curve refers to residual values.

The following part focuses on predicting Russia/Czechia balance of trade in the future. The previous part dealt with the prediction ability of individual neural networks, giving actual data until the beginning of 2020 as an example. Now, we will aim at predicting the balance of trade values from the end of 2020 until the end of 2022. The definite predictions will again involve 5 retained neural structures. The first neural network, 1. MLP 18-6-1, predicting Russia/Czechia balance of trade, indicates a slight drop in the predicted balance of trade value by USD 0.0001 mil. from the beginning of June 2021 until the end of August 2021. However, the balance of trade will be going back to its original value USD 38.1758 mil. at the beginning of September 2021. We will be seeing the same decline from the end of May 2022 until the end of August 2022; in this case, the drop will be bigger by USD 0.0002 mil. The second network predicts a slow climb in the balance of trade value by USD 2.5 mil. from the beginning of April 2021 and until the beginning of September. However, the trend goes back to the original value USD 38 mil. by the beginning of September. Yet, we will be witnessing the same rise from the beginning of April 2022 until the beginning of October 2022. The third network suggests a plunge of the balance of trade value by USD 30 mil. from the end of April 2021 until the beginning of August 2021. Yet, the curve begins to move upwards to its original value USD 43 mil. at the beginning of August 2021. However, the period between the beginning of May 2022 until the beginning of August 2022 will be seeing the same dramatic fall (Fig. 6.77).

Graphical development 100 predicts a steep decline in the balance of trade value by USD 20 mil. from the end of March 2021 until the end of June 2021, yet soaring to the original value USD 50 mil. by the beginning of June 2021. We will be witnessing the same plunge from the end of March 2022 until the beginning of July 2022.

The aforementioned graphical predictions imply that all the tested networks can roughly predict the actual movement of Russia/Czechia balance of trade and are able to detect local minimums and maximums, indicating a good practical use. As far as future predictions go, the networks make relatively uniform predictions of the balance of trade value. However, the actual success rate of these networks will be subject to further research, comparing the actual Russia/Czechia balance of trade development with the balance predictions made by the retained neural structures.

6.17 Balance 12b

It follows from Table 6.24 that the best results were achieved only by the MLP networks, with 3–6 neurons in the hidden layer. All retained networks were generated using the training algorithm BFGS. The networks generated by means of the BFGS algorithm use the logistic function; only one of the networks generated by means of BFGS algorithm uses the Tangent function. The output function of the networks are Logistic function (two networks), Tangent function (two networks), and Sine (one network).

The weight values of the individual retained networks are different. The network performance achieves positive values. We are searching for the values as close to 1.0 as possible. In this context, the best performance is shown in the validation data set, achieving the value of 0.67. The other two data sets show the values ranging from 0.61 to 0.75. Based on the data, the best network of this data set appears to be the second network MLP 36-3-1.

The largest residuals in the networks 1.MLP 36-6-1, 3.MLP 36-4-1, and 4.MLP 36-3-1 are recorded in the testing data set, which contains the biggest volume of data. In the case of the networks 2. MLP 36-3-1 and 5.MLP 36-5-1 are in the validation data set.

A monthly mean value was USD 39,086.88, while the mean value for a year was USD 2006.485.

Fig. 6.78 shows that the network tries to capture the local minimum, yet not very successfully, as seen from the green curve of residuals. Other networks were able to capture the export time series relatively well in the period of the 2008–2009 economic crisis; however, they only roughly copy the actual development.

Fig. 6.79 shows that the retained networks are able to copy the actual development of the balance roughly only, they are unable to capture the local extremes and smaller or sometimes even larger deviations of the actual value of the balance. Both this graph and the graphs of smoothed time series according to the individual neural structures indicate that all the retained networks are very similar to each other in terms of their performance and their ability to smooth the actual export time series.

The first network predicts the value of the balance in the monitored period in the range of USD 36 mil.—USD 42 mil. The maximum predicted value is recorded at the end of November 2022 (Fig. 6.80).

The value of the balance in the monitored period predicted by this network is USD 267,410 mil.

The third network shows the predicted value of the balance, which is divided into roughly annual cycles. The network thus predicts gradually increasing and

Table 6.24 Summary of active networks_E2_balance 12b

Index	Net. name	Training perf.	Test perf.	Validation perf.	Training error	Test error	Validation error	Training algorithm	Error function	Hidden activation	Output activation
1	MLP 36-6-1	0.693891	0.627292	0.664155	2143.226	3664.665	1953.601	BFGS 31	SOS	Logistic	Logistic
2	MLP 36-3-1	0.668225	0.727911	0.672466	2309.050	2884.890	1865.378	BFGS 19	SOS	Tanh	Logistic
3	MLP 36-4-1	0.662566	0.614178	0.666472	2319.289	3780.035	1891.430	BFGS 31	SOS	Logistic	Tanh
4	MLP 36-3-1	0.694224	0.641110	0.670805	2141.018	3545.475	1987.349	BFGS 34	SOS	Logistic	Tanh
5	MLP 36-5-1	0.699296	0.750441	0.665845	2111.779	2759.128	1913.935	BFGS 84	SOS	Logistic	Sine

Source: Authors

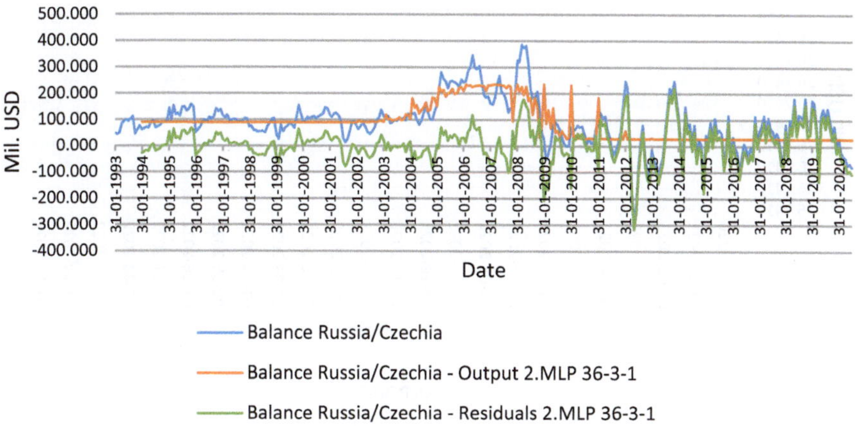

Fig. 6.78 Time series prediction—2. MLP 36-3-1_E2_balance 12b. Source: Authors

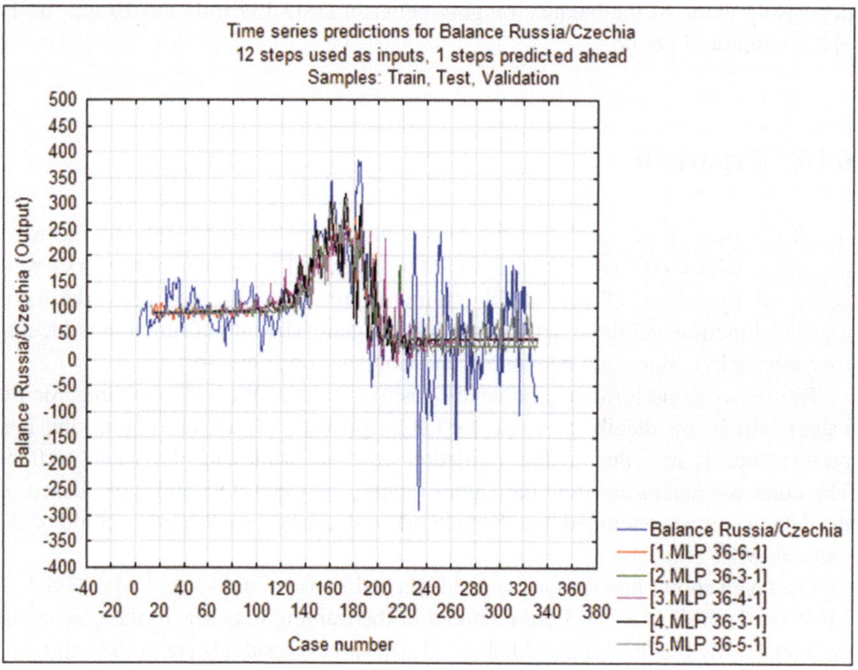

Fig. 6.79 Time series predictions_E2_balance 12b. Source: Authors

decreasing value of the balance ranging between USD 42 mil. and 40 mil. in the monitored period. In the monitored period, the value of the balance predicted by the network no. 4 is approx. USD 40 mil., with the maximum predicted value being recorded in April 2021. The fifth network predicts gradually increasing and

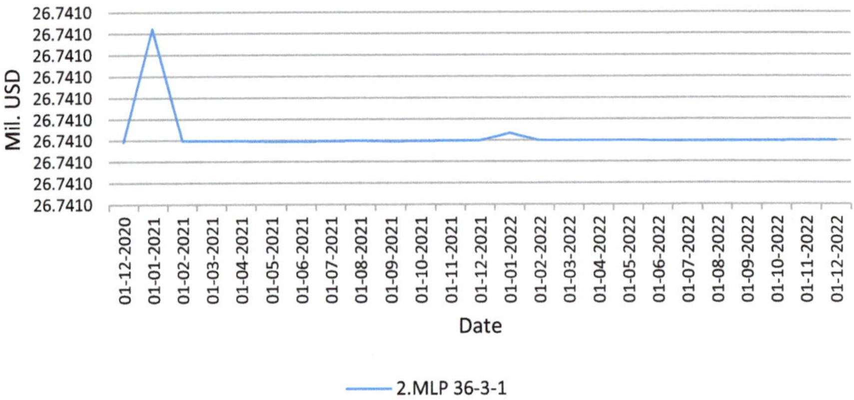

Fig. 6.80 Balance prediction—2. MLP 36-3-1_E2_balance 12b. Source: Authors

decreasing value of the balance ranging between USD 137 mil. and 19 mil. in the given monitored period.

6.18 Export 1b

It follows from Table 6.25 that the best results were achieved only by the MLP networks, with 6–10 neurons in the hidden layer. All the retained networks were generated by means of the BFGS training algorithm, with two networks using logistics function and three networks using Tangent. The output function is Identity (two networks), Sine (two networks), and Logistic (one network).

The network performance achieves positive values. We are searching for the values which are ideally as close to 1.0 as possible. In terms of this, the best performance is recorded in the validation data set, achieving the value of 0.89. The other two data sets show the values ranging between 0.83 and 0.93. Based on the data, it can be concluded that the network with the best performance could be the network MLP 3-6-1.

The result shows that the largest residuals in the case of networks 1.MLP 3-8-1, 2. MLP 3-6-1, 4.MLP 3-7-1 3 are recorded in the training data set. In the case of the networks 3.MLP 3-10-1 and 5.MLP 3-9-1, the largest residuals are in the validation data set.

The monthly mean value was USD 39,086.88, while the yearly mean value was USD 2006.485.

Fig. 6.81 shows the ability of the second neural network to roughly copy the development of the actual values of the export. However, it is only able to react to large changes in terms of years, not to smaller fluctuations in the shorter periods.

Fig. 6.82 clearly shows the fact that the retained networks are only able to copy the actual development of the export very roughly; they are not able to capture the

Table 6.25 Summary of active networks_E2_export 1b

Index	Net. name	Training perf.	Test perf.	Validation perf.	Training error	Test error	Validation error	Training algorithm	Error function	Hidden activation	Output activation
1	MLP 3-8-1	0.916835	0.879220	0.876122	1670.140	2372.434	2519.291	BFGS 176	SOS	Tanh	Identity
2	MLP 3-6-1	0.863833	0.840086	0.892784	2659.382	2596.237	2198.446	BFGS 153	SOS	Logistic	Identity
3	MLP 3-10-1	0.923934	0.894216	0.890579	1535.217	2170.598	2407.542	BFGS 152	SOS	Logistic	Sine
4	MLP 3-7-1	0.851013	0.835155	0.882432	2888.666	2640.980	2389.456	BFGS 66	SOS	Tanh	Sine
5	MLP 3-9-1	0.933198	0.920135	0.883038	1355.490	1536.270	2486.527	BFGS 129	SOS	Tanh	Logistic

Source: Authors

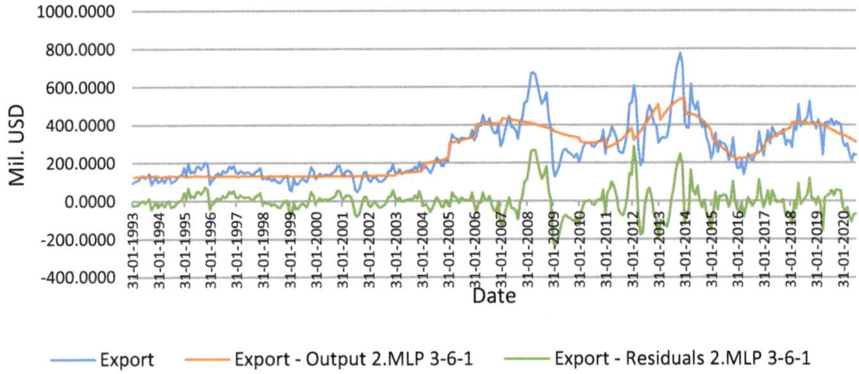

Fig. 6.81 Time series prediction—2. MLP 3-6-1_E2_export 1b. Source: Authors

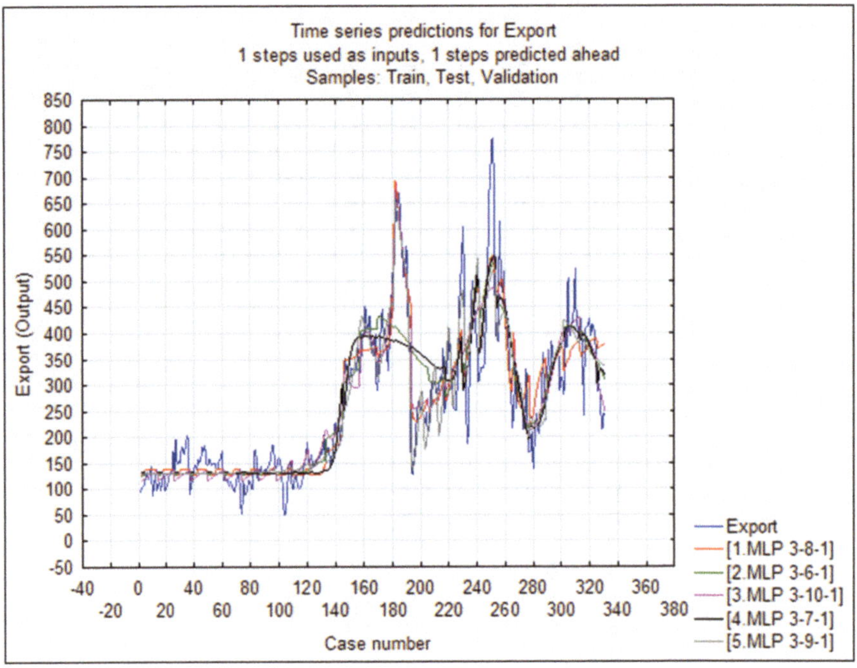

Fig. 6.82 Time series predictions_E2_export 1b. Source: Authors

local extremes and smaller or often greater deviations of the actual value of the Balance. Based on this graph as well as the graphs of the smoothed time series of the individual neural structures, it can be concluded that all the retained networks are very similar to each other in terms of their performance and ability to smooth the actual time series of the export.

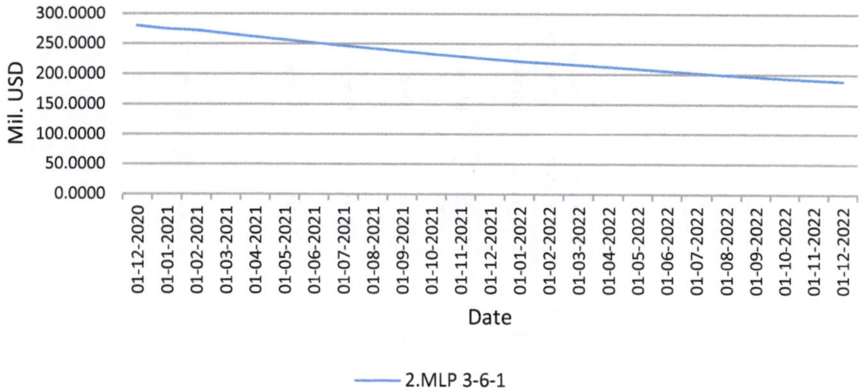

Fig. 6.83 Export prediction—2. MLP 3-6-1_E2_export 1b. Source: Authors

The value of the export predicted by the first network for the monitored period ranges between USD 377 mil. and 394 mil. The maximum value is predicted at the end of December 2022, while the minimum predicted value is in February 2021 (Fig. 6.83).

The value of the export predicted by the second network in the monitored period ranges between USD 279 mil. and 188 mil., with the maximum value being predicted at the end of December 2020 and the minimum value at the end of December 2022.

The third network predicted values of the export divided roughly in annual cycles. It can be seen that the curve is repeated about after a year; the only difference is that the peaks of the local maximum and minimum are by approx. USD 200 mil. lower each year. The fourth network predicted values of the export divided roughly in annual cycles. It can be seen that the curve is repeated about after a year; the only difference is that the peaks of the local maximum and minimum are by approx. USD 60 mil. each year. The value of the export predicted by the fifth network in the monitored period ranges between USD 327 mil. and 315 mil., with the maximum value being predicted at the end of December 2020, while the minimum value at the beginning of December 2022.

6.19 Export 3b

It follows from Table 6.26 that the best results are achieved only by the MLP networks containing 5–8 neurons in the hidden layer. All the retained networks were generated by means of the SOS training algorithm. Four of the retained networks use the Tangent function; the output activation functions used are Identity, Sine, Logistic, and Tangent. One retained network uses the Logistic function and the Identity function as the output function.

Table 6.26 Summary of active networks_E2_export 3b

Index	Net. name	Training perf.	Test perf.	Validation perf.	Training error	Test error	Validation error	Training algorithm	Error function	Hidden activation	Output activation
1	MLP 9-7-1	0.867433	0.761567	0.767661	2574.349	3734.427	4682.036	BFGS 99	SOS	Logistic	Identity
2	MLP 9-8-1	0.837726	0.743999	0.764739	3089.085	4160.395	4810.604	BFGS 84	SOS	Tanh	Identity
3	MLP 9-6-1	0.850863	0.764020	0.767202	2858.667	3829.032	4532.573	BFGS 105	SOS	Tanh	Sine
4	MLP 9-5-1	0.911547	0.761016	0.876048	1749.977	3804.017	2620.851	BFGS 162	SOS	Tanh	Logistic
5	MLP 9-5-1	0.876319	0.847340	0.824919	2421.066	2643.317	3935.578	BFGS 88	SOS	Tanh	Tanh

Source: Authors

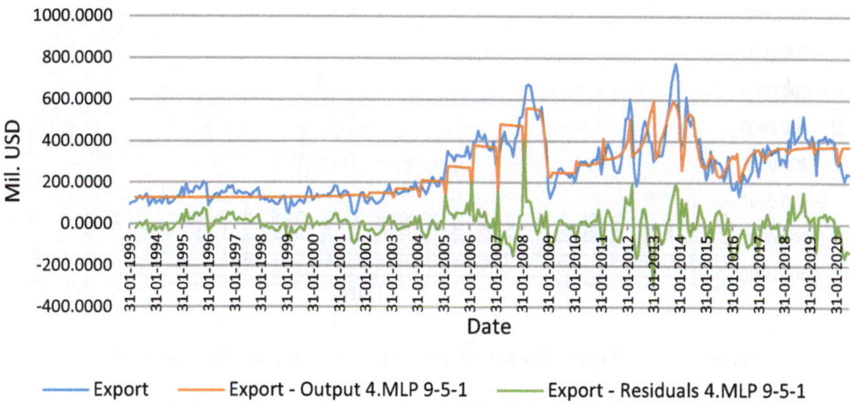

Fig. 6.84 Time series prediction—4. MLP 9-5-1_E2_export 3b. Source: Authors

The network performance achieves relatively positive values. We are searching ideally for the values as close to 1.0 as possible. In terms of this, the best performance is recorded in the validation data set, achieving the value of 0.87. The remaining two data sets achieve the values ranging from 0.74 to 0.91. Based on the data, it can be said that the best performance could be the fourth network MLP 9-5-1 or fifth MLP 9-5-1.

The largest residuals in the case of networks 1.MLP 9-7-1 and 4.MLP 9-5-1 are recorded in the testing data set, which contains the largest volume of data. In the case of the networks 2.MLP 9-8-1, 3.MLP 9-6-1, and 5.MLP 9-5-1, the largest residuals can be seen in the validation data set.

The monthly mean value was USD 39,086.88, while the yearly mean value was USD 2006.485.

This Fig. 6.84 shows the ability of the fourth neural network to roughly copy the development of the actual export values. However, it is only able to respond to larger changes in terms of years, not to smaller fluctuations in the export values in shorter periods.

This Fig. 6.85 shows the ability of the fifth neural network to roughly copy the development of the actual export values. However, it is only able to respond to larger changes in terms of years, not to smaller fluctuations in the export values in shorter periods (Fig. 6.86).

These networks are closer to the actual development of the export—it follows from the graph that the network curves cross and follow the blue curve representing the actual development of the export.

The first network predicted export values divided into approximately yearly cycles. The curves and the local minimum show the same values. The second network also predicted value of export divided into approximately yearly cycles. The only difference being the fact that the peaks of the local maximum are by USD 40 mil. higher each year. The values of the local minimum are by USD 4 mil. lower. The third network also predicted value of export divided into approximately yearly

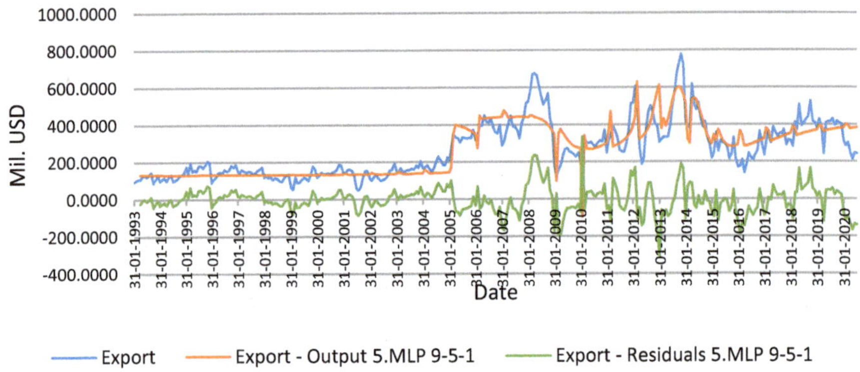

Fig. 6.85 Time series prediction—5. MLP 9-5-1_E2_export 3b. Source: Authors

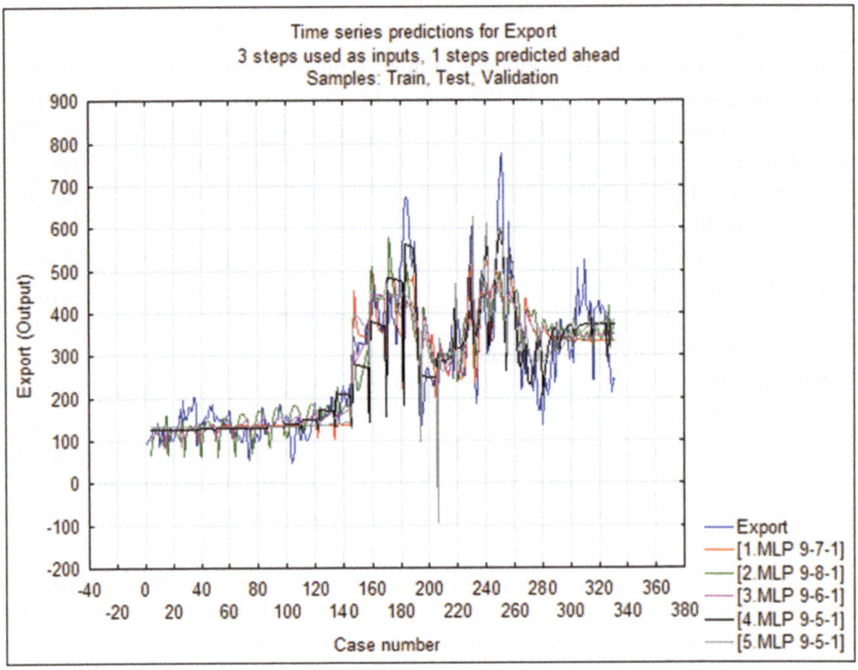

Fig. 6.86 Time series predictions_E2_export 3b. Source: Authors

cycles. The only difference being the fact that the peaks of the local maximum are by USD 8 mil. higher each year.

Fig. 6.87 with fourth neural network shows the predicted value of export divided into approximately yearly cycles. It can be seen that the curve is repeated about after a year, the only difference being the fact that the peaks of the local maximum and minimum are by USD 110 mil. higher each year.

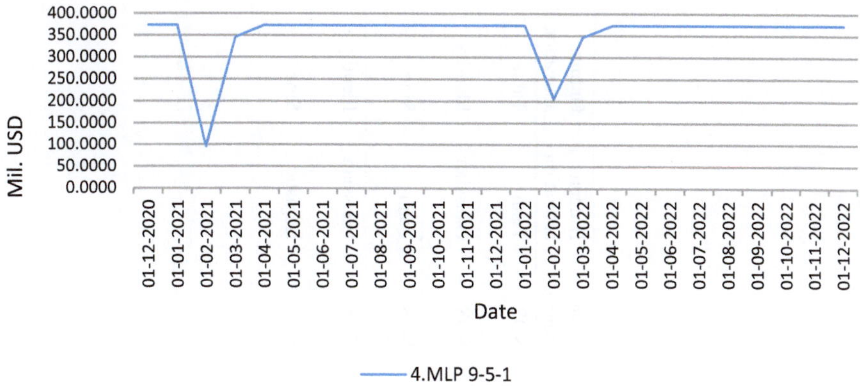

Fig. 6.87 Export prediction—4. MLP 9-5-1_E2_export 3b. Source: Authors

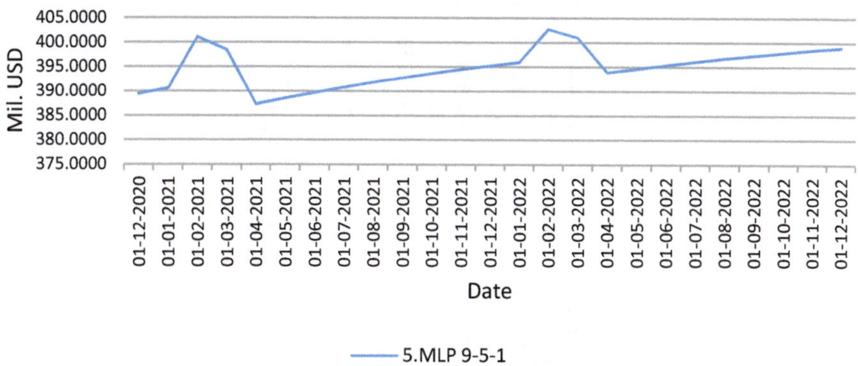

Fig. 6.88 Export prediction—5. MLP 9-5-1_E2_export 3b. Source: Authors

Fig. 6.88 with fifth neural network shows the predicted value of export divided into approximately yearly cycles. It can be seen that the curve is repeated about after a year, the only difference being the fact that the peaks of the local maximum and minimum are by USD 1 mil. higher each year.

6.20 Export 6b

It follows from Table 6.27 that the best results were achieved only by the MLP networks containing 4–28 neurons in the hidden layer. Three of the retained networks were generated using the BFGS algorithm, while the other two by means of RBFT training algorithm. The networks generated by means of the RBFT algorithm use Gaussian function and Identity as the output activation function. Two of the three networks generated using the BFGS training algorithm use hyperbolic tangent in the

Table 6.27 Summary of active networks_E2_export 6b

Index	Net. name	Training perf.	Test perf.	Valid. perf.	Training error	Test error	Validation error	Training algorithm	Error function	Hidden activation	Output activation
1	MLP 18-6-1	0.799710	0.716842	0.713515	3.675523E+03	4.444665E+03	5.421134E+03	BFGS 84	SOS	Tanh	Tanh
2	RBF 18-28-1	0.081382	0.144701	0.720987	1.027487E+19	7.981223E+17	3.479682E+11	RBFT	SOS	Gaussian	Identity
3	MLP 18-4-1	0.795853	0.723706	0.716839	3.738498E+03	4.277692E+03	5.365023E+03	BFGS 66	SOS	Tanh	Sine
4	RBF 18-23-1	0.203614	0.252439	0.716762	1.483828E+11	2.563166E+10	6.514151E+10	RBFT	SOS	Gaussian	Identity
5	MLP 18-4-1	0.796752	0.722824	0.714992	3.723748E+03	4.322723E+03	5.360609E+03	BFGS 97	SOS	Logistic	Sine

Source: Authors

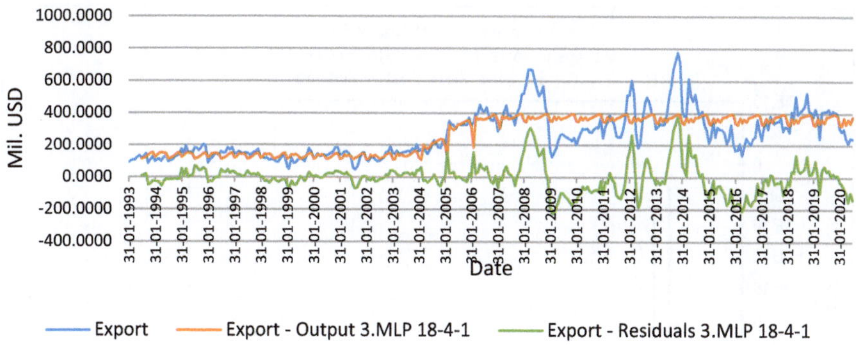

Fig. 6.89 Time series prediction—3. MLP 18-4-1_E2_export 6b. Source: Authors

hidden layer, and one uses the logistic function. Two networks generated by means of the BFGS algorithm use Sine as the output function, while the third one uses Tangent. There is a relatively high performance of the given networks in all data sets.

The network performance achieves relatively positive values. We are searching ideally for the values as close to 1.0 as possible. From this perspective, the best performance is recorded in the validation data set, achieving the value of 0.72. The other two data sets show the values ranging from 0.14 to 0.81. Based on the data, it can be estimated that the third network MLP 18-4-1 could be the best network of this set.

The largest residuals of the networks 1.MLP 18-6-1, 3.MLP 18-4-1, and 5.MLP 18-4-1 are recorded in the validation data set, which contains the greatest volume of data, while in the case of 2.RBF 18-28-1 and 4.RBF 18-23-1, the largest residuals are in the training data set.

The monthly mean value was USD 39,086.88, while the yearly mean value USD 2006.485.

It follows from Fig. 6.89 that the networks are able to predict the rough development of export relatively well, yet they have problems with predicting the local minimum and maximum values (Fig. 6.90).

The first network predicted export values divided into approximately yearly cycles. It can be seen that the curve is repeated after about a year, the only difference being the fact that the peaks of the local minimum and maximum values are by USD 18 mil. higher each year. The network thus predicts gradually increasing and decreasing values of the export ranging between USD 290 mil. and 272 mil. in the given monitored period. The export values predicted by the second network in the monitored period range between USD 205 mil. and 487 mil., with the maximum value being predicted at the end of December 2022 and the minimum value at the end of January 2021.

Fig. 6.91 with the third network shows the predicted export values divided into approximately yearly cycles. It can be seen that the curve is repeated after about a year, with the only difference being the fact that the peaks of the local maximum and minimum values are approx. by USD 5 mil. higher each year.

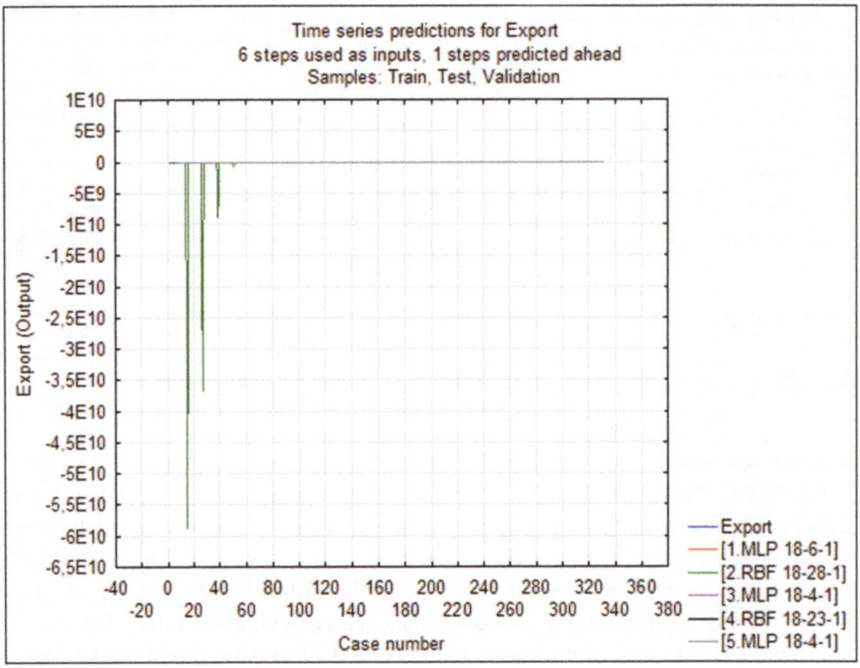

Fig. 6.90 Time series predictions_E2_export 6b. Source: Authors

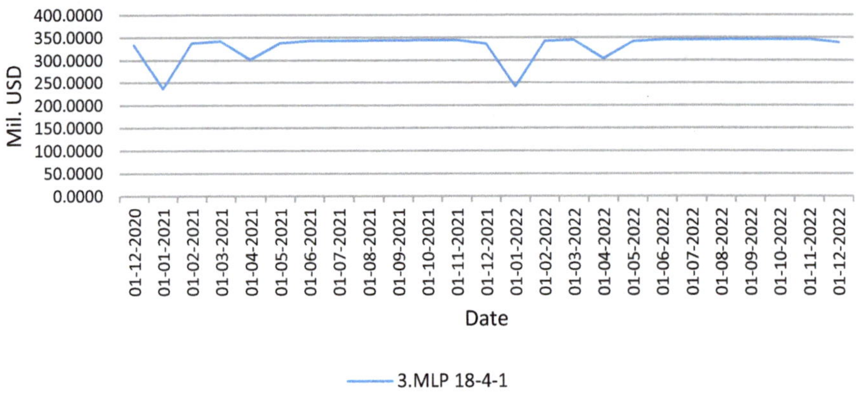

Fig. 6.91 Export prediction—3. MLP 18-4-1_E2_export 6b. Source: Authors

The export values predicted by the fourth network in the monitored period range between USD 320 mil. and 519 mil. The maximum predicted value is recorded at the end of December 2022, while the minimum value is predicted at the end of January 2021. The export values predicted by the fifth network within the monitored period range between USD 310 mil. and 422 mil. The maximum predicted value is recorded at the end of December 2022, while the minimum value is predicted at the end of January 2021.

6.21 Export 12b

It follows from Table 6.28 that the networks are MLP, where three networks contain three neurons in the hidden layer, two networks use seven neurons in the hidden layer. The networks are very similar to each other, since they use the same training algorithm (SOS). Three networks use the Tangent function in the hidden layer, the remaining two use the logistic function. The output activation function is logistic in three cases, Sine (one network), and Exponential function (one network).

The network performance achieves relatively positive values. We are searching ideally for the values as close to 1.0 as possible. In this context, the best performance is recorded in the validation data set, achieving the approximate value of 0.70. The remaining two data sets achieve the values of 0.73–0.79. Based on the data, it can be estimated that the best network of this set could be the fourth retained network, MLP 36-3-1.

That the largest residuals are recorded in the validation data set, which also contains the largest volume of data. The minimum and maximum standard residuals are very close to the ideal value (0) and indicate a relatively accurate prediction.

The data statistics of the Russian and Czech balance of trade for individual data sets divided according to the methodology, i.e., the training data set containing 70% of the input data, while the testing and validation data sets containing 15% of the input data each were presented. The statistical characteristics include the maximum and minimum values, mean, and the standard deviation.

Fig. 6.92 shows possibly the best network, which is able to predict the actual development of the export, often even in the case of local minimum or maximum. Other networks were able to relatively well smooth the export time series in the period of great economic crisis of 2008–2009; however, they are able to copy the actual development very roughly only.

Fig. 6.93 shows that the retained networks are able to copy the actual development of the export very roughly only, they are unable to capture the local extremes and smaller or often greater deviations of the actual export values. Based on this graph, as well as the graphs of the time series smoothed by individual neural networks, it can be concluded that all the retained neural networks are very similar to each other in terms of their performance and ability to smooth the actual export time series.

The first network predicted export values divided into approximately yearly cycles. It can be seen that the curve is repeated about after a year, the only difference being the fact that the peaks of the local minimum and maximum values are by USD 4–5 mil. lower each year. This network thus predicts gradually increasing and decreasing export values ranging from USD 400 mil. to 354 mil. in the given monitored period. The export value in the monitored period predicted by the second

Table 6.28 Summary of active networks_E2_export 12b

Index	Net. name	Training perf.	Test perf.	Validation perf.	Training error	Test error	Validation error	Training algorithm	Error function	Hidden activation	Output activation
1	MLP 36-7-1	0.785699	0.757050	0.703024	3834.727	3619.644	5324.228	BFGS 16	SOS	Logistic	Exponential
2	MLP 36-3-1	0.782051	0.753757	0.704002	3900.359	3746.586	5361.858	BFGS 17	SOS	Logistic	Sine
3	MLP 36-3-1	0.789713	0.757403	0.706311	3770.530	3679.348	5268.022	BFGS 15	SOS	Tanh	Logistic
4	MLP 36-3-1	0.792478	0.757280	0.700720	3724.501	3689.470	5391.746	BFGS 46	SOS	Tanh	Logistic
5	MLP 36-7-1	0.780992	0.732264	0.703603	3914.298	3887.033	5307.367	BFGS 13	SOS	Tanh	Logistic

Source: Authors

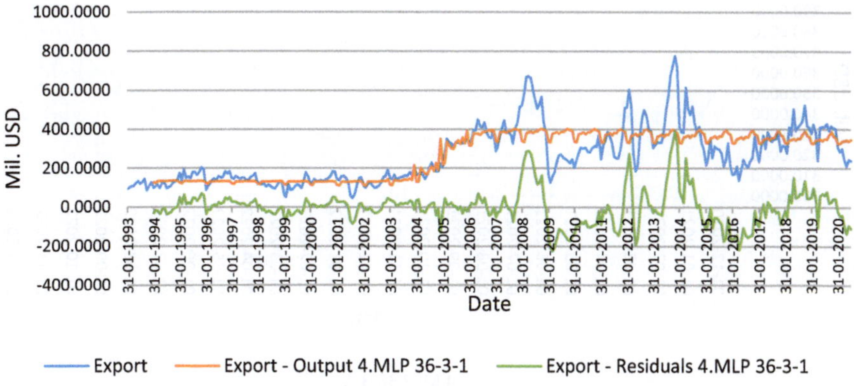

Fig. 6.92 Time series prediction—4. MLP 36-3-1_E2_export 12b. Source: Authors

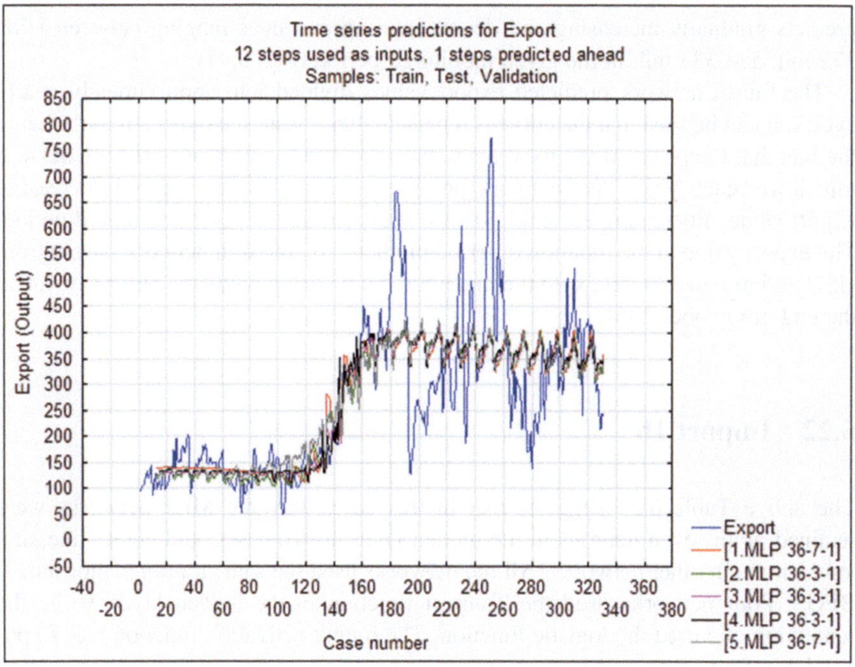

Fig. 6.93 Time series predictions_E2_export 12b. Source: Authors

network ranges from USD 291 mil. to 386 mil., with the maximum value being predicted before the fall at the end of October 2021. The third network predicted export values divided into approximately yearly cycles. It can be seen that the curve is repeated after a year, the only difference being the fact that the peaks of the local maximum and minimum values are by USD 4–5 mil. lower each year. This network

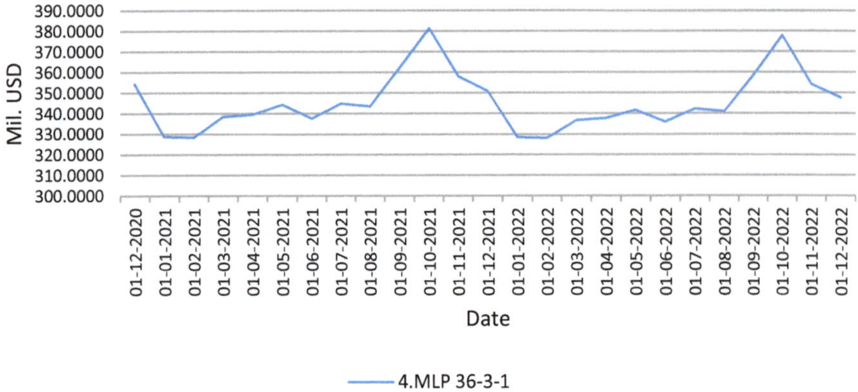

Fig. 6.94 Export prediction—4. MLP 36-3-1_E2_export 12b. Source: Authors

predicts gradually increasing and decreasing export values ranging between USD 372 mil. and 333 mil. in the given monitored period (Fig. 6.94).

The fourth network predicted export values divided into approximately yearly cycles. It can be seen that the curve is repeated after a year, the only difference being the fact that the peaks of the local maximum and minimum values are by USD 4–5 mil. lower each year. This network predicts gradually increasing and decreasing export values fluctuating around USD 381–328 mil. in the given monitored period. The export value in the monitored period predicted by the fifth network ranges from USD 305 mil. to 370 mil., with the maximum value being predicted before the fall at the end of October 2021.

6.22 Import 1b

The above Table 6.29 suggests that in this case, only the MLP networks were retained, with seven neurons in the hidden layer in two cases, and eight, nine, and ten neurons in other networks. All the networks used the same training algorithm—BFGS. Four networks used the Tangent function in the hidden layer, while the remaining one used the logistic function. The output activation function was Exponential in four cases, and Identity in one case.

The network performance achieves relatively positive values. We are searching ideally for the values as close to 1.0 possible. From this perspective, the best performance was achieved in the validation data set, achieving the value of about 0.98. In the two remaining data sets, the values range from 0.97 to 0.98. Based on the data, it can be estimated that the best network of this set could be the second retained network, 2.MLP 3-7-1.

Table 6.29 Summary of active networks_E2_import 1b

Index	Net. name	Training perf.	Test perf.	Validation perf.	Training error	Test error	Validation error	Training algorithm	Error function	Hidden activation	Output activation
1	MLP 3-7-1	0.982398	0.977767	0.988992	350.5575	383.1386	243.4686	BFGS 200	SOS	Tanh	Exponential
2	MLP 3-7-1	0.984930	0.978756	0.988023	299.3180	352.3765	272.5310	BFGS 279	SOS	Tanh	Exponential
3	MLP 3-10-1	0.982310	0.974405	0.989561	351.0180	431.7861	236.0686	BFGS 278	SOS	Tanh	Identity
4	MLP 3-9-1	0.979191	0.972327	0.988156	447.2907	505.5997	271.5707	BFGS 224	SOS	Tanh	Exponential
5	MLP 3-8-1	0.977507	0.971098	0.988489	445.0384	481.3106	262.9241	BFGS 224	SOS	Logistic	Exponential

Source: Authors

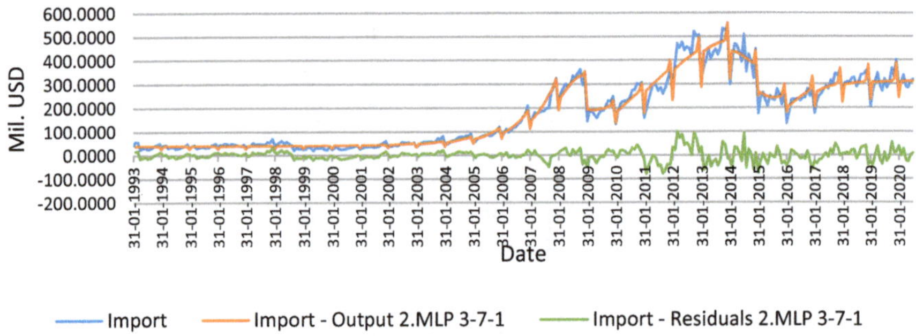

Fig. 6.95 Time series prediction—2. MLP 3-7-1_E2_import 1b. Source: Authors

That the largest residuals are recorded in the training data set, which contains the largest volume of the data. Both minimum and maximum standard residuals are very close to the ideal value of 0, which indicates a relatively accurate prediction.

In the monitored period, the mean monthly import value was USD 39,086.88, while the mean yearly value was USD 2006.485 (Fig. 6.95).

The correlation coefficients indicate a very weak performance of the network.

These very positive characteristics of the retained networks should be reflected in the predictions for the period between the end of 2020 and the end of 2022. It can be seen that it is really reflected in the predictions. All the networks predict that in the monitored period, the value of the import will be positive, significantly above 0. It can also be noted that all the networks predict a sharp decrease in the import values at the beginning of 2022, but in the next months, the value increases again.

The predictions of these networks are close to the actual development of the import. Fig. 6.96 shows that their curves cross and follow the blue curve of the actual development of the import.

The import value predicted by the first network for the monitored period ranges between USB 251 mil. and 386 mil. The maximum value is predicted before the fall at the end of the year 2021 (Fig. 6.97).

The second network predicts a narrower range of the import values (from approx. USD 249 mil. in the fall at the beginning of 2021 to approx. 401 mil. at the end of the monitored period).

The third network predicts a relatively significant decrease in the import values at the beginning of 2021 (by up to USD 131 mil.). For the rest of the monitored period, however, it predicts a relatively stable and significant growth from USD 441 mil. at the beginning of the monitored period to USD 523 mil. The fourth network predicts a narrower range of import values (from approx. USD 274 mil. in the fall at the beginning of the year 2021 to approx. USD 480 mil. at the end of the monitored period). The import values predicted by the fifth network for the monitored period range between approx. USD 248 mil. and 346 mil. The maximum value is predicted at the end of February 2022.

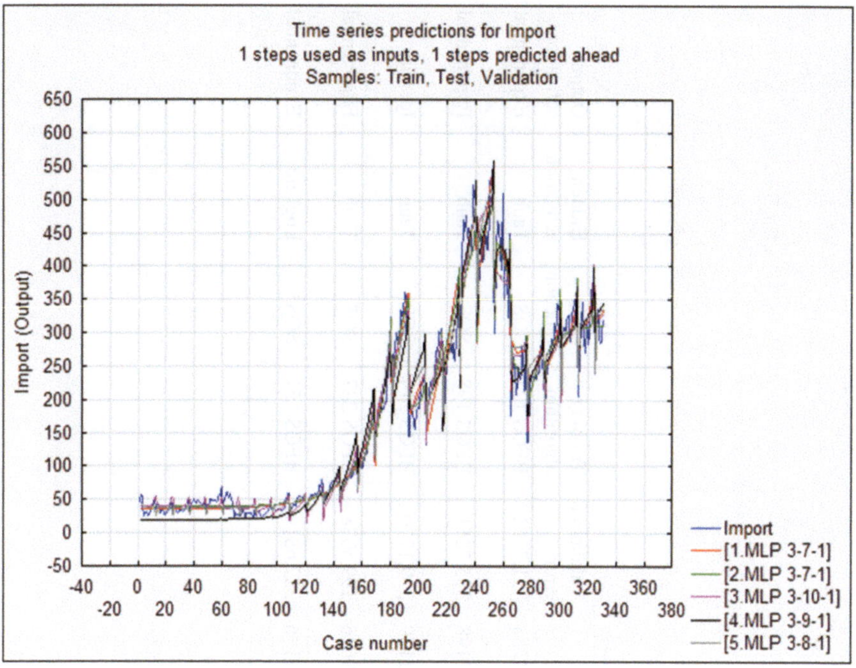

Fig. 6.96 Time series predictions_E2_import 1b. Source: Authors

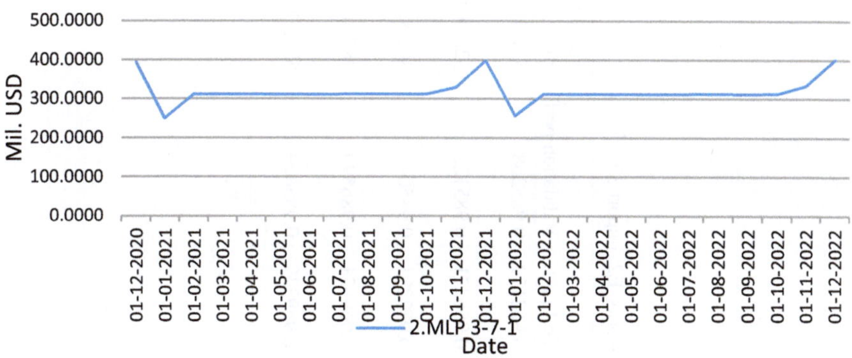

Fig. 6.97 Import prediction—2. MLP 3-7-1_E2_import 1b. Source: Authors

6.23 Import 3b

Table 6.30 indicates that in this case, only the MLP networks were retained. Two of them contain 5–10 neurons in the hidden layer. All the networks used the same training algorithm (BFGS) and the activation function in the hidden layer (Tangent).

Table 6.30 Summary of active networks_E2_import 3b

Index	Net. name	Training perf.	Test perf.	Validation perf.	Training error	Test error	Validation error	Training algorithm	Error function	Hidden activation	Output activation
1	MLP 9-10-1	0.972873	0.962179	0.985268	531.5317	619.1253	331.7822	BFGS 122	SOS	Tanh	Exponential
2	MLP 9-8-1	0.973074	0.956271	0.985123	528.0018	715.2198	335.7851	BFGS 198	SOS	Tanh	Exponential
3	MLP 9-10-1	0.979552	0.972291	0.985042	401.8238	459.1149	339.1770	BFGS 214	SOS	Tanh	Identity
4	MLP 9-5-1	0.985408	0.969921	0.986599	287.4607	511.9626	299.5038	BFGS 227	SOS	Tanh	Exponential
5	MLP 9-8-1	0.970654	0.959339	0.985829	576.3742	678.7146	327.6819	BFGS 151	SOS	Logistic	Exponential

Source: Authors

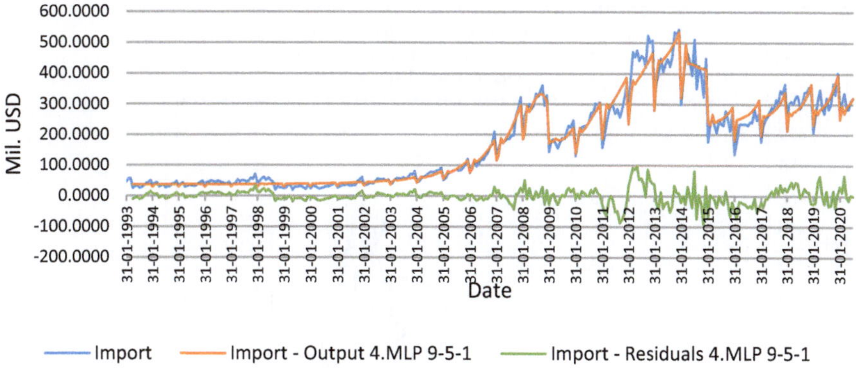

Fig. 6.98 Time series prediction—4. MLP 9-5-1_E2_import 3b. Source: Authors

Only one network uses logistic function. In the output layer, four networks use exponential function, one network uses Identity.

The network performance achieves very positive values. We are searching ideally for the values as close to 1.0 as possible. From this perspective, the best performance is recorded in the validation data set, achieving the value closest to 1. In the two remaining data sets, the values range between 0.95 and 0.98. Based on the data, it can be concluded that the best network of this set could be the fourth retained network, 4.MLP 9-5-1.

The largest residuals are mostly in the testing data set. In the case of the network 3.MLP 9-10-1, the largest residuals are in the training data set (Fig. 6.98).

The given neural network is only able to roughly copy the development of the import values. It is not able to capture the local minimum and maximum values. Therefore, it is rather inapplicable in practice, as it is able to predict only an approximate value of the import.

Fig. 6.99 presents the smoothed time series. The blue curve represents the actual development of the import; other curves represent the individual retained neural networks, or predictions of the aforementioned balance of trades according to the individual neural structures. It follows from the graph that the retained neural networks are able to copy the actual development of the import well; however, they are unable to capture the local maximum and minimum values.

The first network shows a narrower range of the import values in the monitored period. There can be seen a significant decrease in the values at the beginning of the year 2020 by up to USD 170 mil. and even a larger decrease at the beginning of the year 2022 (by approx. USD 167). Except for the decrease, the import values are stable, fluctuating around USD 300 mil. In the case of the second network, there is a notable decrease in the values at the beginning of 2020 (by approx. USD 92 mil.) and even larger decrease at the beginning of 2022 (by approx. USD 91 mil.). Except for these falls, the import values are stable, fluctuating around USD 350 mil. The import values predicted by the third network in the monitored period range between approx.

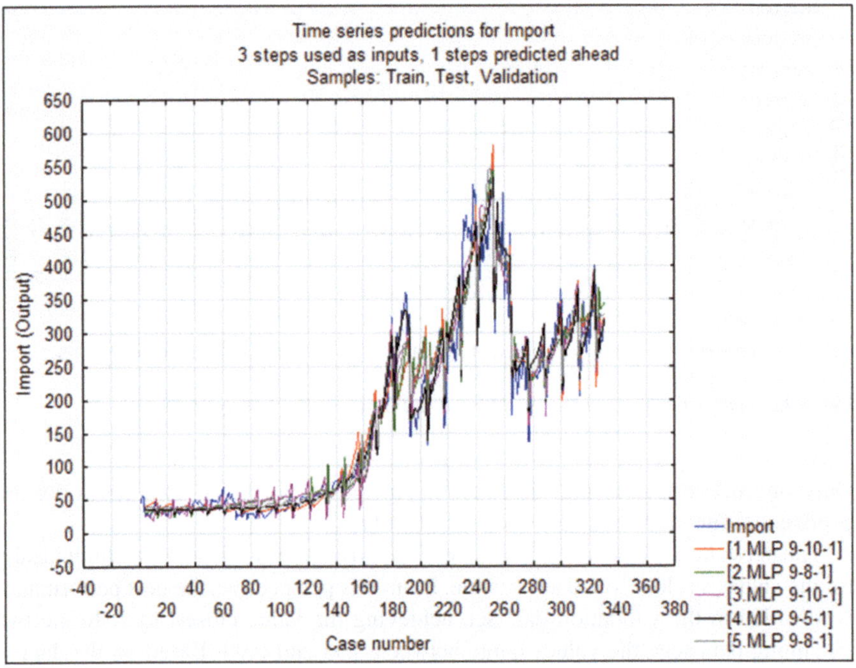

Fig. 6.99 Time series predictions_E2_import 3b. Source: Authors

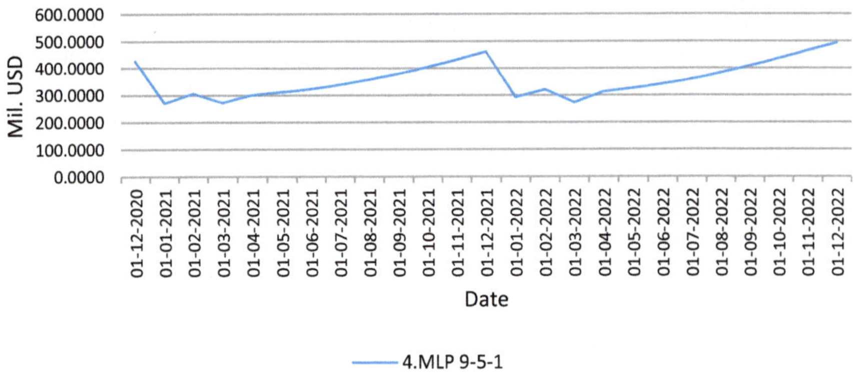

Fig. 6.100 Import prediction—4. MLP 9-5-1_E2_import 3b. Source: Authors

USD 247 mil. and 400 mil. The maximum value is predicted for the end of November 2022.

Fig. 6.100 shows the declared fall in the value of the import, which is expected to grow in the long run (from USD 429 mil. to USD 494 mil.).

The import value predicted by the fifth network for the monitored period ranges between USD 329 mil. to USD 332 mil., with the maximum value being predicted before the fall at the end of the year 2022.

6.24 Import 6b

It follows from Table 6.31 that the best results are achieved by the MLP networks only, with 4–7 neurons in the hidden layer. The retained networks were generated using the BFGS training algorithm. Four networks use Tangent, one uses logistic function. The output activation function is Exponential function. In all data sets, the network performance is relatively high.

It follows from the table that the network performance achieves relatively positive values. We are searching ideally for the values as close to 1.0 as possible. From this perspective, the highest performance is recorded in the validation data set, achieving the value around 0.98. In the remaining two data sets, the range of the values is between 0.91 and 0.97. Based on the data, it can be concluded that the best network of this set can be the third retained network, 3.MLP 18-5-1.

Fig. 6.101 represents the smoothed time series and residuals according to the network 3. MLP 18-5-1. There can be seen a relatively precise prediction and low residual values.

It can be seen from Fig. 6.102 that the networks, although showing a very high performance, are able to predict the value of the Russian/Czech import only roughly. At the beginning of the monitored period, the networks are able to predict the import values relatively accurately, but this is obviously due to the relatively stable development of the import values, which do not show any significant fluctuations in this period. This is confirmed by the graphs of the predictions and residuals of the individual retained networks. This can be seen, e.g., on the example of the most successful (in terms of its performance) network, 2. MLP 18-7-1.

The import values predicted by the first network in the monitored period range between USD 377 mil. and 414 mil. There is a decrease at the beginning of January 2020 (by approx. USD 105 mil.). Another decrease is recorded at the beginning of 2022 (by approx. USD 106 mil.). The maximum value is predicted for the end of the year 2022. In the case of the second network, the range of the import values in the monitored period is narrower, with a significant decrease at the beginning of the year 2021 (by approx. USD 129 mil) and even larger decrease at the end of the year 2022 (by approx. USD 136 mil.).

The import values predicted by this network in the monitored period range between USD 334 mil. and 338 mil. The maximum value is predicted at the beginning of December 2022 (Fig. 6.103).

The import values predicted by the fourth network in the monitored period range between USD 406 mil. and 519 mil. The maximum value is predicted at the end of November 2022. The fifth network predicts a slight decrease in the import values at the beginning of 2021 (by approx. USD 69 mil.). Another slight decrease is expected

Table 6.31 Summary of active networks_E2_import 6b

Index	Net. name	Training perf.	Test perf.	Validation perf.	Training error	Test error	Validation error	Training algorithm	Error function	Hidden activation	Output activation
1	MLP 18-4-1	0.962723	0.943398	0.979176	717.5596	950.965	462.6022	BFGS 177	SOS	Tanh	Exponential
2	MLP 18-7-1	0.963361	0.948958	0.980780	704.0362	849.980	428.8323	BFGS 124	SOS	Tanh	Exponential
3	MLP 18-5-1	0.971191	0.958953	0.979606	551.7400	671.747	519.5734	BFGS 251	SOS	Logistic	Exponential
4	MLP 18-5-1	0.955400	0.911633	0.981080	853.4440	1466.281	448.0234	BFGS 105	SOS	Tanh	Exponential
5	MLP 18-6-1	0.962226	0.946920	0.980864	722.4212	870.759	427.1721	BFGS 138	SOS	Tanh	Exponential

Source: Authors

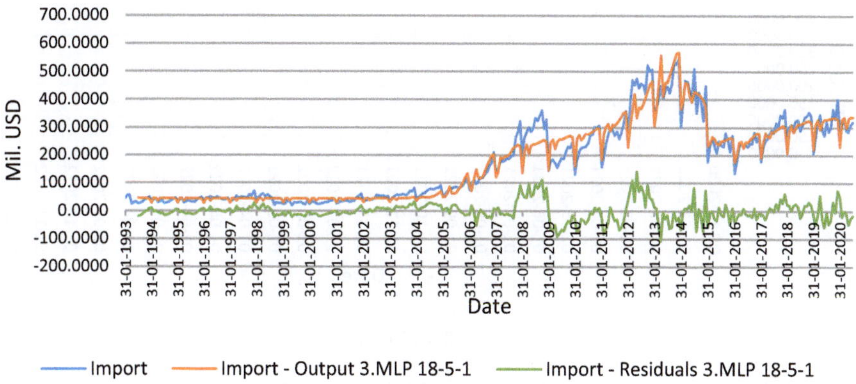

Fig. 6.101 Time series prediction—3. MLP 18-5-1_E2_import 6b. Source: Authors

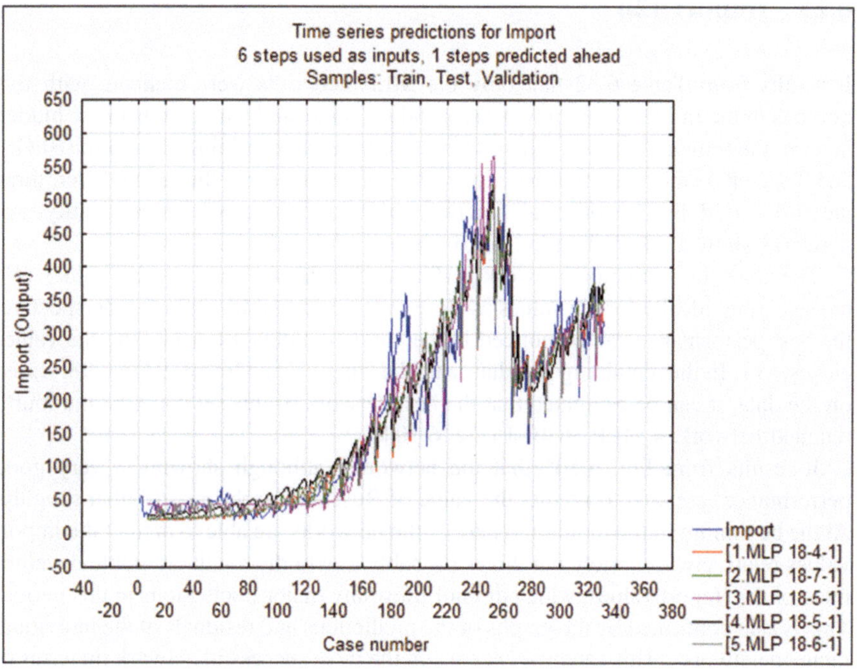

Fig. 6.102 Time series predictions_E2_import 6b. Source: Authors

at the end of November 2022 (by approx. USD 50 mil.). For the rest of the monitored period, constant and significant growth is mostly expected (from approx. USD 379 mil. at the beginning of the monitored period to USD 422 mil.).

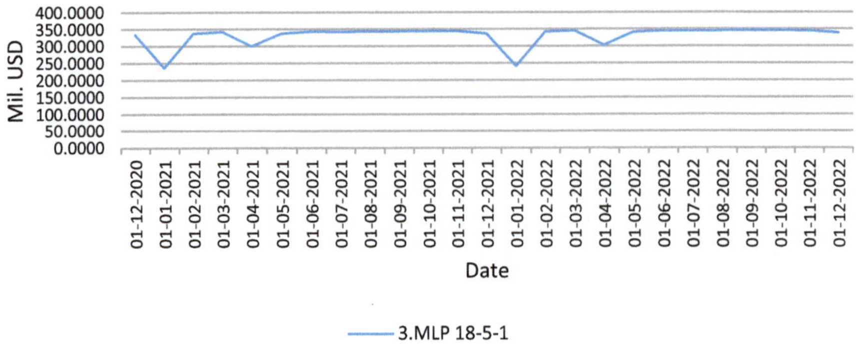

Fig. 6.103 Import prediction—3. MLP 18-5-1_E2_import 6b. Source: Authors

6.25 Import 12b

It results from Table 6.32 that only the MLP networks were retained, with five neurons in the hidden layer in two cases and six, nine, and ten neurons in the hidden layer in the remaining cases. All networks used the same training algorithm (BFGS) and Tangent as the activation function in the hidden layer. In the output layer, three networks used the Exponential function, while two networks used Identity. All networks show a relatively good performance.

The table shows that the network performance achieves very positive values. We are searching ideally for the values as close to 1.0 as possible. From this perspective, the best performance can be noticed in the validation data set, achieving the values closest to 1. In the remaining two data sets, the values range from 0.93 to 0.98. Based on the data, it can be estimated that the best network of this set could be the fourth retained network, 4.MLP 36-10-1 (Fig. 6.104).

It results from Fig. 6.105 that the networks, although showing a very good performance, are able to predict the value of Russian/Czech import rather roughly. At the beginning of the monitored period, the networks are able to predict the import values relatively accurately but this is probably due to the relatively stable development of the import values, which did not show any major fluctuations in this period. This is also confirmed by the graphs of the predictions and residuals of the individual retained networks. This can be seen, e.g., on the most successful network (in terms of its performance), 4. MLP 36-10-1. The residual values are low until the period before the great economic crisis of 2008–2009.

The import values predicted by the first network in the monitored period range between USD 283 mil. and 385 mil., with the maximum value being predicted at the beginning of December 2022 and the minimum value at the end of January 2021. The second network shows a limited range of import values in the monitored period, with a clear decrease in the values at the beginning of February 2021 (by approx. USD 32 mil.). Another smaller decrease is estimated at the beginning of 2022 (by approx. USD 19 mil.). In the rest of the monitored period, the values fluctuate

Table 6.32 Summary of active networks_E2_import 12b

Index	Net. name	Training perf.	Test perf.	Validation perf.	Training error	Test error	Validation error	Training algorithm	Error function	Hidden activation	Output activation
1	MLP 36-5-1	0.976233	0.957675	0.974387	442.3025	676.8800	570.6880	BFGS 60	SOS	Tanh	Identity
2	MLP 36-9-1	0.974538	0.947657	0.973248	474.4410	862.2535	630.0556	BFGS 68	SOS	Tanh	Exponential
3	MLP 36-5-1	0.965525	0.939444	0.974494	643.5617	984.2052	554.2234	BFGS 77	SOS	Tanh	Identity
4	MLP 36-10-1	0.981597	0.978149	0.971385	340.7703	348.8056	613.3890	BFGS 78	SOS	Tanh	Exponential
5	MLP 36-6-1	0.976364	0.959432	0.968817	440.1182	652.6702	689.3416	BFGS 68	SOS	Tanh	Exponential

Source: Authors

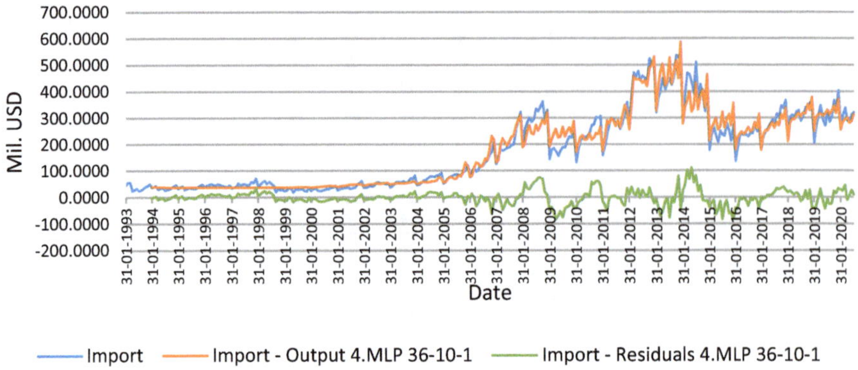

Fig. 6.104 Time series prediction—4. MLP 36-10-1_E2_import 12b. Source: Authors

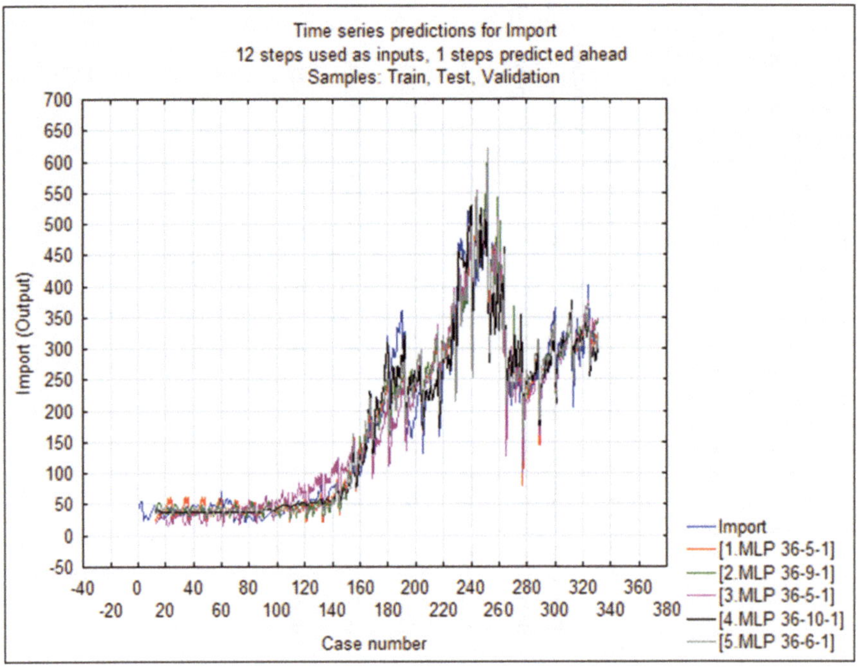

Fig. 6.105 Time series predictions_E2_import 12b. Source: Authors

around USD 350 mil. The import values predicted by the third network in the monitored period range between USD 308 mil. and 416 mil. The maximum value is predicted for the beginning of December 2022; the minimum value, at the end of January 2021.

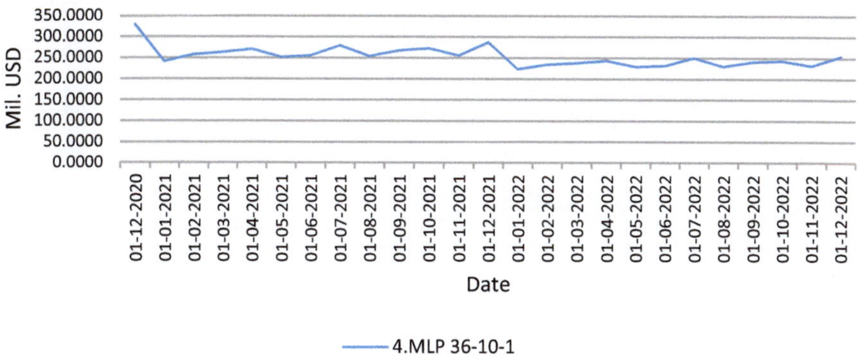

Fig. 6.106 Import prediction—4. MLP 36-10-1_E2_import 12b. Source: Authors

This network predicts a narrower range of import values (between USD 223 mil. in the fall at the end of January 2022 and USD 329 mil. at the beginning of the monitored period) (Fig. 6.106).

In the case of the fifth network, the network also predicts a limited range of import values in the monitored period. There is a clear decrease in the value at the beginning of 2022 (by approx. USD 87 mil.) and a larger decrease at the beginning of 2021 (by approx. USD 96 mil.). In the rest of the monitored period, the import values fluctuate around USD 300 mil.

Chapter 7
Conclusion

There is no doubt that international trade is an important part of the economy of any country and everyday life. International trade ensures a large number of jobs and provides consumers a wide choice. It is considered to be a driving force for the prosperity of countries around the world, leading also to the expansion of their consumption potential. As an example, the European Union has benefited greatly from the interconnected global economy, as evidenced by the fact that the international trade of the EU accounts for almost 35% of its GDP and the value of the direct foreign investments in the EU in relation to the GDP is 40%. Before the coronavirus crisis, the openness of the EU was one of the greatest in the world, with 35 million jobs depending on export and other 16 million jobs depending on foreign investments. In other words, every seventh job depends on export, which is two thirds more than in the year 2000. International trade is very important also for small- and medium-sized enterprises, which account for 87% of all exporting enterprises in the EU and are the driving force behind its export performance.

As already mentioned several times, the COVID-19 pandemic and the related global recession have had a devastating impact on the international trade. Despite the fact that currently the virus seems to be globally under control and economies are slowly recovering, this issue must not be neglected. The future of international trade is still uncertain, demanding, and precise predictions of its development or specifics are very difficult to make. Most likely, there will be some permanent changes in the future. As an example, there will be a change in the demand structure. People in the developed countries will be able to work from home more often, which will result in the reduced demand for cars and petrol. In this context, there might also be a reduction in the demand for office and business premises. These changes are likely to put downward pressure on the prices of commodities and the volume of trades. The demand for electronics, health care, childcare, and care of the elderly is expected to rise, while lower demand is expected in the case of cars and clothing. It follows from current predictions that the volume of global trade in goods is expected to rise by 10.8% in the year 2021 and by 4.7% in 2022. The growth is expected to slow

J. Horák et al., *Development of World Trade in the Context of the COVID-19 Pandemic*, Contributions to Economics,
https://doi.org/10.1007/978-3-031-27257-8_7

down, since trade in goods is now approaching its long-term trend before the pandemic. Supply-side problems, such as semiconductor shortage and problems in harbours, can burden supply chains and trade in certain areas; however, they are not likely to have a greater impact on the global aggregates. The greatest risks of negative development arise from the pandemic itself. Nevertheless, there are significant differences between individual countries behind the overall strong trade growth, with some developing regions not achieving the global average. The economic divergence between the regions is exacerbated mainly by the unfair approach to vaccine distribution.

In terms of forecasting the development of trade specifically between the CR and Russia, it can be quite logically concluded that the current situation will not positively contribute to the potential export to Russia, which represents a very interesting destination and large market for Czech companies. The mutual ratio of export and import between the Czech Republic and Russia is balanced, although the balance of trade is gradually changing in favour of the Czech Republic, to the foreign trade of the Czech Republic with Russia, with regard to the current situation. However, the export items are different on each side. On the side of Russia, it is mainly commodities; on the Czech side, goods from various industries. The dependence of the Czech Republic on Russia in terms of raw materials is not sustainable in the long run; however, a political and business consensus, as well as a long-term investment plan is needed to address it. There are also Czech companies actively operating in Russia, especially in engineering, automotive, energy, or food industry. Certain decrease in the demand on the side of Russian customers can be expected; however, there will be no fatal cessation of bilateral trade relations.

This was expected before the outbreak of the Russian-Ukrainian conflict. Without this fact, we already predicted that the dependence of the Czech Republic on Russia in the field of raw materials is not sustainable. This was confirmed during the year 2022 after the outbreak of said conflict. Not only the government of the Czech Republic, but also other governments of the world are trying to do something about a similar problem. The conflict essentially stopped trade with the Russian Federation, and in the second half of 2022 it is very difficult to predict future developments. It will greatly depend on the development of the Russian-Ukrainian conflict.

MIX
Papier aus verantwortungsvollen Quellen
Paper from responsible sources
FSC® C105338

If you have any concerns about our products,
you can contact us on
ProductSafety@springernature.com

In case Publisher is established outside the EU,
the EU authorized representative is:
Springer Nature Customer Service Center GmbH
Europaplatz 3, 69115 Heidelberg, Germany

Printed by Libri Plureos GmbH
in Hamburg, Germany